Changing Shades of Orange and Green

Perspectives in British–Irish Studies
General Editors: JOHN COAKLEY AND JENNIFER TODD

# Changing Shades of Orange and Green

*Redefining the Union and the Nation in Contemporary Ireland*

edited by
**John Coakley**

University College Dublin Press
Preas Choláiste Ollscoile
Bhaile Átha Cliath

First published 2002
by University College Dublin Press
Newman House
86 St Stephen's Green
Dublin 2
Ireland

www.ucdpress.ie

ISBN 1–900621–83–5
ISSN 1649–2390

Cataloguing in Publication data
available from the British Library

Typeset in Ireland in Adobe Garamond and Trade Gothic
by Elaine Shiels, Bantry, Co. Cork
Text design by Lyn Davies
Printed in Ireland on acid-free paper by ColourBooks, Dublin

# Contents

# Contributors to this volume

PAUL ARTHUR is Professor of Politics at the University of Ulster. He has published extensively on Northern Ireland politics, and his recent books include *Special relationships: Britain, Ireland and the Northern Ireland problem* (Blackstaff, 2001); *Northern Ireland since 1968* (2nd ed., Blackwell, 1988), with Keith Jeffrey; and *Government and politics of Northern Ireland* (4th ed., Longman, 1994).

JOHN COAKLEY is senior lecturer in politics at University College Dublin and director of the Institute for British–Irish Studies. He has edited *The social origins of nationalist movements* (Sage, 1992); *The territorial management of ethnic conflict* (Frank Cass, 1993); and *Politics in the Republic of Ireland* (with Michael Gallagher, 3rd ed., Routledge, 1999).

RICHARD ENGLISH is Professor of Politics at Queen's University, Belfast. His books include *Ernie O'Malley: IRA intellectual* (Oxford University Press, 1998) and (with Graham Walker) *Unionism in modern Ireland: new perspectives on politics and culture* (Macmillan, 1996).

DAVID ERVINE, MLA, is leader of the Progressive Unionist Party in the Northern Ireland Assembly and a former member of the Northern Ireland Forum for Political Dialogue (1996–8). He was elected to Belfast City Council in 1997, and has been active in loyalist politics since the 1970s.

TOM GARVIN is Professor and Head of the Department of Politics at University College Dublin. He has published extensively on Irish politics, and is author of *The evolution of Irish nationalist politics* (Gill & Macmillan, 1981), *Nationalist revolutionaries in Ireland 1858–1928* (Clarendon, 1987) and *1922: the birth of Irish democracy* (Gill & Macmillan, 1996).

JAMES W. MCAULEY is Professor of Political Sociology and Irish Studies in the Department of Sociology and Psychology at the University of Huddersfield. He has published extensively on the theme of loyalist politics, and is the author of *The politics of identity: a loyalist community in Belfast* (Avebury, 1994).

MITCHEL MCLAUGHLIN, MLA, has been a member of the Northern Ireland Assembly since 1998. He was a member of the Sinn Féin talks team at Castle Buildings in 1997–8 and served on Derry City Council from 1985 to 1999. He is National Chairman of Sinn Féin.

ALBAN MAGINNESS, MLA, has been a member of the Northern Ireland Assembly since 1998. He was elected to Belfast City Council in 1985, and served as Lord Mayor in 1997–8. He was chairman of the SDLP, 1985–91, a member of the SDLP delegation at the Brooke and Mayhew talks (1991), of the Dublin Forum for Peace and Reconciliation (1994–5) and of the Northern Ireland Forum for Political Dialogue (1996).

DERMOT NESBITT, MLA, has been a member of the Northern Ireland Assembly since 1998 and is Junior Minister at the Office of the First Minister and Deputy First Minister. A university lecturer by profession, he was a member of the Northern Ireland Forum for Political Dialogue and of the Ulster Unionist talks team at Castle Buildings in 1996–8.

DESMOND O'MALLEY was a Dáil deputy from 1968 to 2002. He served as Minister for Justice and as Minister for Industry and Commerce in Fianna Fáil governments, but was expelled from the party in 1985 for condemning party policy on family planning. He established a new party, the Progressive Democrats, in 1985, and was party leader until 1993.

JENNIFER TODD lectures in politics at University College Dublin. She has published extensively on Northern Ireland politics and on comparative ethnic conflict, and her recent books include *The dynamics of conflict in Northern Ireland: power, conflict and emancipation* (co-author; Cambridge University Press, 1996); and *After the Good Friday Agreement: analysing political change in Northern Ireland* (co-editor, UCD Press, 1999).

# Foreword

The warm welcome and, indeed, deep sense of relief with which the Northern Ireland peace process and the 1998 agreement were greeted pervaded all sections of Irish society. For the university sector, as for others, these developments raised new opportunities for the creation of a better life for all, but they also created new challenges. For political leaders, the challenge was one of implementing and consolidating the agreement. The universities, of course, have played their own role, both directly and indirectly, in this task; but they also have an additional responsibility. The factors that led to the agreement, and the dynamics associated with it, need to be analysed in a reflective and detached manner. This analysis, in turn, needs to be informed by active contact with those most centrally involved in the process of political change.

For these reasons, the Conference of University Rectors in Ireland (CRI) took an important initiative in conjunction with UCD's Institute for British–Irish Studies: the launch of a lecture series on the theme 'Redefining the union and the nation'. A set of well-received public lectures took place during the year 2000, and it is on these that the present book is substantially based. The lecture series, like this book, had a double aim: to offer a wide-ranging analysis of change in the perspectives of Ireland's major political traditions, and to ensure interaction between the world of politics and the public sector, on the one hand, and the world of the university and academic research on the other.

It is therefore a pleasure to welcome the appearance of this book, an important contribution to our understanding of the major shifts in thinking that have permitted a political settlement to this island's problems. It is also refreshing to note that with this volume the publishers, UCD Press, are launching a new series entitled Perspectives in British–Irish Studies. Indeed, it is singularly appropriate that this university be associated with such a series, given the central role that it has played in the definition of the British–Irish relationship through the extensive involvement in political life of its staff and former students.

It is to be hoped that in the years to come we shall see this series develop, and that it will add to the growing corpus of works that analyse a problem that was once seen as intractable.

ART COSGROVE
*President, University College Dublin*
*Chair, Conference of University Rectors in Ireland (2001)*

# Preface

Since a complex settlement designed to resolve Ireland's long-running political conflict was hammered out in 1998, the new institutions set up under its provisions have rarely been out of the limelight. The political face of Northern Ireland has been transformed, but the permanence of this transformation has been regularly questioned. The word 'crisis' has frequently, and justifiably, been invoked to describe the latest events. Whatever the future may hold for the new institutions, the very fact that they were created in the first place bears eloquent testimony to the new flexibility that was a characteristic of the major political traditions as the twentieth century drew to a close.

Largely with a view to providing a forum through which academics, policy makers and opinion formers could jointly analyse issues of this kind, the Institute for British–Irish Studies was established in University College Dublin in 1999. It joined forces the following year with the Conference of University Rectors in Ireland – itself a new expression of shared North–South interests – to sponsor a series of public lectures that addressed the nature of the remarkable changes that had been taking place in the political traditions of the island. The present book arises from that lecture series, and seeks to provide a more permanent record of the conclusions to which speakers came. The revised texts of the lectures have been supplemented by an introduction, a conclusion and an appendix that reproduces extracts from significant documents.

As always in the case of volumes of this kind, some very considerable debts have been accumulated. Thanks are due in the first instance to the Conference of University Rectors in Ireland, whose project director, Francis McGeogh, played a leading role in the launch of the lecture series, and whose successive chairs, Dr Séamus Smyth (President, National University of Ireland, Maynooth) and Dr Art Cosgrove (President, University College Dublin) provided important moral and practical support. Thanks are also due to four other UCD colleagues who chaired sessions in the course of the lecture series: Dr Caroline Hussey, Registrar, and Professors Ronan Fanning, Brigid Laffan and Stephen Mennell. A particular debt of gratitude is owed to those whose work caused the lecture series to run smoothly or who have contributed in other ways to the preparation of this book: to Carmel Coyle, who was responsible for getting the series off the ground; to Karen Lang, who provided invaluable administrative support; and to Jean Brennan, Kevin Howard, Michael Kennedy, Claire Mitchell, Brid Reason and Anna Visser. Finally, a word of thanks is due to Barbara Mennell of UCD Press for the care with which she piloted this book through its production stage and, in particular, to the authors for their patience in putting up with editorial queries and for their commitment in taking time out of busy schedules to work on the contributions now presented here.

JOHN COAKLEY

*Director, Institute for British–Irish Studies, University College Dublin*

*September 2002*

**Chapter 1**

# Constitutional innovation and political change in twentieth-century Ireland

John Coakley

## Introduction

On the morning after a conclusion was reached in the final 36-hour talks marathon in Belfast that resulted in the Good Friday Agreement, *The Irish Times*, in a front-page editorial bearing the historically evocative title 'Easter 1998', paid tribute to 'the peacemakers who buried the quarrel of 400 years inside the grey, prefabricated huts of the Castle Buildings at Stormont'. It reminded its readers that

> The two great traditions of this island have each yielded on the absolutism of their positions. Nationalists have had to swallow the bitter truth that there will be no united Ireland in the foreseeable future and that if it comes, it will only do so with the consent of Northern Ireland's majority. Unionists have had to accept, in the new cross-border structures, that Northern Ireland is not as British as Finchley, as Mrs Thatcher once put it. And the people of this State will be asked to relinquish the territorial claim to Irish unity which lies at the heart of their political culture and which has been enshrined since 1937 within Articles 2 and 3 of the Constitution (*The Irish Times*, 11 April 1998).

Although this newspaper, like others, warned that the agreement itself was only the beginning of what would be a demanding process, an unprecedented atmosphere of political euphoria developed in the days that followed. The range of areas covered by the agreement and the span of political perspectives that assented to it were truly remarkable. The agreement extended not only over constitutional issues of extraordinary sensitivity and complex institutional provisions for the future government of Northern Ireland, for North–South cooperation and for East–West relations; it also elaborated fundamental principles in the areas of human rights, policing, criminal justice and equality, and made specific transitional provisions in the areas of decommissioning of weapons, demilitarisation, release of prisoners and reconciliation of victims of violence. The parties to the agreement included not just the leaders of the main constitutional nationalist and unionist parties and the parties of the centre; also present were the leaders of the main loyalist and republican movements that had paramilitary wings; the Irish and British prime ministers had staked their personal reputations on a settlement, and worked tirelessly in the negotiations; and the President of the United States made extended interventions by telephone, as well as having given concrete long-term support to the process.

The agreement was the culmination of several years of complex and sensitive discussions on matters of principle, and it was to usher in several years of difficult and delicate negotiations on the details of implementation. Its profound domestic importance and its considerable international significance have deservedly attracted a great deal of attention from academics, journalists and others, and it is worth setting the present book in the context of this broader body of literature. Thoughtful and wide-ranging analyses of the general background to the problem that the agreement sought to resolve – the character of the political system of Northern Ireland in its domestic and its wider geopolitical settings – are readily available (see Whyte, 1990; McGarry and O'Leary, 1995; Ruane and Todd, 1996). So, too, are more specific discussions of the Northern Ireland political background (Bew, Gibbon and Patterson, 1996; Aughey and Morrow, 1996; Mitchell and Wilford, 1998), as are detailed chronologies (Bew and Gillespie, 1999; CAIN, 2002a) and sources of general reference material on the Northern Ireland problem (Elliott and Flackes, 1999; CAIN 2002b). The peace process itself has predictably received a great deal of attention. Some early works examine this as it unfolded before the agreement (Gilligan and Tonge, 1997; Mallie and McKittrick, 1997); others have had a chance to consider not only the peace process and the agreement itself, but also issues of implementation (Ruane and Todd, 1999; Cox, Guelke and Stephen, 2000; Hennessey, 2000; de Bréadún, 2001; Wilford, 2001).[1] The agreement has also been set in the broader historical context of relations between North and South and between Ireland and Great Britain (Arthur, 2000), and it has been examined in a comparative perspective (McGarry, 2001). More specific accounts of the functioning of the institutions set up under the agreement are also available (Wilson, 2001), as are monitoring reports that examine developments in Northern Ireland in the context of devolution within the United Kingdom (Wilford and Wilson, 2000; Wilson and Wilford, 2001; Constitution Unit, 2002).

The aim of the present volume is to supplement this already rich literature by focusing on a cross-cutting theme, that of a type of ideological shift that has formed the backdrop to the institutional transformation of politics in Ireland, North and South. Perceptive studies of change within particular political traditions have, of course, appeared (for example, Cochrane, 1997, on unionism and Todd, 1999, on republicanism and nationalism), but there is a case for a more systematic effort to juxtapose analyses of changes in each of the major traditions with a view to facilitating comparison and examining the interplay between them in the context of evolving political compromise and agreement.

The object of this book is, then, to examine this domain of ideas – the changing character of the main political traditions in Ireland at the end of the twentieth century. This introductory chapter seeks to describe the institutional context of this pattern of change. The scene may be set, as in the case of theatre in its narrower sense, by considering three features: the stage, the actors and the content of the drama. Placing political bones on this metaphor, we need to consider the constitutional setting within which political interaction has been taking place, the background of the principal political players, and the outworking of the vivid piece of political theatre in which they have been engaged in recent years.

## The constitutional context

The first and most general feature that has formed the backdrop to ideological change has been the evolving constitutional and institutional nature of the United Kingdom and of its Irish offspring. First, the character of the United Kingdom changed steadily in the twentieth century, as provisions for the government of Great Britain and of its neighbouring island were overhauled and its relationship with its former colonies was redefined. Second, the creation of a new Irish state – though this was caught initially in a geopolitical dilemma between the pursuit of independence from Great Britain and of domination over Northern Ireland – proved to be a valuable contribution to the longer-term stability of these islands, as the Republic's relations with both London and Belfast were normalised. Third, the appearance of an autonomous political system in Belfast raised the prospect of a thoroughgoing hibernicisation of Britain's old Irish question, but the ethnic dynamics of Northern Ireland prevented this outcome, and indeed created the very circumstances that led to the Good Friday Agreement. Let us consider these features in turn.

### The British–Irish union and its aftermath
While the British–Irish union of 1800 may have represented the culmination of several centuries of domination by the larger island over the smaller, it is striking that western Europe's most effective imperial power was its least successful state builder. At the same time as much of the globe was being painted red, the United Kingdom's own back yard was reverting to green.

The secession of the Irish Free State in 1922 was much more traumatic for the parent kingdom than the secession of Norway from Sweden in 1905 (the only comparable case in twentieth-century western Europe before Iceland seceded from Denmark in 1944). Ireland's relationship with Great Britain extended over a much longer period (centuries rather then decades), its level of economic, social and cultural dependence was much higher (not qualified by influence from another power, as in the case of long-standing Danish rather than Swedish cultural influence in Norway), and its strategic importance for Great Britain was incomparably greater (not just because of its geographical position, but because of the far-reaching consequences for the empire of being seen to allow the Irish to tweak the tail of the British lion). By any standards, then, the establishment of the Irish Free State in 1922 was a remarkable political achievement for those who brought it about and a profound reversal for those who resisted it.

As the British Empire became transmuted into the British Commonwealth, it was a sensible strategy to disguise the blow to the heart of the empire that Irish secession represented by emphasising the 'different' character of the Irish Free State. The member of the Commonwealth that was most intimately linked by geography and history to the mother country became the Commonwealth's errant child, and was so indulged by its parent. In breach of Commonwealth norms, its first governor-general was not a British nobleman but a native commoner. Its second governor-general was forced to resign ignominiously in 1932 in a politically calculated manoeuvre, linked to a drive in Dublin for further independence. Its third governor-general, his occupation as a Maynooth shopkeeper horrifying to the British establishment, saw his power whittled away and his office eventually abolished in 1936. These changes corresponded to a steady loosening of the bonds of the Commonwealth, but the Irish Free State strayed much further from the centre than its other members. Its new constitution in 1937 invoked the authority of the people (rather than the will of king and parliament) as its source of legitimacy, renamed the state 'Ireland' and endowed itself with a directly elected president for domestic purposes. Finally, in 1949 the president became in effect head of state, as the king's role as formal head of the Irish executive – carefully disguised in article 29.4 of the new constitution – ended, and Ireland departed from the Commonwealth.

Managing the relationship with Ireland was a continuing concern of successive British governments. During the early years of the Irish Free State, conventional Commonwealth structures were relied upon, but with the advent of a more independent-minded Fianna Fáil government in 1932 particular attention had to be paid to the issue. One response was the creation in 1932 of a cabinet Irish Situation Committee, which monitored a range of bilateral contacts with Dublin. Although these failed to prevent the adoption of a quasi-republican constitution in 1937, a considerable rapprochement was attained in the Anglo-Irish agreements of 1938, under which Britain ceded military facilities at the 'treaty ports', favourable trade conditions and an end to conflict over land annuities, in return for good relations (McMahon, 1984: 237–84). But the improved political atmosphere was not sufficient to persuade Ireland to enter the war on Britain's side in 1939, nor to stay in the Commonwealth ten years later; and these two episodes – Ireland's wartime neutrality and departure from the Commonwealth in 1949 – caused a dark cloud to spread over the British–Irish relationship.

One consequence of the more fraught relationship between the British and the South was a warmer British relationship with the North. The initial difference in status between the two new Irish regimes was symbolised in the fact that the Irish Free State was the responsibility of the Dominions Office, whereas Northern Ireland came under the oversight of the Home Office. But the latter jurisdiction was exercised with a light touch. It became clear as early as 1922 that Northern Ireland was being allowed the substance of autonomy in devolved matters: under intense pressure from the Unionist government, the Home Office backed down on its decision to withhold the royal assent from a bill abolishing proportional representation in local elections, setting a precedent that was not subsequently breached (Birrell and Murie, 1980: 9). Furthermore, following Ireland's departure from the Commonwealth, the Ireland Act (1949) provided Northern Ireland with its most solemn guarantee to that point of the permanence of its position within the United Kingdom: it was affirmed that 'in no event will Northern Ireland or any part thereof cease to be part of His Majesty's dominions and of the United Kingdom without the consent of the Parliament of Northern Ireland'.

The outbreak of civil unrest in 1968 that was followed quickly by inter-communal clashes and paramilitary violence led, as is well known, to a steady reversal of this 'hands-off' policy. In a number of stages, the British government progressively assumed responsibility for the government of Northern Ireland: through steadily increasing political pressure from November 1968, direct intervention in August 1969, to direct rule in March 1972. Subsequent experiments in devolution (1973–4 and since 1998), in the pursuit of a locally generated settlement through a constitutional convention (1975–6), assembly (1982–6) and forum (1996–8), and in granting a consultative voice to the Irish government (since 1985), have not overridden the constitutional reality that ultimate authority lay, at least until 1998, in Westminster.

Over the same period, British policy in regard to the Republic has changed fundamentally. It is true that the Anglo-Irish free trade agreement of 1965 signalled a further thaw in the British–Irish relationship; but attempts by the Irish government to assert its interest in Northern Ireland were firmly rebuffed by the British after the troubles broke out in 1969 (Fanning, 2001). However, the importance of Dublin's role was quickly recognised and, although British governments varied in their openness to Irish government views, Irish influence grew over the decades. A new era began in 1985 with a formal institution-alisation of the 'Irish dimension' to the problem. It is to be assumed that this also reflected longer-term British interests. There is a fundamental tension between Britain's debt of sentiment and honour to the unionists of Northern Ireland, on the one hand, and the imperative of maintaining good relations with the much larger nationalist population of the island, on the other. While the former have a significant voice at Westminster, this has been declining in relative significance in recent years;[2] but the latter have an independent voice in Europe and internationally, providing a powerful argument for heeding the advice of their leaders. In this context, the pledge of Peter Brooke in November 1990 – its punctuation (the absent comma) as significant as its overt content – that Britain had no 'selfish strategic or economic' interest in Northern Ireland, later underwritten by the Good Friday Agreement, is not implausible: it is Dublin rather than Belfast that is likely to carry more weight in terms of Britain's long-term strategic (and other) self-interest.

The final aspect of the 'British dimension' that we need to note is the set of territorial reforms launched after the new Labour government took office in 1997. Devolution to Scotland and the creation of a Welsh assembly intro-duced a new complexity to the already unconventional system of government of the United Kingdom (whose central administration has traditionally tolerated a wide but uneven measure of autonomy on the part of the authorities in Edinburgh, Cardiff and Belfast, and which has failed to absorb its adjacent crown territories of the Isle of Man, Jersey and Guernsey). These reforms meant, in turn, that Ireland's 'British dimension' would have to be seen in a new light, not just from Belfast but also from Dublin: London would continue to be the overwhelmingly important political focus to the East, but some account would also have to be taken of new repositories of devolved power.[3]

### Irish independence and its consequences

The constitutional view from Dublin has, of course, been rather different from that from London. It was originally intended that the Government of Ireland Act of 1920 would serve as a political framework for all of the island and as the constitution of 'Southern Ireland', the name proposed by the British for the 26-county state on which they intended to confer home rule following partition. This arrangement was superseded by the Anglo-Irish treaty of 1921, which conceded dominion status to the South. The constitution of the new Irish Free State (1922) was thus based on a compromise between Irish nationalists and the British government, and enacted at Westminster. By the end of its life it was a very different document; especially after 1932, it was amended in such a way as to erode the significance of the remaining elements of actual or symbolic British influence.

The new constitution of 1937 represented not just a further stage in the loosening of the links between Ireland and Great Britain; it also sought to redefine the relationship with Northern Ireland. The Government of Ireland Act had introduced new all-Irish institutions (notably, a council of Ireland) and presupposed the continuation of certain all-Irish offices, including those of Lord Lieutenant and Lord Chancellor, as well as of the Irish privy council. But the existing offices were swept away when the South acquired dominion status in 1922, and the provisions for the council of Ireland were dropped by agreement between London, Dublin and Belfast in 1925. Given the enthusiasm that was to be found decades later in the Republic for the idea of a council of this kind, it is worth noting that in 1925 the concept had few friends. During a debate on the issue in the Dáil, leading speakers from the government side (William Cosgrave, Kevin O'Higgins and Desmond FitzGerald) were dismissive of the council; northerner Ernest Blythe described it as 'an artificial method of imposing certain political machinery on the country'; and Richard Mulcahy was the only speaker from the government side to hint at momentary misgivings at its abolition (which he managed to overcome). Expressions of support for the Council of Ireland were few and brief, and were confined to the opposition benches (though these did not, at the time, include the large group led by de Valera, which also substantially ignored the abolition of the council).[4] In the decades that followed, contact between the northern and southern governments was minimal, and was restricted to a few areas, such as hydroelectric power on the Erne and the railway system, where the logic of cooperation was unanswerable (see Kennedy, 2000). This seemed to mirror a pronounced tendency for southern society and its leaders to substantially ignore Northern Ireland, notwithstanding the vehemence of irredentist rhetoric (see O'Halloran, 1987; Fanning, 2001; Kennedy, 2001).

Given this trend, the insertion of an inclusive definition of the 'national territory' in the 1937 constitution was surprising. The relevant articles read:

ARTICLE 2. The national territory consists of the whole island of Ireland, its islands and the territorial seas.

ARTICLE 3. Pending the re-integration of the national territory, and without prejudice to the right of the Parliament and Government established by this Constitution to exercise jurisdiction over the whole of that territory, the laws enacted by that Parliament shall have the like area and extent of application as the laws of Saorstát Éireann [the Irish Free State] and the like extra-territorial effect.

The precise legal significance of these articles is unclear, but the dominant view among constitutional lawyers up to 1990 was that they constituted a political statement that was aspirational in form (see Forde, 1987: 36–7, 50–3; for an alternative perspective, Carty, 1998). A Supreme Court ruling in 1990 offered a much starker interpretation, seeing these articles as a claim of legal right over Northern Ireland (Kelly, 1994: 12–14).

The Good Friday Agreement, however, led to a fundamental change: the substance of articles 2 and 3 was not only removed from the constitution, but an important guarantee to northern unionists was incorporated in it. The wording of the new article 3.1 gives explicit constitutional recognition to the right of Northern Ireland to opt out of a united Ireland, and provides supporters of partition with a powerful weapon by specifying two new constitutional conditions required for unity (explicit consent of majorities on either side of the border): 'a united Ireland shall be brought about only by peaceful means with the consent of a majority of the people, democratically expressed, in both jurisdictions in the island'.

### Northern Irish autonomy and the government of a divided society

Unlike the position in the South, the Government of Ireland Act of 1920 came into effect in Northern Ireland in 1921 and, indeed, constituted its fundamental law for 51 years. As is well known, it provided for majoritarian structures of government for a deeply divided society: governments were formed from parliamentary majorities on the Westminster model. Indeed, the majoritarian tendency of the system was accentuated by change in the electoral system in 1929, when proportional representation was replaced by the British-style plurality system in Stormont elections. At the 12 elections from 1921 to 1969 the Unionist majority in the House of Commons averaged 69.9% of the membership of the house and never fell below 61.5%; the Unionist majority in the Senate was even more decisive; and the Northern Ireland government was entirely dominated by Unionists.[5] But it was precisely in this dominance, in the extent of Unionist control over local government and in Catholic grievances in the areas of employment, housing and policing that the seeds of the downfall of this system lay.

The reality was that Northern Ireland's 'minority problem' was much more acute than that of the South. According to the 1911 census, the area that was to become the Irish Free State had a Protestant minority – overwhelmingly unionist in political orientation – of 10.4%; by 1926, this had dropped to 7.4%, and it had fallen to approximately 3.2% by 1991 (Coakley, 1998: 89). But this has been dubbed a 'silent' minority; it is true that it complained little of its treatment in the new state, and it was certainly never subject to the kind of collective political mobilisation that was so characteristic of its northern counterpart. In Northern Ireland, by contrast, what was a Catholic minority of 34.4% in 1911 remained substantially at this level for the next 50 years. Since then, it has risen steadily, to more than 42% by 1991. But this was not just a demographically potent minority; it was also marked by the heritage of disproportionate socio-economic underprivilege and by a strong tradition of mobilisation behind anti-system parties.

It was, indeed, precisely this mobilisation that was responsible for the collapse of the old regime in 1972, after more than three years of civil unrest. Since then, ultimate power in Northern Ireland has been the responsibility of a new member of the British cabinet, the Secretary of State for Northern Ireland, whose office not only absorbed the powers of the prime minister of Northern Ireland but also extended to the management of the very considerable reserved powers that had never been devolved to the Northern Ireland administration. Ultimate responsibility for security policy has been the most important of these, and this power has remained in the hands of the Secretary of State even during the two periods (in 1973–4, and since 1999) during which a separate Northern Irish executive has existed.

## The political context

The constitutional context sketched in the last section is the outcome of a long-term struggle between particular political actors, or sets of actors. The most obvious of these, as was to be seen clearly in the talks that led up to the agreement and that, indeed, continued on after it, have been the British government, the Irish government and the Northern Irish parties. The role played by the two governments was decisive in the talks process; but for purposes of this book our focus is on the process of ideological reassessment that facilitated compromise rather than on the necessarily constrained bargaining positions of the governments.

The position of the British government was not, of course, a function purely of international commitments and expectations, of long-standing domestic understandings and promises, of bureaucratically imposed guidelines or limits, and of the other restrictions that routinely condition policy initiatives; it also derived from a change in government in the United Kingdom and from a policy shift in the Labour Party. Long-term change in both main British parties indeed constituted an important backdrop for the pursuit of a settlement in Northern Ireland. But this important subject is too large to be given adequate attention in the present volume, forming, as it does, part of the transformation in thinking about the territorial management of the United Kingdom that was also to lead to new political structures in Scotland and Wales.

If we narrow the focus to the dramatic ideological changes on the island of Ireland, we have to consider similarly the diversity of perspectives that is obvious in Northern Ireland but that is sometimes disguised in the Republic by the lower salience of the Northern Ireland issue and, on the government side, the constraints of coalition power sharing. In assessing the policy orientations of these parties, it is useful to group them into two great but far from monolithic political traditions – unionism and nationalism. The resonance of these traditions for the part of Ireland that became independent in 1922 diminished considerably over the decades that followed, as new political realities asserted themselves, making it appropriate to give separate consideration to the evolution of the main political forces in the South. In reviewing developments within these domains, it is important also to seek to measure the extent to which the competing perspectives have enjoyed a popular following, and this issue – electoral support for the major political traditions – is addressed at the end of this section. It should be pointed out that in this context the metaphor of political theatre needs to be carefully defined: the political parties (or actors) may be grouped within particular 'traditions', but the characters they play out are complex – sometimes schizophrenic, and always developing over time.

### Unionism and its variants

In its classical sense, unionism referred to a commitment to maintain the union of 1800 between Ireland and Great Britain. But it was clear already in the nineteenth century that unionism meant much more than this: that its adherents also stood for defence of the traditional values of the British state, including the Protestant monarchy, the empire and the privileges of the ruling class. When the marshalling of the forces of Irish nationalism in the late nineteenth and early twentieth centuries rendered the integral preservation of the union politically unrealistic, Irish unionism underwent a fundamental redefinition. Its northern components embarked on a new project: to maintain as much as possible of Ireland within the United Kingdom, while letting the South go its own way. Ultimately, this meant arguing for a six-county Northern Ireland and leaving southern unionists to fend for themselves, a departure that had been anticipated for some time in the electoral organisation of unionism.[6]

The central concern of the unionist movement – preservation of the union with Great Britain – suffered a double setback in 1921: not only was the South bent on leaving the United Kingdom, but 'home rule' was thrust on the new state of Northern Ireland itself. Although unionists quickly came to see merit in having their own institutions of government in Belfast, this development established an enduring tension, whose significance has waxed and waned over the years, between supporters of complete integration with the United Kingdom and defenders of devolved institutions in Belfast. Though the correspondence is not perfect, this tension may be related to a distinction between two ideological tendencies within unionism, those which have been labelled 'Ulster British' and 'Ulster loyalist' (Todd, 1987). In tracing the evolution of unionism, then, it is useful to look first at the unionist 'mainstream' (which has by and large sought to camouflage the tension between the 'British' and 'loyalist' positions) and then to examine evidence of separate strands:

British-style conservative unionism and a more populist form of Ulster loyalism that frequently finds expression in religious terms.

### *'Mainstream' unionism*

The great *Ulster Unionist Party* of the twentieth century was one Europe's most remarkable electoral phenomena. Its close linkage to the state over half a century invites comparison with other one-party regimes, and it would be unwise to ignore entirely the distinctive features that comparative analysis identifies in intimate party-state relationships of this kind.[7] But the reality is that Ulster unionism's political hegemony arose not from the kind of stage-managed elections that were so characteristic of Communist systems, but from the numerical superiority of the ethnic bloc which constituted its power base, and from its capacity to manage a comprehensive popular mobilisation within this bloc. After the abolition of proportional representation in 1929, it became increasingly difficult for its dominance within this bloc to be challenged. The re-introduction of proportional representation in 1973 had the reverse effect, facilitating significant defections from the party; but it is probable that the end of Northern Ireland's system of devolved government in 1972 (which undermined the imperative of political cohesion in a governing party, since there was none) and the political turmoil of the early 1970s also played a major role in encouraging internal divisions.

Much of the battle for the soul of unionism crystallised into a struggle for control of the Ulster Unionist Party, or, more specifically, of the Ulster Unionist Council (UUC), which since 1905 has acted as an intermediary between the parliamentary group and the unionist electorate (the UUC comprises representatives of local unionist associations and other unionist groups as well as of the Orange Order). Relatively quiescent (predictably enough) during the years of unquestioned Unionist rule, the UUC acquired a new significance in the early 1970s, as opponents of the party leadership sought to use this structure to force a change in direction. Thus, the leadership of Brian Faulkner (1971–4) came to an end when the UUC rejected the Sunningdale compromise, and his successors, Harry West (1974–9) and James Molyneaux (1979–6), sought to implement the new party policy: restoration of devolved government to Northern Ireland without enforced power sharing, and good-neighbourly relations with the Republic rather than an institutionalised Irish dimension.

Of course, there were variations in emphasis within the party in terms of the priority given to particular political objectives, and policy itself evolved steadily. Thus, James Molyneaux was noted for his interest in the British dimension, and regarded fuller integration within the United Kingdom as a potentially valuable guarantee for unionists. But it was also under Molyneaux's leadership that the possible endorsement of power sharing was again raised in the late 1980s. The capacity of the party to compromise on such issues, in return for important gains in other areas, was illustrated most vividly in 1998, when the new party leader, David Trimble negotiated a historic deal with nationalists.

### 'British' conservative unionism

From the very beginning, the Ulster Unionist Party has been deeply imbued by a strand that defines itself, essentially but not explicitly, as British nationalist. Indeed, the party's best-known leader, Sir Edward Carson (1910–21), was one of those to articulate this position most clearly, and it is likely that his immediate successors and their colleagues shared much of this thinking. This is especially likely to have been the case with Northern Ireland's early prime ministers, whose personal class and business interests bound them closely to Great Britain: Sir James Craig (1921–40), John Andrews (1940–3), Sir Basil Brooke (1943–63), Terence O'Neill (1963–9) and James Chichester Clark (1969–71).

The Unionist Party has been a sufficiently broad church to be able to accommodate this strand of opinion in more recent decades, though it is likely that some of the more committed secular 'British nationalists' may have left to support other parties. Some may have found refuge in the *Alliance Party*; although that party has consciously striven to maintain its biconfessional status since its formation in 1970, it did manage to attract a sizeable ex-unionist vote (and, indeed, an ex-nationalist one too). A more notable haemor-rhage took place in 1974 when Brian Faulkner led his supporters out of the party to form the new *Unionist Party of Northern Ireland*; but successive electoral setbacks led to the dissolution of this party in 1981. The *Conservative Party*, which has been contesting elections in Northern Ireland with declining success since 1989, has sought to appeal to a similar constituency. In addition, in 1995 there appeared the strongly integrationist *United Kingdom Unionist Party* (UKUP), led by a prominent former UUP member, Robert McCartney. Most of its assembly members broke away in January 1999 to form the *Northern Ireland Unionist Party*, which shares with its parent party a strong opposition to the Good Friday Agreement.

### Ulster loyalism

Although the term 'loyalist' is now commonly used in contradistinction to 'unionist' to signify a more robust ideology, it may also be seen as yet another strand that has been present from the beginning within the Ulster Unionist Party. It is worth examining this alternative to mainstream unionism in terms of three dimensions: political radicalism, religious fundamentalism and tactical militancy.

Any conservative movement that seeks to mobilise the support of the urban working class is likely also to create a tension within its own ranks between the interests of this class and the main thrust of party policy; and the greater its success in this mobilisation, the more acute this tension is likely to be. Ulster unionism indeed succeeded in enlisting the great bulk of the Protestant working class in support of its cause, and was relatively successful in beating off the appeal of left-wing politics. Although the Northern Ireland Labour Party enjoyed modest success from 1925 onwards in Belfast constituencies, the Protestant working class remained, by and large, loyal to unionism. The creation in 1918 of a labour wing within the Ulster Unionist Party was a significant instrument in maintaining this relationship and in keeping a brake on potential radical threats. There is some evidence of the existence of 'populist'-style opposition within the Unionist Party itself: analysis of division lists from 1921 to 1972 shows a relatively high degree of backbench revolt, with complaints that the government was not doing enough for the socially disadvantaged as a recurring (but not the only) theme (Whyte, 1973).

Although the Protestant character of Ulster unionism was undoubted, and was reflected in the party's close links with the Orange Order, fundamentalist Protestantism constituted a more formidable threat to the party's dominance than political radicalism. This had been articulated at various levels inside and outside the world of politics since the nineteenth century, and received its most concrete expression in 1903 when the breakaway Independent Orange Order parted with the official movement. Although the initial motive for this departure was religious, Independent Orangeism quickly moved to a position of political radicalism, attacking the social conservatism of official unionism (Boyle, 1962). This marriage of Protestantism and radicalism enjoyed limited electoral success before the First World War, but it has been argued that its more open and democratic appearance was largely confined to the character of its leader, Lindsay Crawford (Patterson, 1980). Similar expressions of Protestant radicalism were to be found after the establishment of Northern Ireland, with the upsurge in electoral support for 'Progressive unionism' in 1938 as a significant example (Harbinson, 1973: 219–22). Interestingly, the Independent Orange Order was later revived, with the Rev. Ian Paisley as its most celebrated personality after 1962; and the characteristic linkage between fundamentalism and political radicalism was apparent in Paisley's *Protestant Unionist Party* from 1969, and was even more pronounced after this party was reconstituted as the *Democratic Unionist Party* (DUP) in 1971. Indeed, the DUP was to become the foremost exponent of this distinctive political blend, adding to the mainstream unionist message a suspicion alike of the Vatican and its alleged agents and of mainstream unionism and its privileged leaders.

A disposition to contemplate militant forms of political protest has also been a long-standing characteristic even of mainstream unionism. The creation of the Ulster Volunteer Force (UVF) in 1913 indeed signalled the movement's willingness to engage in violent resistance to home rule. Such reliance on extra-constitutional paramilitary force was unnecessary after 1921, when unionism gained control of the apparatus of the new state of Northern Ireland and of its domestic security forces. But even before the fall of Stormont, loyalist militancy was reborn: a new underground UVF was created in 1966, and a large loyalist paramilitary body, the Ulster Defence Association (UDA), appeared five years later. While these were pro-union forces that identified Northern Ireland's nationalists as the main enemy, they also contained radical political elements that eventually brought much original thinking to bear on the problems of Northern Ireland. This was especially clear in the *Progressive Unionist Party*, the political wing that grew out of the UVF in 1979; but it was also to be seen in the *Ulster Democratic Party*, born out of the UDA in 1989 but winding itself up in an atmosphere of sectarian tension in November 2001.

### Nationalism and its variants

Although divisions on the nationalist side corresponded in important respects with those on the unionist side (for example, in the tendency for diverging priorities on policy and strategy to be translated into party political divisions), there were important differences between the two sides. Bitterly though the divisions between the main unionist parties may be articulated, it is not possible to distinguish unambiguously between them in terms of fundamental policy (integration versus devolution), ideological orientation (conservative versus radical), religious perspective (secular versus fundamentalist) or political strategy (conventional versus militant). One party or other may, of course, be identified with distinctive positions on these dimensions, as the DUP is with Protestant fundamentalism, but neither is defined exclusively in terms of any of these. Although the two main nationalist parties have also always had their own internal ideological divisions, they tend to be distinguished from each other by more consistent policy and strategic priorities. One tradition, commonly labelled constitutional nationalism, has always had a reformist political programme and, apart from deviations around 1914 and 1968, has been strongly wedded to conventional politics. The other, normally labelled republicanism, has had a separatist (and, later, irredentist) political programme and has relied on paramilitary methods as a major strategic resource. Because of the historically relatively underprivileged character of the community from which both of these traditions draw their support, both tend to be left leaning. In the case of constitutional nationalism this was clearest in the late nineteenth and early twentieth centuries, when agrarian reform was on the top of the agenda, but it is striking that the contemporary expression of constitutional nationalism was baptised the Social Democratic and Labour Party in 1970 and that it affiliated to the Socialist International. Flirtation with socialism was for long a characteristic of republicanism, though this was not the only ideology with which the movement was linked in the past; and since the 1970s this relationship seems to have deepened.

*Constitutional nationalism*

The birth of contemporary Irish constitutional nationalism may be dated to the 1880s, though its gestation had lasted for over 50 years. The party of Parnell captured much of Ulster and all of the rest of Ireland in the general election of 1885. Although southern Ireland was later to go its own way, the results of the 1885 election continued to be reproduced in what is now Northern Ireland for a further 80 years. But the old nationalist party, a modern political machine that stood for home rule for all of Ireland, was transformed after 1921 in Northern Ireland into an elite-led movement with little continuous organisation engaged in a long, futile struggle against partition and in defence of the community from which it had sprung (see Phoenix, 1994). Efforts to modernise the party and broaden its appeal were relatively unsuccessful, and it was to perish after 1969; a new, radically different party, the *Social Democratic and Labour Party* (SDLP), arose out of its ashes (Lynn, 1997: 210–22; Staunton, 2001: 255–77). The SDLP not only managed to create and sustain the structure of a modern party; it also redefined the constitutional nationalist agenda. No longer was the ending of partition to be seen as a panacea, though Irish unity remained a formal objective; the party formulated policies covering the whole gamut of public policy, and quickly adopted a distinctive dual policy on the future of Northern Ireland (McAllister, 1977: 55–9). This represented a significant softening of the traditional nationalist line, emphasising the need for any future Northern Ireland administration to be based on the principle of power sharing, and the imperative that the 'Irish dimension' to the problem be given institutional recognition in formal North–South political structures. Under the influence of the party's leading thinker and strategist, John Hume (who took over as party leader following the resignation of the SDLP's founding leader, Gerry Fitt, in 1979), the party developed a more complex and subtle interpretation of the problem, setting it in a broader geopolitical context (Murray, 1998: 209–39).

*Militant republicanism*

Modern Irish republicanism has been most persistently identified with Sinn Féin, and it is worth using the development of this movement as a framework for describing the evolution of republicanism. Part of the story is deferred until later, since offshoots of Sinn Féin were to make up the core of the party system in the South, but historically the movement may be seen as having proceeded through a number of phases. One influential article suggested that by the late 1920s no fewer than four separate Sinn Féins had appeared in succession, each differentiated from the others in terms of leadership, membership, aims, and means of attaining these; reflecting policy differences, they have been labelled respectively monarchical, nationalist, republican, and extremist or fundamentalist (Pyne, 1969). From the perspective of the early twenty-first century, it is necessary to note that this process has continued: even before 1970, when the party split again, Sinn Féin had already changed character to such an extent that it might have been termed a 'new' party, and after it shed its nationalist militants in that year it might indeed be labelled the fifth Sinn Féin; while the secessionists of 1970 merit the label 'sixth' Sinn Féin (indeed, an additional 'seventh' Sinn Féin may also be identified). For clarity, these developments may be categorised schematically.

*The first Sinn Féin*, 1905–17, was a small party founded by the nationalist journalist Arthur Griffith, and consisted of a coalition of political views, with Griffith's own 'dual monarchist' stance and abstentionist policy as its most characteristic positions (Davis, 1974).

*The second Sinn Féin*, 1917–22, was dramatically successful electorally, winning decisive majorities in parliamentary elections in 1918 and 1921 (Eamon de Valera, senior surviving commandant of the 1916 rising, replaced Griffith as president in 1917); the policy orientation of the party was more distinctly republican and pro-force, but retained sufficient ambiguity to continue to attract 'dual monarchists' (Laffan, 1999).

*The third Sinn Féin*, 1922–6, comprised those who rejected the treaty of 1921 but was defeated in the elections of 1922 and 1923; still led by de Valera, its objective was the 're-establishment' of the Republic declared in 1919 (Pyne, 1969).

*The fourth Sinn Féin*, 1926–70, comprised the remnants of the party, following the withdrawal of de Valera and his supporters in 1926 to create Fianna Fáil, and was electorally marginal.

*The fifth ('Official') Sinn Féin*, since 1970, was led by left-leaning activists, headed by Tomás Mac Giolla, who steered the party in a socialist and increasingly anti-nationalist direction; it suffered a further split in 1974, following which the *Irish Republican Socialist Party* (IRSP) was founded; it renamed itself *Sinn Féin The Workers' Party* in 1977, and simply the *Workers' Party* in 1982; and in 1992 most of its parliamentary wing broke away to form *Democratic Left*, whose members joined the Irish Labour Party in 1999.

*The sixth ('Provisional') Sinn Féin*, since 1970, comprised those who withdrew from the 'official' party in January 1970 under the leadership of Ruairí Ó Brádaigh (replaced in 1983 by Gerry Adams, in a move that reflected increasing northern influence) and went on to become the main challenger to the SDLP for the nationalist vote in Northern Ireland and to establish a growing electoral presence in the South.

*The seventh, 'Republican', Sinn Féin,* since 1986, was set up by a funda-mentalist group led by Ruairi Ó Brádaigh that broke with the parent party as it moved towards more pragmatic policies; rather than joining this group, those who broke with the party as Sinn Féin became involved in all-party talks set up a separate *Thirty Two County Sovereignty Committee* in 1997.[8]

Just as the SDLP sought to bridge the gap between formal commitment to Irish unity and a policy of de facto reform of the Northern Ireland state, so too did (the sixth) Sinn Féin try to straddle the gap between left and right, between a 'new Ireland' and an unambiguously united Ireland, and between parliamentary and militaristic methods. Indeed, the history of the overt political movement is only part of the story of Irish republicanism. Its paramilitary dimension may be traced back to 1858, the year in which the Irish Republican Brotherhood (IRB) was founded (Ó Broin, 1976). The IRB's military history was unimpressive before 1916, though it infiltrated several nationalist organi-sations. One of these was the Irish Volunteers, founded in 1914, a section of which spearheaded the 1916 rising and had become known as the Irish Republican Army (IRA) by the truce of 1921. The IRA subsequently under-went divisions parallel to those in Sinn Féin, notably in 1922 and 1970. The Official IRA (as the main organisation was known after 1970) divided again in 1974, when the Irish National Liberation Army (INLA) broke away along with the IRSP; and the secessions from the *Provisional IRA* in 1986 and 1997 are believed to have been associated respectively with the creation of the *Continuity IRA* and the *Real IRA*.[9] Indeed, there were important respects in which the IRA 'tail' wagged the Sinn Féin 'dog'; there is evidence that signifi-cant ideological shifts in Sinn Féin have been preceded – and sanctioned in advance – by fundamental policy re-orientation within the IRA army council.

### Party politics in the Republic of Ireland
The struggles within nationalism that have just been discussed took place within the context of the island of Ireland, but the strands that have been identified are represented in most characteristic form in Northern Ireland, where they account for the significant political forces within the nationalist community. There are three principal respects in which politics in the South departs from this pattern. First, at least in a narrow genealogical sense, the constitutional nationalist tradition perished in the South after 1918, leaving Sinn Féin to dominate the electoral marketplace. Second, there is an important sense in which the core of the new party system of the South consisted essen-tially of offshoots of Sinn Féin that had 'gone constitutional'. Third, however, the electoral supremacy of the post-Sinn Féin parties was not altogether complete: it left space for the appearance of other parties emphasising alternative dimensions of political activism.

When the second Sinn Féin broke up in 1922, a majority of its parliamentary party went on to form the first government of the Irish Free State. Although the civil war of 1922–3 had elements of a conflict between democratic supporters of the treaty and fundamentalist opponents, it could also be seen, at least at the level of the leaders on the two sides, as a power struggle between pragmatists and ideologues (Garvin, 1996: 139–57). Although being realistic and winning elections do not of themselves turn victors into democrats, it seems that by the end of the civil war the pro-treaty side was well down the road towards wholehearted support for conventional politics, and the fact that the constitution of the new state was largely its own creation (though subject to the terms of the 1921 treaty) also helped it to become a 'constitutional' party. Reorganised as Cumann na nGaedheal in 1923, it left office following its defeat at the 1932 election and the next year merged with two smaller groups, the National Centre Party and the National Guard (Blueshirts), to form Fine Gael.

The path towards constitutional politics was necessarily slower on the anti-treaty side. The first decisive step was de Valera's break with Sinn Féin in 1926 and the foundation of Fianna Fáil; the second was Fianna Fáil's decision to take its seats in the Dáil in 1927, thus affording de facto recognition to the institutions of the state; and the third was the party's capture of these institutions, when it became the governing party after the 1932 election. The transfer of power in 1932, incidentally, symbolised not only Fianna Fáil's increasingly unreserved identification with the state but also Cumann na nGaedheal's full acceptance of constitutional principles (its surrender of power to its electorally victorious opponents was not seen at the time as a foregone conclusion; see Regan, 1999: 279–304). Both of the major parties that grew out of the second Sinn Féin suffered occasionally from minor and ephemeral secessions by disillusioned supporters, but one major division overshadowed the others. This occurred in 1985, when Desmond O'Malley was expelled from Fianna Fáil and went on to form the Progressive Democrats.

But focusing on parties descended from Sinn Féin will tell us only part of the story of electoral politics in the South. Other interests periodically mounted strong challenges to the domination of the system by the two major parties: agrarian movements in the 1920s (the Farmers' Party) and the 1940s (Clann na Talmhan), independent republicans in the 1940s (Clann na Poblachta) and the Green Party in the 1990s. But the most consistent third force has always been the Labour Party, which since 1922 has completed the picture of an essentially triangular party system. It is worth considering briefly the characteristics of the four most important of these parties.

*Fianna Fáil*

The party's full name (the expression 'the republican party' was added as a subtitle) points to its historical concern with the 'national question' – with establishing full Irish independence and unity with Northern Ireland. These concerns were articulated most consistently by the party's first leader, Eamon de Valera (1926–59), though it has been suggested that he regarded unity as 'inevitable but postponable', and that like many southern nationalists he saw it as a long-term aspiration rather than an urgent goal (Bowman, 1982: 305–15). The two leaders who followed, Sean Lemass (1959–66) and Jack Lynch (1966–79) have been credited with guiding the party in a less nationalist direction, focusing more on domestic economic and social problems and offering de facto recognition to partition. Although the rhetoric of their successor, Charles Haughey (1979–92) had a more nationalist tone, he continued substantially the same policies; and his successors, Albert Reynolds (1992–4) and Bertie Ahern (since 1994) presided over a fundamental shift in official policy on Northern Ireland, one that was a prerequisite to the Good Friday Agreement.

*Fine Gael*

Like its main rival, this party's original subtitle ('the United Ireland Party') pointed in the direction of its policy on the national question. In its early years, indeed, the party was more commonly known by its subtitle (the UIP). But its policy on unity was traditionally less insistent than that of Fianna Fáil and, until 1948, it envisaged this as being brought about within a Commonwealth context. Early leaders of the party, including William T. Cosgrave (1935–44; leader of Cumann na nGaedheal, 1923–33) and Richard Mulcahy (1944–59) were themselves veterans of the independence movement, and subscribed to broad nationalist objectives, though giving little priority to Northern Ireland. The next leader, James Dillon (1959–65), was more strongly associated with the traditional constitutional nationalism of the old Nationalist Party, and his successor, Liam Cosgrave (1965–77), belonged to a new generation; for both, the problems of the Republic took priority over those of the North. The position shifted under Garret FitzGerald (1977–87), who had a committed and well-informed interest in the affairs of Northern Ireland, prompted both by personal inclination and by the need to find a solution in a context of deteriorating political circumstances (FitzGerald, 1991: 11–12). The party was in opposition for most of the term of his successors Alan Dukes (1987–90), John Bruton (1990–2001) and Michael Noonan (2001–2), but John Bruton played a significant role as Taoiseach in the period immediately after the 1994 ceasefires (when he attracted both praise and criticism for his capacity to empathise with the unionist position).

### The Labour Party

Although the Labour Party had always presented itself as providing an alternative to the sterility of post-civil war politics and was more concerned with economic and social issues than with constitutional ones, it could not avoid the question of Northern Ireland. In its early years it sought to sidestep the issue, though typically adopting a relatively nationalist position. When Irish unity was written into the party's statement of aims in 1930, it was emphasised that this should be 'by mutual agreement', and that Northern Ireland should be allowed autonomy. The party entered a more nationalist phase under its long-term leader William Norton (1932–60), whose position on the issue was not greatly different from that of Fianna Fáil. The party constitution was amended in 1934 to call for the establishment of a 32-county 'workers' republic'; although reference to the workers' republic was dropped subsequently, the emphasis on unity remained. Under the leadership of Brendan Corish (1960–77) party policy shifted fundamentally. This was less a consequence of change on Corish's part than of the entry of new personalities to the party and a reconsideration of traditional policy in the light of developments in Northern Ireland. Especially under the influence of Conor Cruise O'Brien in the early 1970s, the party became more open to unionist perspectives and less committed to the nationalist position (Gallagher 1982: 124–53).[10] Later leaders, Frank Cluskey (1977–81), Michael O'Leary (1981–2), Dick Spring (1982–97) and Ruairi Quinn (since 1997) followed broadly the same path. Spring's term of office coincided with major developments in the peace process, and his role as foreign minister in 1993–7 placed him in a crucial position in relation to Northern Ireland policy in this formative period.

### The Progressive Democrats

Though the party's origins lay largely in disagreement over the nature of the Fianna Fáil leadership (the party's founding leader, Desmond O'Malley, was a long-term critic of Charles Haughey, and so were many of the party's early activists), the Progressive Democrats also represented a new ideological departure (Lyne, 1987). They articulated much more clearly than any other party a set of new principles similar to those of southern European liberalism: a suspicion alike of church interference in civil matters and of state intervention in the economy. The party was also explicitly committed to unity only by consent, and emphasised the need for the Republic to put its own house in order rather than interfering in Northern Ireland affairs. This more restrained policy has been continued by the party's second leader, Mary Harney (since 1993); but since the party has been in government almost continuously since 1989 as a junior coalition partner it has had a significant influence on the formulation of Northern Ireland policy.

## The electoral balance sheet

The political traditions and parties that have been described above are, of course, of unequal importance. It is necessary now to look at their relative weight as players on Ireland's political stage. Historically, the position has been exceptionally straightforward in Northern Ireland, where two parties have entirely overshadowed all others. The dominance of these parties over the period 1921–69 is illustrated in table 1.1.

Table 1.1 **Average support for main parties in Northern Ireland by period, 1921–98**

| Party | 1921–69 | 1973–82 | 1996–8 |
|---|---|---|---|
| Ulster Unionist Party | 69.6 | 28.3 | 22.8 |
| Democratic Unionist Party | — | 16.2 | 19.7 |
| Other unionists | 3.4 | 16.5 | 9.2 |
| | | | |
| Nationalist Party / SDLP | 15.7 | 21.5 | 20.4 |
| Sinn Féin | 1.0 | 3.4 | 16.6 |
| Other nationalists | 3.9 | 2.7 | 0.0 |
| | | | |
| Other | 6.4 | 11.4 | 11.4 |
| | | | |
| Total | 100.0 | 100.0 | 100.0 |

Note: the first column refers to the distribution of seats in 12 elections to the House of Commons of Northern Ireland; the second to the first preference votes in three elections (to the Assemblies of 1973 and 1982 and the Convention of 1975); and the third to the party list vote in the election to the Forum (1996) and to the first preference vote in the election to the Assembly (1998). 'Nationalist Party / SDLP' refers to the Nationalist Party to 1969 and to the SDLP since then. The most important 'other' parties, with average support over the whole of the period in question, are: first period: Northern Ireland Labour Party (3.4%); second and third periods, Alliance Party (9.4% and 6.5% respectively). The largest 'other unionist' party in the second period was the Vanguard Unionist Progressive Party (1973–5, 7.7% on average for the whole period).

Sources: calculated from Walker, 1992; Elliott, 1997, 1999.

During this period, the Unionist Party won almost 70% of all seats in the Northern Ireland House of Commons, leaving the Nationalist Party in control of most of the remainder. Indeed, this pattern can be projected back to the late nineteenth century: in the nine elections from 1885 to 1918, the Unionist Party won 70% of all seats in the present territory of Northern Ireland, to the Nationalists' 26%. More recently, though, this pattern has been decisively broken. On the unionist side, the UUP was challenged from two directions, with the rise of the DUP and of the Alliance party. By 1975 the party itself had split: opponents of power sharing (including, it is interesting to note, David Trimble and Reg Empey) had followed William Craig into the

Vanguard Unionist Progressive Party in 1973, while supporters of the ousted Brian Faulkner (including many of the former UUP elite) followed him in 1974 into the Unionist Party of Northern Ireland (UPNI). In the 1975 convention elections, then, the pro-union vote was divided between five significant parties. By the early 1980s, though, the pattern of the early 1970s had reasserted itself: the UUP, now rather weaker, was wedged between the DUP on one side and the Alliance Party on the other, VUPP and UPNI having disappeared. On the nationalist side, politics followed a rather different pattern, one of electoral consolidation rather than fragmentation. It is true that the SDLP, like the UUP, had to compete with the Alliance Party in the narrow terrain of the centre, but its main challenger was the new-style Sinn Féin movement that emerged in the wake of the hunger strikes of 1981. Since then, the SDLP–Sinn Féin contest for the nationalist vote has mirrored that of the UUP and the DUP on the unionist side.

*Table 1.2* **Average first preference vote for main parties in Republic of Ireland by period, 1922–2002**

| Party | 1922–69 | 1973–82 | 1987–2002 |
|---|---|---|---|
| Fianna Fáil | 41.7 | 46.9 | 41.7 |
| Fine Gael | 30.9 | 35.7 | 26.2 |
| Labour Party | 11.6 | 10.7 | 11.3 |
| Progressive Democrats | — | — | 6.1 |
| Sinn Féin | 0.7 | 0.7 | 2.7 |
| Other | 15.0 | 5.9 | 12.0 |
| Total | 100.0 | 100.0 | 100.0 |

*Note*: the first column covers 17 elections to Dáil Eireann; the second, five; and the third, five. 'Fianna Fáil' includes the Anti-Treaty Sinn Féin vote in 1922. 'Fine Gael' includes the Pro-Treaty Sinn Féin vote in 1922 and Cumann na nGaedheal from 1923 to 1933. Sinn Féin support in the first period refers only to the elections of June 1927, 1954, 1957 and 1961; in the second period it includes support for the National H-Block Committee in 1981 and for Sinn Féin in February 1982. The most important 'other' parties, with average support over the whole of the period in question, are: first period: the Farmers' Party (1922–32, 2.8%), Clann na Talmhan (1943–61, 2.3%) and Clann na Poblachta (1948–65, 1.5%); second period: 'Official' Sinn Féin and Sinn Féin The Workers' Party (2.3%); third period, Workers' Party (2.0%), Green Party (1.9%) and Democratic Left (1992–7, 1.0%).

*Source*: calculated from Coakley and Gallagher, 1999: 367; *The Irish Times*, 20 May 2002.

In the South, the party system that appeared in 1922 proved to be remarkably stable, though it showed a striking break with the pattern of pre-1922 politics (nationalists of various hues had won 96% of all seats in the eight elections of the 1885–1910 period; in 1918–21, Sinn Féin won 96%). Fianna Fáil's dominance and Fine Gael's position as second party have been confirmed at all elections since 1932, leaving the Labour Party to fight for third place. From 1932 to 2002 the share of the vote won by these parties has been remarkably stable, with Fianna Fáil on an average of 45.3%, Fine Gael on 30.1% and Labour on 11.0%. The rise of the Progressive Democrats in the 1980s put a dent – albeit a small one – on this pattern; and the extent to which Sinn Féin's recent growth will pose a challenge to the existing party system is as yet unclear. It should be noted that in this table, as in table 1.1, the technique of averaging support across a range of elections necessarily understates the strength at particular elections of smaller parties, which might have peaked at certain elections at a level well above their average for the period.

## The dimensions of change

The final step in exploring the background to the shifts in orientation of the major political traditions on the island of Ireland requires us to consider the immediate political background: the various sets of political circumstance that both gave momentum to attitudinal change and were influenced by it. The first and most obvious of these is the pursuit of a new constitutional dispensation for Northern Ireland following the collapse of the old institutions of government in 1972. The second is the set of ceasefires in autumn 1994 that ushered in an unprecedented atmosphere of peace and which was associated with a shift in direction by the major paramilitary groups and a more inclusive approach to negotiation, leading ultimately to the Good Friday Agreement. Finally, the consolidation of this process as the agreement has settled down provided an impetus for further change.

### Political vacuum in Northern Ireland, 1972–94

When a period of more than 50 years of self-government for Northern Ireland ended in 1972, the search began for new institutions to replace those that had been suspended. It quickly became clear that British policy had embraced two principles close to the heart of the SDLP: that any new system of government must be based on inter-bloc power sharing, and that the 'Irish dimension' to the problem should be institutionally recognised. Both of these principles were embodied in the first and most ambitious experiment in devolution to Northern Ireland until the 1990s. As part of the scheme, a new assembly was elected in June 1973 by proportional representation; following inter-party negotiations, agreement was reached on a three-party coalition of the UUP, the SDLP and the Alliance Party; and, following a further agreement between this coalition and the British and Irish governments at Sunningdale in December 1973 on the establishment of a Council of Ireland, the new government took office on 1 January 1974.

The fate of this imaginative experiment was to haunt politicians for decades: Brian Faulkner lost both the leadership of his party (January 1974) and his position as head of government when it collapsed in the face of a loyalist-organised general strike (May 1974). Later initiatives designed to move in the direction of devolved government were more cautious. A constitutional convention was elected in 1975 but failed to reach a consensus (its report, based on the voting strength of its unionist majority, recommended a modified version of the pre-1972 system). A constitutional conference of the main parties was convened by the secretary of state in 1980, but again disagreed on the principle of power sharing. An assembly was elected in 1982 as part of a 'rolling devolution' plan, under which power could be devolved to it if requested by a qualified majority of 70 per cent; but only the DUP and the Alliance party attended consistently, making consensus impossible (O'Leary, Elliott and Wilford, 1988).

Notwithstanding the failure of devolved government to take root, significant progress was made on another front. The British and Irish governments agreed on the establishment of a formal mechanism for co-operation, within the context of which issues related to Northern Ireland could be discussed: in 1981 there appeared the Anglo-Irish Intergovernmental Council. This provided a framework for frequent meetings at ministerial and official level, and provided a forum for discussion and exchange of views. A further step was taken with the signing of the Anglo-Irish Agreement in November 1985. This established a second body in the context of the first, an Anglo-Irish Inter-governmental Conference with a specific focus on Northern Ireland, with a standing joint secretariat made up of civil servants from the two jurisdictions. A parliamentary tier envisaged in the 1981 arrangements, the British–Irish Inter-Parliamentary Body, was finally created in 1990. Though effectively guaranteeing Northern Ireland's status within the United Kingdom, the emphasis in the Anglo-Irish Agreement on equality between the two traditions in Northern Ireland and the voice it gave the Irish government in Northern Ireland's internal affairs antagonised unionists deeply. This antagonism was accentuated by the strictly inter-governmental nature of the agreement; unlike the position in 1974, there was no executive which could be delegitimised at the polls or intimidated by direct action.

### The peace process and inter-party negotiations, 1994–8
The Anglo-Irish Agreement of 1985 placed particular pressure on the unionist parties and on Sinn Féin. It gave the former a vested interest in negotiation, since it quickly became clear that the most effective way of undermining the agreement would be to reach an accommodation with nationalists on new structures of devolved government (the agreement provided that in these circumstances devolved matters would no longer fall under the remit of the

Anglo-Irish institutions). But to the extent that it represented a gain for moderate nationalism, it helped the SDLP in its electoral struggle with Sinn Féin.

In addition to the strategic options dictated to the parties by the logic of the agreement, other pressures encouraged negotiation. The bloody paramilitary campaigns that had been waged since the 1970s seemed increasingly to have failed to deliver political dividends. By the end of 1993, almost 3,500 people had been killed in incidents related to the troubles, most of them uninvolved civilians (the security forces accounted for 1,009 of the deaths, and among paramilitary organisations, 108 loyalists and 422 republicans had been killed; calculated from Smyth, 2000: 121). Yet it was by no means clear that any of the parties to the conflict could demonstrate that they had advanced their positions in any way commensurate with the suffering they had experienced and inflicted. Combined with this, conciliatory signals from Dublin and London appeared to offer republicans the prospect of significant advance by the political route. The 'Downing Street declaration' by Taoiseach Reynolds and Prime Minister Major on 15 December 1993 was a landmark along this route; it referred (admittedly, ambiguously) to the 'right of self-determination' of the Irish people, and held out the prospect of negotiating the political future to 'democratically mandated parties which establish a commitment to exclusively peaceful methods and which have shown that they abide by the democratic process'.[11] This, and further signals that Washington, too, was more likely to be an ally to republicans than a neutral bystander, eased the way towards an IRA ceasefire, declared on 31 August 1994. Similar but less dramatic reconsiderations were taking place on the loyalist side and, now that the IRA threat was on hold, a ceasefire by the Combined Loyalist Military Command (an umbrella body linking loyalist organisations, of which the UDA and the UVF were the most significant) was announced on 13 October 1994.

The expectation that talks involving parties with paramilitary links would follow quickly on the ceasefires turned out not to be realistic. Although government-sponsored 'Framework documents' outlining a blueprint for further discussions on 22 February 1995 were interpreted as a further gesture towards republicans, an explicit precondition on participation in talks was imposed on 7 March 1995 by Secretary of State Mayhew: progress on 'decommissioning' of paramilitary weapons. Far from responding positively, the IRA eventually abandoned its ceasefire on 9 February 1996; it was to be restored only on 20 July 1997. In the meantime, elections had taken place to a new Northern Ireland Forum on 30 May 1996 (the election results were intended also to give a mandate to political groups to engage in inter-party negotiations), and the British Conservative government had been replaced by a Labour administration following the election of 1 May 1997. On

9 September 1997 Sinn Féin was allowed to join the inter-party talks (which had begun on 10 June 1996), precipitating the withdrawal of the DUP and the UKUP.

In the talks that followed, culminating in the Good Friday Agreement of 10 April 1998, the extent to which the various groups were prepared to compromise and horse-trade is well known. It should be noted, of course, that the very decision to enter into talks already implied a softening of attitudes and a willingness to reconsider standpoints that had for long been regarded as sacrosanct. External agencies also had a profound impact. Agreement, however, could occur only if the parties to it had sufficient ideological latitude to permit them to enter it; and, remarkably, they appear to have had – just about – precisely such latitude.

### The agreement and its implementation, 1998–2002

The fundamental compromises on all sides that were characteristic features of the Good Friday Agreement were hailed at the time as evidence of the capacity of party leaders to accept unpalatable changes in some areas in return for long-term gains in others. In this, it appeared as if the leaders had substantial public support. Notwithstanding committed opposition by the DUP and the UKUP, the UUP endorsed the agreement by a comfortable margin, and Sinn Féin moved slowly towards acceptance. Public opinion polls showed strong support, and this was underwritten in the results of referenda on 22 May 1998 (71 per cent voted in favour of the agreement in Northern Ireland and 94 per cent in the Republic), and of the general election to the new assembly on 25 June 1998.

Abstract principles can, however, translate into painful practice, and the extent to which parties with radically different perspectives had compromised became clear to their supporters as the provisions of the agreement began to be implemented. Indeed, it was not until 2 December 1999 that the Northern Ireland executive took office and the new institutions came into existence (with the first meeting of the North/South Ministerial Council on 13 December and the first meeting of the British–Irish Council four days later). Even at that, the institutions had a shaky existence, and were altogether suspended by Secretary of State Mandelson from 11 February to 30 May 2000. The resignation of First Minister Trimble on 1 July 2001, followed by the remaining unionist ministers on 18 October, risked bringing the whole agreement to an end; but following significant IRA decommissioning on 23 October the ministers resumed their posts and Trimble was re-elected First Minister (though not without difficulty) on 6 November 2001.

For unionists, the spectacle of the release of IRA prisoners, the sight of Sinn Féin ministers in office in Stormont (aggravated by the prolonged absence of decommissioning) and the transformation of the Royal Ulster Constabulary into the Police Service of Northern Ireland were unpleasant indicators of what the small print of the agreement implied. Northern Ireland's place within the union might have been guaranteed for the foreseeable future and its main enemies, the IRA, might have been neutralised, but it would be a different, less 'British' union. Furthermore, even the guarantees about the need for Northern Ireland's consent for any change in constitutional status were being undermined by the demographic advance of the Catholic population, leading to intercommunal tension in certain areas of pronounced Protestant decline, such as Portadown and North Belfast.

By implying a perception of nationalist 'victory', this unionist discomfiture ironically but classically made the burden of compromise easier for republicans. Sinn Féin might have yielded on the principle of collective self-determination for the people of the whole island of Ireland, but this was not of immediate practical significance. Sinn Féin's working acceptance of partition – symbolised in the party's willingness to take up not just seats in the assembly but also places in the executive – could, similarly, be presented as a pragmatic, short-term position rather than a fundamental, long-term principle. But the issue of decommissioning was a more overt, inescapable sign of how far republicans had compromised: it signalled explicit acceptance that the struggle was over, implying in turn either that republicans had surrendered or that they had achieved their aims. This dilemma – the debate as to whether the IRA leadership comprised 'traitors' or 'victors' – caused profound unease among grassroots activists, unwilling to accept that they might have been betrayed, but faced with unmistakable evidence that the war had not been won.

But it was not only the two main protagonists, unionists and republicans, that experienced difficulty with the implementation of the agreement. So too did the groups in the middle. For the SDLP, the agreement was close to being the ideal path towards political accommodation. But there was a price to be paid for bringing republicans in from the cold: as Sinn Féin became increasingly 'slightly constitutional' (to quote Sean Lemass's famous description of Fianna Fáil in 1928[12]), it posed a greater electoral challenge to the SDLP. Just as voters in the Irish Free State in the 1930s had migrated from moderate constitutional nationalism to determined constitutional nationalism (in switching from Cumann na nGaedheal to Fianna Fáil), might not their Northern Ireland counterparts make a parallel switch, from the SDLP to Sinn Féin?[13] For the Alliance Party, similarly, the agreement represented an ideological victory but a strategic defeat. To the extent that it was broadly consociational, it was compatible with the party's long-term objectives; but in following the logic of consociationalism and placing a premium on membership of one or other of the two main blocs it undermined the very middle ground on and for which Alliance stood. The erosion of this middle ground was to be seen in Alliance's declining support; and the political marginalisation of the party was reflected in procedures for cross-community voting in the assembly, procedures that ultimately forced several of the party's members to re-designate themselves by bloc.[14]

## Conclusion

This account of the constitutional development of the island of Ireland, of the evolution of political forces in both parts of the island and of recent political changes that have had implications for – and been affected by – both of these is intended to provide a background for the more specific analysis of the shifting political priorities of Ireland's major political traditions. It has drawn attention to the extent to which major political groups have constituted fluid political coalitions, with priorities changing over time and with continuing competition between different tendencies. The reality is that no party – in Ireland or elsewhere – has managed in practice to assert its ideological hegemony over all of its supporters behind a programme of unchanging orthodoxy. Parties not only fail to agree with each other; each is itself a forum for policy debate and disagreement.

This chapter has also sought to describe the constitutional and political contexts that have set the parameters for political debate. The constitutional position, subject to vigorous challenge from the 1880s to the 1920s, appeared then to have stabilised, apart from ongoing tension between Dublin and London that took another couple of decades to resolve. This stability seemed to provide a predictable background for political discourse and rhetorical confrontation, one to which the major political traditions would be constrained to adapt. But the troubles that began in the late 1960s gave rise ultimately to fundamental constitutional questions, and significant developments in 1985 and 1998 sought once again to redefine the relationships between London, Dublin and Belfast. In particular, the open-ended nature of the 1998 agreement raised the prospect of further constitutional change, depending on the evolution of demographic and political forces in Northern Ireland.

In the chapters that follow, then, the theme of change within the major political traditions is explored in detail. Ideological change (or even ideological conservatism disguised as change for tactical reasons) is important because of its impact on the negotiation process in the 1990s that permitted the creation of the 1998 agreement. Change, or its absence, defined the constraints within which the various political elites could operate. But the very existence of the agreement, and of the wide package of constitutional and institutional reforms to which it gave rise, is likely to have had a considerable impact on the parties themselves. This was calculated to promote further development in the thinking of all parties, including even those most hostile to the new political arrangements.

In describing these changes, this book adopts a dual approach. First, a set of leading politicians examines the theme of change within particular traditions. This is matched by a corresponding set of contributions by academic observers. Change has been especially marked in the constitutional nationalist tradition within Northern Ireland, which is examined from different perspectives by Alban Maginness and Jennifer Todd. But it has been even more pronounced in the republican tradition, where it is discussed from the standpoint of a politician and of an academic commentator by Mitchel McLaughlin and Paul Arthur, respectively. Two strands of unionism are analysed using the same formula. Thus, Dermot Nesbitt and Richard English focus on the complex and fascinating pattern of change within Ulster unionism from the standpoints in turn of the practicing politician and the involved academic. The even more remarkable shift in direction within militant loyalism is assessed by one of its main architects, David Ervine, and by academic analyst James McAuley. Finally, Desmond O'Malley and Tom Garvin examine the pattern of change in the south, again from complementary political and academic perspectives.

But these contributions can necessarily tell only part of the story. Apart from the conscious omission, for reasons mentioned above, of the highly significant changes that have been taking place in Great Britain, there are important components in the political map of Northern Ireland that have not been discussed, since they do not fit into the theme of ideological change. On the one hand, there are strands within republicanism and unionism (represented respectively by Republican Sinn Féin and by the DUP and its allies) that have taken pride in *not* having changed. Similarly, there are new political groups (such as the Alliance Party and the Women's Coalition) whose very existence is a *consequence* of change, rather than themselves having been transformed ideologically as political circumstances have evolved. Since these are not discussed elsewhere, their perspectives are assessed in a concluding chapter, and an appendix reproduces the text of certain documents that bear eloquent witness to the speed and extent of change.

Having set the constitutional stage, then, and outlined the political story that was to unfold on it, it is time to turn to the political actors themselves for their assessments of change within their individual political traditions.

# Part 1

# Political perspectives

**Chapter 2**

# Redefining northern nationalism

Alban Maginness

I

The great historical legacy of the SDLP, and of John Hume in particular, lies in redefining Irish nationalism. I deliberately do not say Northern nationalism, as I believe the SDLP has radically changed the thinking of the mainstream political parties in the South, as well as the broad mass of constitutional nationalist thinking in both North and South. Not only do I make that wider claim, but I also further claim that the SDLP has radically changed the thinking of physical force nationalism or republicanism as well.

II

The SDLP was an outworking of the civil rights movement of the late 1960s. The civil rights movement was a non-violent reaction to the grave social and economic injustice and inequalities visited upon the Catholic community since partition. It arose out of a sense of frustration within the Catholic community at its plight at the hands of a seemingly all-powerful and monolithic Unionist Party hegemony. Equally frustrating was the ineffectual political opposition of the moribund so-called Nationalist Party which was certainly not a party and probably not very nationalist either.

Belfast's Catholic population was traditionally and not surprisingly labour-leaning in its political orientation, though what that meant in the reality of Belfast's sectarian political cauldron was little more than trying to mitigate the oppressive nature of unionist rule at Stormont and in particular the unionist-dominated Belfast City Hall. Catholic politics in Belfast was historically fragmented and factionalised, leading to great political frustration and even despair. Furthermore its practical separation and isolation from the rest of the Catholic population and politics throughout the six counties weakened and divided the already diminished strength of the Catholic minority within the partitioned state. Conversely, unionist politics grew from strength to strength, prospering on the weakness and divisions of the Catholic opposition. The abstentionist or semi-abstentionist nature of the nationalist political opposition at Stormont further illustrated the ineffectiveness of the traditional nationalist approach to politics. The desire for a united, effective political opposition both inside and outside Stormont became a latent aspiration among Catholics and other anti-unionists, and that aspiration became a realistic proposition following the rise of the civil rights movement. For most Catholics this was achieved through the setting up of the Social Democratic and Labour Party (SDLP). Support for the SDLP from a comfortable and steady majority of the Catholic community was to be a recurrent feature of elections from 1970 onwards.

Since the foundation of the northern state, sporadic republican campaigns of violence were all equally ineffectual, and in time became discredited as a form of political opposition even among those who formerly supported this strategy. Indeed, not only were the campaigns ineffective, but they were also militarily incompetent and at times risible. They also consistently failed to generate popular support among the Catholic community. They were comprehensively and easily defeated militarily by the RUC and provided plentiful propaganda for the unionist leadership to consolidate its support among Protestants and to further marginalise and oppress the Catholic community. These campaigns therefore played into the unionists' hands, further strengthening the unionist hegemony and demoralising the Catholic community.

The very success of the civil rights movement in undermining unionist rule was a lesson in itself, and it must be understood that without the civil rights agitation Stormont would surely have continued to survive. The key to the success of this movement was the fact that the agitation was on the basis of accepting that Northern Ireland existed, and that the campaign was about the internal rights of Catholic citizens within Northern Ireland. The argument for civil rights was manifestly reasonable and was logically irresistible, especially within a unionist, or British, political context. The national question was therefore not at issue, and to reintroduce that question, as the Provisional campaign certainly went on to do, was to undermine and through abhorrent and counter-productive paramilitary violence, ultimately subvert the civil rights movement. Physical force republicanism, while paying lip service to the civil rights campaign, saw it simply as a way of creating political unrest, on the back of which it could reintroduce the unresolved national question. It saw a successful civil rights movement as being antipathetic to its traditional aim of a united Ireland on a territorial basis.

The reality was that the prevailing political outlook within the Catholic community was characterised by a sense of gross injustice, a desire for equality and a rising tide of political and economic expectation among a well-educated young Catholic community. Nationalism was a secondary consideration, a long term aspiration, and the prevailing traditional view that a united Ireland would ultimately solve all problems was also beginning to become a discredited notion, if only because people were not prepared to wait for a notional united Ireland at some indeterminate date in the future.

From the very beginning, although the SDLP was an anti-partitionist party, its emphasis was on eradicating injustice and creating equality within Northern Ireland. Its constitution redefined anti-partitionism on the basis of unity of the Irish people – not the unity of Irish territory. From the very beginning, the consent principle became the founding principle upon which, in SDLP eyes, constitutional change could take place in the future.

But this was not merely theorising on the part of the SDLP; it informed its basic thinking and consequent political action. The fact that the party received popular approval in successive elections from the Catholic community was important in terms of reshaping the political consciousness of that community. This basic outlook orientated the party towards thinking creatively about alternative, non-traditional methods of addressing the problem of a divided community in Northern Ireland and by extension the problem of a divided people in Ireland. Out of this arose the guiding principle of partnership, which has been central to the political thinking of the party through the past three decades. This principle has shaped and informed the political thinking and policies of the party.

## III

This, in my view, has culminated in the Good Friday Agreement, which I believe is the outstanding achievement of the SDLP. The agreement is a roll call of SDLP demands and proposals. Its very structures shadow and reflect the analysis of the party for many years. Its insistence that all the pertinent relationships be addressed together, in an interlocking fashion, so that the complexity of the problem can be fully explored and addressed, was SDLP dogma. The three strands around which the pre-agreement talks centred – the Catholic–Protestant or nationalist–unionist relationship within Northern Ireland, the North–South relationship, and the British–Irish relationship – were all part of SDLP thinking. The basic institutions of the agreement reflect the political need to tackle these relationships: the Northern Ireland Assembly and power sharing Executive, the North/South implementation bodies and the North/South Ministerial Council, and the British–Irish Council.

So much for the past; we now have the opportunity and challenge of the present. We have constructed the Good Friday Agreement, which seeks to repair and heal the fractured relationships between nationalists and unionists in Ireland both within the North and between North and South, and, quite as important, between Ireland and Britain. This latter relationship will be addressed within the British–Irish Council, which, in my view, despite being largely deliberative, has a significant role to play in the building of a new, warm and dynamic relationship between our two islands. We share many things in common: a common history, a common geography, a common weather and even the English language, which, given the rapid development of the global economy, is now an undoubted benefit to the Irish people.

There would have been no successful European Union without the dynamic core relationship between Germany and France, begun by Adenauer and de Gaulle and refined by Mitterand and Kohl. That relationship is at the heart of Europe, and has contributed enormously to peace in the post-war period. We can construct a similar relationship that can repair the damage of history and heal the wounds that have festered for too long between our two neighbouring islands – a relationship based on friendship instead of hostility, a relationship based on trust instead of fear, a relationship based on partnership not rivalry, and a relationship based on equality not on superiority. This is a new multidimensional relationship centred on people, not on territory or on the outmoded concept of sovereignty, rooted in the nineteenth century, that has blighted political thinking in twentieth century.

We should now realise that we live in a world in which sovereignty is pooled among and sometimes between nations. Sovereignty is shared within the European Union, within NATO, and within the context of the International Convention on Human Rights and other international agreements, which include provisions to prosecute war crimes extra-territorially. Parallel with those developments is rapidly increasing globalisation in the economic domain. The trend towards greater and closer interdependence and interrelationships amongst the world economies since the end of the Second World War has now become an irresistible dynamic in international relations. It continues at a rapid pace irrespective of language, race and, more importantly, political ideology, be it of the right or the left. It is therefore within that wider global context that one should see the separate, though not unique, development of institutions within the Good Friday Agreement. As a consequence, Northern Ireland does not remain wholly within the control of Britain, but rather develops a new and imaginative relationship simultaneously with both Britain and the Republic of Ireland.

The ultimate aim of the agreement is to achieve one overall goal – the reconciliation of the people of Ireland, and of the people of Ireland and Britain. It is people-based, not land-based. It does not seek to join territory, or reinforce territory, but to create a partnership within Northern Ireland between nationalists and unionists in which trust can be built through working together, and to create a partnership between the people of North and South, also through working together. In that way trust can be built on many fronts and will allow a genuine and sustained reconciliation to take place. What the people will determine in future will be entirely up to them in a free and democratic manner. Their choice probably will not conform to any of our traditional models.

## IV

Wherefore the agreement, now? There are a number of very positive factors that I believe will assist and strengthen it. These fall into two main areas, political and economic. The political front is dominated by the nature of the institutional reforms that have followed from or have been associated with the agreement itself. The reality is that despite every twist and turn of the political dice the Assembly has displayed a remarkable resilience and has withstood the seriously destructive power of anti-Agreement forces both within and without the Assembly. In part, this is due to the tacit acceptance by most of the anti-Agreement unionists of the institution of the Assembly and its operations, for a variety of reasons both self-interested and otherwise.

Similarly and perhaps even more remarkably, the Northern Ireland Executive has survived well, despite the stop-start nature of its history and despite the fact that its collegiate character is more notional than real. Imperfect though it may be as an institution, it has worked in a reasonably impressive form, agreeing successive budgets and programmes for government and achieving cross-community support for both within the Assembly. It has also successfully steered through the Assembly at least 23 pieces of Executive-initiated legislation. The Democratic Unionist ministers' boycott of Executive meetings has been a serious inconvenience rather than a disability, and has certainly not been a fatal blow to the operational effectiveness of the Executive. It has admittedly been less than successful in achieving a collective character akin to any recognisable government or executive body elsewhere. The First and Deputy First Ministers are not yet popularly perceived as joint prime ministers. Other ministers are seen as stand-alone officers, not as part of a fully joined-up government. The Executive is seen as a series of political silos loosely connected by weekly meetings. The sense of partnership government has not yet emerged sufficiently to engage the public's imagination. Indeed some might continue to view the Executive as an arena where the two communities pit their wits in an attempt to wrestle political power from one another. Instead of sharing power, the contestants jealously prize their ministerial power and compete for more influence in order to assert the rights of their respective communities.

However imperfect the Assembly and the Executive may be, their very existence over a sustained but very difficult period will further encourage an atmosphere of political normality and acceptance of the Agreement's institutions. The operation of the Assembly committee system in a virtually non-partisan, uncontroversial fashion creates further confidence in the Assembly and its other operations. Related to this is the prospect of the development of non-sectarian cross-community politics on a limited range of issues. One can see this already, in putative form, in a degree of cross-party opposition to Minister de Brún and her health department's policies and in opposition to Minister Foster and his legislative proposals for best value for local government. The opposition in both of these instances is to the respective ministers' policy positions, not to their party political allegiances. Once any system becomes institutionally entrenched it is much harder to undermine or weaken, and this is what has been happening within the Assembly itself.

Furthermore, the new beginning to policing based on the implementation of the Patten Report has the capacity to attract widespread cross community support for the Police Service of Northern Ireland (PSNI). Even the once-controversial name change from Royal Ulster Constabulary to Police Service of Northern Ireland has been accepted with little resistance. The subsequent agreements by the policing board regarding the new police badge and on the Omagh bomb investigation have secured the cross community authority of the board itself. For an institution that many observers believed had little chance of success, it has remarkably confounded its critics and successfully ploughed a way forward in one of the most difficult areas of politics, namely security. While there are many difficulties ahead, the start to the new dispensation has been good, and if this continues it will bring about greater security and political stability within the community.

The implementation of the reform of the criminal justice system, allied to the introduction of a human rights bill for Northern Ireland, will undoubtedly radically alter our domestic jurisprudence, building a rights-based legal culture and thus putting to rest the security-type legal culture that we have endured for so long. Additionally, the United Kingdom Human Rights Act, 1999, will have a very positive contribution in developing the rights-based culture I referred to earlier.

But aside from these institutional changes and reforms there are other political changes that are likely to be of great significance. One such is the maintenance of peace following the end of large-scale paramilitary violence, acutely symbolised by the start to Provisional IRA decommissioning, ushering in a new atmosphere of enhanced confidence between the communities. Such a situation provides the government and others with the opportunity to engage communities at a local level and to actively promote the development of positive community relations. While the sectarian clashes surrounding the Holy Cross Girls' Primary School in Ardoyne would suggest that relative peace has done little to reduce the endemic sectarianism of northern society, yet it has served to remind all that beneath the political superstructure, which is functioning reasonably well, lies a substructure at a community level which is quite dysfunctional in terms of the relationship between two local communities.

On the economic front the continued dynamism of the Republic's economy, despite the slowdown after 11 September and the rationalisation within the telecommunications sector, has a significant beneficial spillover effect on Northern Ireland. The Republic's economic success and growth are important in themselves, as they act as a model of what a new Northern Ireland economy could be like. The northern economy is also, of course, enjoying significant growth and development, and because of its character has very largely been insulated from the adverse impact of 11 September. There thus lies great promise for further and sustained economic development of the northern economy, and thereby a happier electorate and a more stable political situation. All this is taking place in a context of deepening European integration, a development whose importance is accentuated by the fact that the EU is not just an economic union, but also a political union. The likely prospect that Britain will join the European currency zone in the short to medium term will strengthen the impact of these economic trends and emphasis in a practical way the need for cooperation between North and South.

## V

On the other hand there are a number of strong negative factors that are at work, some of which run counter to the positive factors outlined above. The implementation of the new institutions has experienced great difficulty, and the stop-start nature of the implementation process has been corrosive and demoralising. There continues to be a disillusionment and unhappiness about the Agreement in certain sectors, particularly within the unionist community – a deeply worrying and potentially destabilising factor.

The setting up of the new police service has not won universal support, particularly within the Catholic community. While the jury is still out as far as many Catholics are concerned regarding the PSNI, there is always a danger that something unanticipated might happen that could derail the whole project at this very early stage. But the gravest danger is constant political tension, whether produced by accident or design. Though in an obvious sense less damaging than paramilitary violence, this can lead to a state of constant crisis that debilitates the whole body politic. To some extent this has been eased by the start of Provisional IRA decommissioning of weaponry. The continued fragmentation within loyalism and its paramilitary organisations has increased the likelihood of violence, as has the disintegration of loyalist paramilitary organisations into ghettoised gangs with no political agenda at all, save anti-Catholic sectarianism and the retention through purely criminal means of local power, control or influence. If this trend were to continue, working-class loyalist communities could be deprived of strong and authoritative leadership and descend into anarchic subcultures.

The decline of economic fortunes as a consequence of the unexpected – for example the foot-and-mouth crisis and the events of 11 September – could, if repeated in other guises, impact badly on Northern Ireland. If, for example, the British decided against joining the Euro zone, this could both in the medium and long term adversely affect the Northern Ireland economy.

Continued political instability could also have an adverse impact, forcing nervous prospective foreign investors to the conclusion that Northern Ireland was still a high-risk area for investment, one that should be avoided.

Recurrent, bitter inter-communal violence and tension at a local level provide us with a reminder of the deep sectarian undercurrents that continue in our society, though fortunately they remain for the most part below the surface. Though localised, incidents of this kind are highly destabilising and demoralising, and represent a grave danger for the foreseeable future.

## VI

Our task now is to implement the agreement fully and faithfully, and in a spirit of reconciliation. To simply create a system of mere coexistence, a cold unfriendly peace, would be wasteful. One recognises, given the depth of our recent and previous history, that no instant remedy will wipe away the damage done over the centuries. The healing process must begin, and begin now. Old prejudices and hatreds will then progressively dissolve. What is required is a real and vibrant spirit of reconciliation, though it is by no means clear that leadership in this direction is forthcoming on all sides in Northern Ireland.

In the future, an agreed, post-nationalist European Ireland will, it is hoped, emerge to play an even fuller part in the world. For the moment, implementing the Good Friday Agreement is our duty, and a most onerous and demanding challenge.

**Chapter 3**

# Redefining Republicanism

Mitchel McLaughlin

I

It was James Connolly who said of Wolfe Tone that he united 'the hopes of the new revolutionary faith and the ancient aspirations of an oppressed people'. Irish republicanism in the new century must perform a similar task. We need to identify the best in the republican tradition that we have inherited and to develop republicanism to meet the needs of our own time.

Irish republicanism is based on a number of core principles that are still relevant today. Simply restated they are:

- the commitment to the sovereignty of the people, to democracy in its fullest sense;

- the commitment to unity of Catholic, Protestant and Dissenter and the rejection of sectarianism of any kind;

- the commitment to the unity of this island and its people, national self-determination, an end to partition and the establishment of a sovereign 32-county Irish Republic.

These are still the basic principles that motivate Irish republicans today. The term 'Irish republicans' is often used in a narrow sense to describe members and supporters of Sinn Féin. I think a broader definition is required – one that embraces all who share the commitment to the complete freedom of the people of Ireland.

Flowing naturally from the basic principles I have outlined are other commitments. Our historical experience gave us an affinity with other peoples who are struggling for national self-determination. Thus Irish republicans have embraced anti-imperialism and internationalism.

Belief in what Patrick Pearse described as 'the sovereign people' has led republicans to seek social and economic democracy as well as national political democracy. James Connolly's measurement of freedom – as expressed in 1915 – is just as relevant today: 'In the long run the freedom of a nation is measured by the freedom of its lowest class; every upward step of that class to the possibility of possessing higher things raises the standard of the nation in the scale of civilisation.'

We cannot divorce these core republican principles from the struggle that they have inspired. We enter the new century at what is the end of the longest period of continued organised resistance to British rule in the history of Ireland. This has taken the form of armed struggle, civil disobedience, street campaigning, prison struggle, hunger strikes to the death, electoral politics, the mobilisation of international opinion and long and tortuous negotiations.

Through building political alliances, through dialogue and debate, through engagement with our political opponents and with our political enemies, republicans helped to chart a course which – if managed properly – will finally lead away from armed conflict and towards the peaceful resolution of the causes of the conflict. That is the basis of the peace process and of the Good Friday Agreement.

## II

The institutions established under the agreement create an all-Ireland framework within which the common interests of all who share this country can be addressed. They need to be developed and defended from those who are attempting to erode and inhibit the outworkings of the agreement. There are many challenges for republicans in the new century, and we need all the resourcefulness and commitment that has been shown by republicans in all the phases of our struggle to ensure that the agreement does indeed provide the vehicle for real change.

The story of the 26-county state is a story of how the hopes and promises of the years 1916 to 1921 were abused by those who claimed to honour them. The 1916 Proclamation's promise to 'cherish all the children of the nation equally' has not been delivered. We must not allow this new opportunity to be lost. The challenge for Irish republicanism in the new century is to offer an alternative to the corruption among sections of the political elite that has been exposed in this state as never before. The root of this corruption is the cosy relationship between big business and the major political parties. Is it any wonder that there is an unprecedented level of public cynicism about politics and apathy among voters?

We need to build a real coalition between republicans, in the broadest sense of the term, and all those campaigning for real and lasting change in our country. This implies that we need:

- a coalition of all those seeking to end poverty and inequality through the sharing of the wealth in our economy;

- a coalition of people across sectarian and racial divisions and an end to racism and sectarianism in all their forms;

- a coalition of those in rural and urban communities who have not been allowed to take full advantage of increased prosperity;

- a coalition of environmentalists who will make the aim of a green, clean Ireland a reality; and

- a coalition of those who cherish Irish neutrality and the sovereignty of the people of Ireland and wish to see them enhanced and not eroded through the gradual creation of an EU super-state.

Republicanism in the new century needs to embrace these diverse but progressive forces. It also needs to have a clear view of our place in the world. Are we to completely submerge Irish foreign policy within a giant EU state? Will we pursue an independent course, meeting as equals the poorer, formerly colonised nations with which we have so much in common? Or will we help to exploit them as part of one of the world's economic and political power blocs?

## III

To Irish republicans, the Republic has always meant more than a form of political administration. The vision of the Irish Republic that we seek encompasses all of Ireland and its entire people. It involves social and economic equality as well as political freedom. It values the Irish language and Irish culture while embracing cultural diversity in Ireland and internationally. Many people have sacrificed much to make this vision and this ideal a reality. I believe that our children will live in that Republic – all the children of the nation, equally. If we, as Irish republicans, are to understand anything about the struggle for freedom and independence, and if we are to advance and achieve our republican objectives, we must have a firm sense of what we are. This has to be rooted in our republican ideology, as well as our historical and collective experience, and it has to be always looking forward while drawing from the lessons of the past to build the future. It lies in the words and deeds of Tone, McCracken and Emmett; of Lalor, Pearse, Clarke and Connolly; and of many others. It lies in the words and deeds of Maire Drumm, of Bobby Sands and Mairead Farrell.

For me, it especially lies in the words of the 1916 Proclamation – almost 100 years old, but as advanced and as radical a political programme as you are likely to find anywhere in the world today. In 1916 Irish republicans produced a document that proclaims and guarantees 'religious and civil liberty, equal rights and equal opportunities to all its citizens' and which speaks of 'cherishing all the children of the nation equally'.

Let us, then, look into our future. What sort of future can it be? The Sinn Féin vision is of an Ireland in which there is no more war, no more conflict; an Ireland in which all the guns and the bombs are silent, forever; an Ireland in which the words of hate are silent, forever; an Ireland in which all the people of this island are at peace with each other and with our neighbours in Britain. It is a vision of an Ireland wherein nationalists and unionists are united by a process of healing and national reconciliation.

The Sinn Féin vision is of the people of this island free from division, foreign occupation, injustice and conflict; a vision of the five million people of this small island applying our collective energy, our wisdom and our intelligence to building the future; a vision of an island economy thriving, working hard to produce the wealth that can reduce unemployment and improve the quality of life of all our people. It is a vision of an Ireland using that wealth to eradicate poverty, to build homes, to improve education, to protect the environment, to heal the sick, to help the weak, the aged – all the children of the nation.

George Bernard Shaw once said: 'Some people see things as they are and ask why? I dream things that never were and ask why not?' Idealism is not dead in Ireland. It is alive and well and thriving within Irish republicanism. It is idealism with a vision for a better future. Caoimhghín Ó Caoláin a few years ago described Sinn Féin as the 'voice of an idea'. It is an idea, an idealism that is both republican and labour, the idea of a free Ireland and a sovereign people.

## IV

In the last few years, for the first time in over two decades, people right across this country are hearing of this new idea and recognising this idealism. But we need to build on our vision right across this island so that the democratic re-conquest of Ireland is realised in all of its social, economic, and cultural manifestations as well as in the political field. Our task must be to articulate and to develop the core republican positions in a way that is reasonable and attractive to the broad mass of the people of Ireland. Citizens have the right to a real future as equals. But this will not happen unless Irish republicans and others grasp the challenge, take the lead and make it happen.

The core of republicanism, both philosophically and ideologically, is the people. The people are sovereign. That means government of the people by the people. But what ultimately is the point of republicanism unless it signifies not only political democracy, but also the maximum welfare of the maximum number? We seek an economic democracy as well as a political democracy. A genuine republic must entail not alone a new political dispensation, but a new social and economic order.

We should not, of course, lose sight of the internationalist dimension of republicanism. Our struggle is not only about winning independence from Britain; it is about asserting our sovereignty in terms of the promotion of an independent foreign policy and positive Irish neutrality. It is about standing alongside our impoverished and oppressed brothers and sisters throughout the world who face the burden of foreign debt and the daily reality of starvation, malnutrition and disease. According to the UN, 134,000 children die each week from malnutrition and preventable disease. We have a responsibility to do all that we can to help them, and to promote the principles of democracy, justice, equality and human rights globally.

But how do we do all of this? And how do we get our national democracy? What is our strategy? And how specifically does that strategy stand regarding the criterion that there can be no internal settlement to the conflict in the North? The constitutional reality is that the British still hold jurisdiction over a part of Ireland, although that has been significantly qualified by the repealing of the Government of Ireland Act. The political reality if we are to attain our goals requires a process of transition to a united Ireland.

As a consequence of the Good Friday Agreement we now have all-Ireland institutions and structures established, as ratified by the people, which we believe can lead to that end. But this will not happen of its own accord. Politics is never static. It will only happen if we make it happen. The Good Friday Agreement is not for Irish republicans an end in itself, but an agreement with the potential to deliver a full national democracy in Ireland. It is an all-Ireland agreement with all-Ireland structures and institutions. Sinn Féin cannot bring about all the changes in politics and in society that are required on our own. Therefore we must link up with like-minded forces and individuals, in other parties and in pressure groups, to put together an alliance for a new Ireland – one which is free of corruption, and characterised by civic virtue and social justice.

## V

We have mapped out a course for the future, and we are taking the lead in charting that course. But let no one misrepresent what we mean by ending British interference in Ireland. Because Sinn Féin rejects the British government's interference in Ireland, some unionists have said that their presence is under attack. That is no more correct now than it ever was.

Republicans have no desire to drive unionists out, or to prevent whoever on this island wishes to designate himself or herself as British from doing so. Nor would we prevent or even discourage anyone who so wishes from endeavouring to promote their cultural identity socially, culturally or politically by any legitimate and democratic method, including the possession of British or any other citizenship. We have the right to pursue our goals politically and democratically. Unionists clearly have the same right.

Rejecting British government interference signifies opposition to the assertion of sovereignty by the British government and parliament over any part of Ireland. We believe that that assertion of sovereignty by the British government is contrary to the democratic wishes of a majority of the people of Ireland. Irish sovereignty is a fact in its own right and quite separate from the entitlements of unionists and those who categorise themselves as British. At the same time as unionists increasingly become disillusioned and suspicious of London's intentions (and indeed they act as though they have as little faith in the British government as republicans) more and more will come to see the benefit of asserting their rights as 20 per cent of an Irish national democracy rather than remaining as two per cent of the United Kingdom. The Good Friday Agreement is the foundation upon which new relationships between unionists and nationalists and republicans can be forged. Working the new institutions together harmoniously will be for the good of all the people of this island. This engagement, properly functioning, will lead in time to a genuine process of national reconciliation.

## VI

Sinn Féin aims to reach out to everybody on this island on the basis of equality and the sovereignty of the people in order to persuade them of the value of an agreed Ireland with agreed institutions. Sinn Féin will undertake its full part in that process, especially given the lack of real choice that the electorates face otherwise. There are already all-Ireland dynamics in operation and structures have now been erected to foster and expand them. It is, however, a matter of political fact that it is not enough for us to will the end, the goal, the objective; we must also will the means. This calls upon all the creativity, principle, and determination that we can muster as a people. What is essential is no less than a vision. Those who fought for an independent Ireland in the last century had one. We must map out ours in this century, appropriate to the circumstances in which we find ourselves.

The Ireland of the new millennium will be more outward looking, and have a mix of civic and cultural Irishness. It will be pluralist, urban, multi-lingual, and, going on current immigration trends, also multi-racial. The republican concept of citizenship has always been inclusive. Republicans totally repudiate the hostile and racist attitude being shown to asylum seekers, mainly in the 26 counties. Those who complain the loudest about refugees seem to have forgotten our own history. In years gone by we suffered racist abuse in our own country from colonial occupiers, and we were subjected to racial discrimination in other lands. It is not so long ago that signs saying: 'No Irish – No Blacks' were displayed on boarding houses in England and America. It is not so long ago that thousands of young people of Ireland departed our shores for the US to work illegally. But it is important to point out that racism does not grow of its own accord. Everywhere it has taken hold, it is because some unscrupulous people in politics and other spheres have nurtured it for their own cynical short-term interests. They must be opposed.

## VII

Lastly, I have referred to civic and cultural Irishness. By civic Irishness, I mean commitment as a citizen to an Irish society that is one of responsibility and not narrow individualism, of ethical standards rather than greed and venality, of a self-governing community through structures of empowerment, of reward by worth and not birth. Beyond that, cultural Irishness is a matter of choosing among a number of influences. Sinn Féin is wedded to the Gaelic as a primary, but not sole, font of inspiration, and not in an exclusionist or supremacist way. It seeks to convince, not to compel. Such civic and cultural Irishness can also be another bridge to unionists. It allows for acceptance of an Irish democracy, without insisting on cultural sameness. Clearly, it is an Irish democracy in which unionists can play a role out of all proportion to any they have played in these islands over the past 80 years. In other words, what is entailed is the construction of a new and inclusive nation with varied, but not incompatible, definitions within it. How that will evolve over time, only history can tell.

In working towards this we must keep sight of where we want to go and avoid the dangers of being mesmerised by the day-to-day tactical or other considerations of struggle. We are living through a time of great hope, great risk, and great opportunity. But it is a time also to remember, as Seamus Heaney puts it, 'that a further shore is reachable from here'.

**Chapter 4**

# Redefining unionism

Dermot Nesbitt

**I**

In one scene of the famous musical *Les misérables*, the star, Jean Valjean, asks in song 'Who am I?' One telling line is 'If I speak I am condemned, if I stay silent I am damned.' Too often the easy road is to say nothing. Indeed I have often been asked why I am in politics. My answer is simple – I enjoy politics. But as often as I am asked that question I am told what I should do – 'don't give in', 'stand firm', 'you live in history, think of the future' – to name but a few words of advice.

However, involvement in politics is not just about enjoyment – there must be hope for a better future for all. We cannot subscribe to that phrase of Oscar Wilde, 'Something was dead in all of us and what was dead was hope.' Not so indeed, unionism has come a long way over the past decades. The following are the questions that I address here. What has been the traditional position of the Ulster Unionist Party? What reasons have there been for change? What main changes have there been in recent years? And, finally, what are the implications for relations within these islands?

**II**

The initial position of the Ulster Unionist Party (properly called the Ulster Unionist Council) before 1920 had been to reject any form of devolved (or self-) government. However, the Northern Ireland parliament (Stormont) became in due course, as viewed by unionists, a bulwark for the Union – even though it was accepted by unionists at the outset that Northern Ireland was being marginalised from mainstream politics. Also, some non-unionists hoped that the separate parliament would lead to a united Ireland.

Unionists therefore sought for many years the return of a parliament which, in their view, had been unfairly removed in March 1972. From that time there was much debate within unionism as to the best way forward – devolution/integration, majority rule/power sharing. Such continued debate was to the detriment of the unionist case and it could be contended, with some justification, that for many years after 1972 unionism did not have a clear and focused policy, argued with consistency, conviction and clarity, to match the case presented by nationalists.

Nationalists' position seemed clear. In 1978 the SDLP document *Facing reality* stated:

> the British Government should enter into immediate discussion with the Irish Government in order to promote jointly matters of common concern to both parts of Ireland. They should also develop jointly a programme for the harmonisation of the laws and services on both sides of the border.

The 'devolution/integration' debate had been a very divisive issue within unionism. In reality, however, these words lack precision. Any form of government below the Westminster level is devolved government. Equally, within certain parameters, there is no one unique form of government called 'integration'. Essentially, the difference between the two views, when used in political debate, refers to whether or not an elected body at Stormont should or should not have the authority to make some of its own laws, as Stormont had between 1921 and 1972.

It is worth noting that the Government of Ireland Act (1920) gave no guarantee that Stormont would have the finance available to provide services comparable with Great Britain. At the time of the home rule bills it was estimated that there would be a financial surplus of income over expenditure of £5.7m and £1.9m for Southern Ireland and Northern Ireland respectively. Northern Ireland's predicted surplus in reality turned out to be a deficit, and public provision in general fell below standards in Great Britain, not because Northern Ireland people were conservative but because the government was chronically short of money. Unionism believed, however, that the political gains of self-government more than outweighed any financial constraint.

In the 1970s and 1980s what were the perceptions? Certainly, unionist policy has always been aimed at securing and enhancing the Union. It was broadly accepted that social disobedience or a 'unionist' terrorist campaign would not preserve the Union, and thus clear policies were essential that would be reasonable, achievable, believable and convincing. It was not a rarity for unionists to say: 'we're finished', 'we've been sold down the river', or 'you're not worth voting for'.

Throughout the period 1974–95, there were at least eight significant attempts to restore accountable democracy in Northern Ireland. These ranged from the power sharing executive of 1974 (headed by the late Brian Faulkner) to the *Frameworks document* of 1995. Though most Ulster Unionist Party leaders during this period were called 'traitor' by some, I believe each leader did his best given the circumstances. On each occasion the package was rejected by some grouping – governments, nationalists or unionists. On each occasion unionism was worse off next time.

An indication of thinking in the 1970s and 1980s can be obtained from the following quotes from leading politicians of the day.

> It would be improper and highly dangerous to our case for any party member to suggest or volunteer or hint at any deviation from or amendment to the main principles of our scheme . . . and these do not include administrative devolution, a single elected regional council as an upper tier of local government or total integration.

> The number one policy in our books is the return of a devolved government to Northern Ireland. Yes indeed, we are looking for the big one here. We must insist that the devolved government that was taken away from us several years ago be given back to us.

> The obvious alternative is a strong devolved government based on the principles of democracy and majority rule. Such a development would be a hammer blow to the morale of the IRA.

These unionist politicians shall remain anonymous, but none is active now in politics.

## III

Unionism began in 1987 to recognise that new thinking was needed. A document entitled *An End to Drift* was published in June 1987. This was prepared by a unionist cross-party group and presented to both Mr Molyneaux and Dr Paisley. It contemplated that unionists should not be 'ashamed to adapt to changing circumstances' and that both parties perhaps abandon 'pure majority rule'. This represented new thinking. It should be remembered that this was against a recent background not only of a boycott of elected institutions by unionists but also of various petitions – for retention of the office of Governor, or rejection of the Anglo-Irish Agreement – and in a context in which all unionist MPs had resigned their seats and fought by-elections. Over 400,000 votes returned the unionist MPs to Westminster on an anti-Anglo-Irish Agreement 'ticket' – a substantial number in the context of Northern Ireland. From a unionist perspective, none of these actions had any measurable impact on the situation. From a personal viewpoint I can accept that government proposals of these kinds for the future of Northern Ireland required agreement among the participating parties (including unionists). But a consensus requirement does not imply that the package in question is an appropriate one – what matters is the content of the package, in terms of its principles and their implementation. To make clear my point, a decision on purchasing a car will depend on how the car performs, not on the fact that the sale requires agreement between buyer and seller. In short, it was absolutely irrelevant that, at regular intervals throughout the 1995 *Frameworks document*, it was stated that agreement by all parties was needed, as if this would make the proposals somehow more acceptable to unionists.

Entering the 1990s, as unionism was rethinking its strategy, other events – on a grander scale – were beginning to have an impact upon thought processes. Indeed, the world is ever changing, and it is never without problems to solve – Northern Ireland is not alone in this context. In this ever-changing world there are from time to time new paradigms. One such paradigm, I believe, was the collapse of the USSR after 1989, a major consequence of which was that the threat to peace and stability within Europe became more intra-state than inter-state. The major governments in Europe turned anew to the problem of accommodating diversity within states. The last time this had been addressed had been before 1939. The issue of intra-state conflict within the European context today arises over and above other problems, such as the transition from totalitarianism to pluralist democracy and the social and economic move from centrally planned economies to market economies.

The solution of intra-state conflict has often been referred to as 'group accommodation' or 'minority protection'. Indeed, a former senior member of the SDLP, Mr Austin Currie – later to become a member of Dáil Éireann – had described our problem in this context as follows:

> Fundamentally the Northern Ireland conundrum is one of conflicting national identities between those who believe themselves Irish and those who believe themselves British. There are religious, social, cultural, political and other dimensions to the problem but they are only dimensions of that central issue.

## IV

Furthermore, my opponents have also defined the problem in the context of 'rights' and 'equality'. Pat Doherty, Sinn Féin Vice-President, writing in the *Belfast Telegraph*, 25 February 2000, stated that:

> Probably more significant is the lack of product on the human rights front. While the Human Rights Commission has been established, none of the many obligations in the Agreement has been honoured. We have yet to produce and ratify a Bill of Rights. We have yet to incorporate the European Convention of Human Rights into local law.

I believe this represents a position constantly adopted by Sinn Fein, namely an expressed concern regarding the 'rights' (or perceived lack of 'rights') of the nationalist/republican community.

I fully agree that 'rights' should be protected. The basic requirements for order in any democratic society today are found within international human rights law. In the context of Northern Ireland there is no more important issue to be addressed than how we organise our society with respect to human rights. The protection of rights is a central part in the establishment and functioning of democracy. International standards of human rights go to the very heart of democratic values. Failure to abide by these universally accepted human rights standards within a state brings into question whether or not that state is democratic. Mr Ahern referred in an *Irish Times* article (2 May 2000), in respect of the problem of asylum seekers, to his government's obligations to international human rights standards. These rights embrace a number of categories: civil, political, economic, social, religious and cultural. The question has been how we can manage the differences that exist in Northern Ireland in ways consistent with democratic values and human rights.

This commitment to human rights reflects much more than a personal obligation on my part; it should be an obligation on all involved to subscribe to international human rights norms. The Irish government, in the 1990s, convened a Forum for Peace and Reconciliation. Like similar forums elsewhere, this forum heard evidence and commissioned studies.

Professors Kevin Boyle (a leading civil rights activist in Northern Ireland in the 1960s), Colm Campbell and Tom Hadden wrote for the Forum in May 1996 the following:

> Decisions on what should constitute fundamental human rights can no longer be regarded as a matter for people in individual states to decide as best they can. The substance of fundamental human rights is now determined by international consensus.

A clear framework such as that found today within international human rights law provides a coherent approach that should give a consistent thread to both words and deeds by both unionists and nationalists/republicans. Without such a clear framework, policy could veer first one way and then another. I am happy to redefine unionism in a rights/equality framework. In trying to do so, an understanding of the word 'minority' is required. I remember very well during the talks process the first time that I mentioned 'minority rights'. I was abruptly told by a senior member of the SDLP that, and I quote, 'I don't ever again want to hear you use the word minority in these talks when you are referring to nationalists.' I have learned to under-stand that the word 'minority' carries with it an implication of being somewhat less in importance. The Council of Europe is the foremost organisation regarding the implementation of human rights – it is responsible for the European Court of Human Rights and the European Convention on Human Rights. The Council has referred to a national minority as a group of persons within a state 'who display distinctive ethnic, cultural, religious or linguistic characteristics' and are 'motivated by a concern to preserve together that which constitutes their common identity'. Such a national minority is to be 'sufficiently representative, although smaller in number than the rest of the population of that state or a region of that state'. This reflects more truly – and sensitively – my concept of a minority; merely smaller in number than other groupings within a state.

Dr Michael Breisky, a former Austrian Ambassador to Ireland, gave a lecture in October 1998 at Queen's University, Belfast, entitled 'Dealing with minorities: a challenge for Europe'. He was very clear on this point. While it is necessary, as a first element, that minorities are protected by the norms of international rules, a second and equally important element requires the breaking down of psychological barriers: the sense of superiority/inferiority must be eliminated. The building of confidence and trust is required.

## V

I appreciate that unionists must convince nationalists/republicans that there will be a fair deal for all within Northern Ireland – that they have a stake in Northern Ireland and can play an important role at each level of government. Equally, unionists must be convinced that all will work within the institutions of government in Northern Ireland in the context of a peaceful environment. This is where real confidence building is required. It goes without saying that others, outside unionism, also need to redefine their thinking. For example, I believe that part of the inherent difficulty in the past was the manner in which previous United Kingdom, and Irish, governments approached the issue of our divided society. It was based on a belief that they faced a unique problem. In February 1995, the *Frameworks document* described Northern Ireland as being in a 'special position'. The then Prime Minister, John Major, described Northern Ireland in the foreword as 'unique'.

The assertion that the central problem in Northern Ireland is unique is not based on objective judgement: there are perhaps a hundred million people across Europe who consider themselves to be on the wrong side of a border. Whether it be Russians in Estonia, Hungarians in Slovakia, Austrians in Italy, or for that matter Muslims in the Philippines – to name but some examples – the dynamics of community division are the same, and thus subject equally to international human rights standards.

I believe that in fully supporting the Belfast Agreement we have at last correctly defined and reflected the concept of 'the totality of relationships', referred to in the various communiqués issued by Mr Haughey and Mrs Thatcher in 1980. There is more in common between the two main islands than there is in division between us. We use the same first language, are joint heirs to a rich Anglo-Irish culture, share many customs and practices, have access to the same media, drive on the same side of the road and have a similar climate which influences many aspects of life. The Belfast Agreement reflects both political and geographic reality. It reflects also best international practice – in a maximalist way – for accommodating diversity.

The Ulster Unionist Party gave its absolute commitment to create an inclusive government – unionist, nationalist and republican – for Northern Ireland. That executive was created in December 1999. For confidence to develop and the process to continue, unionism's continued commitment in word and deed needs to be equally matched by the republican movement regarding a complete end to all violence. This unprecedented commitment to inclusiveness by unionism has in my view been too little acknowledged. The inclusiveness was of course built into the Belfast Agreement to which my colleagues and I agreed as a settlement of Northern Ireland's longstanding conflict. Yet our commitment to inclusivity was not enough to receive a matching commitment concerning an end to violence. Sinn Féin insisted that it be let into government without any certainty or clarity that decommissioning would take place.

Indeed, the point seemed to be little appreciated that without matching commitments and actions by the republican movement, unionists would naturally lose faith with its intentions and come to fear that the republican game plan was not peace and stability in Northern Ireland. Consequently, Stormont was suspended in February 2000. The Executive was reinstated in May 2000, but has been subject to further uncertainty, including the resignation of the First Minister Mr David Trimble on 1 July 2001. It was not until Autumn 2001, when the IRA began the process of putting weapons beyond use, that the Executive was fully restored. Only if all aspects continue to be implemented will the Northern Ireland administration become stable.

I have to say that those of us involved closely in the process were at times disappointed, to put it mildly, at the overt support by the Irish Government for the 'spin' adopted by Sinn Féin. A *Sunday Independent* article on 19 March 2000, written by John A. Murphy, summarises well the Ulster Unionist perception. It commenced: 'De Valera would be alarmed at the propaganda boost Sinn Féin is getting from Fianna Fáil.'

Also, in a much more disturbing vein, I give you a quotation from the *Sunday Business Post* of 26 March 2000. In this paper columnist Tom McGurk wrote:

> For 30 years now we have tried every conceivable political and constitutional arrangement to retain the linkage with Britain in order to placate them. Not only constitutional nationalism but even republicanism has turned itself inside out in ever more radical attempts to show them a face they might accept. But the answer again and again is no.

I am honestly at times left wondering. For all the millions of words written and spoken on the Northern Ireland problem the gulf in comprehension between some remains dauntingly large.

## VI

In conclusion, however, I want to be positive. The Northern Ireland problem is not insoluble. Real progress is truly possible and indeed has occurred, and it must be based on accepted international standards of democracy. As long as all sides subscribe to the same principles of democracy, I firmly believe that we can navigate a path through to political stability. In Northern Ireland, most people wish to live in peace with their neighbours while recognising the right of those neighbours to be different from a cultural, linguistic, educational or religious perspective. Unionists accept the international norms that are appropriate for a divided society. Indeed we have interpreted them in a maximalist fashion, going further to accommodate diversity than in any other European country. While we have moved to the centreline of international best practice and beyond it, the republican movement still remains short of this centreline. Our position is not one of unionism making more demands upon republicanism than are made upon us. Nor is it merely about the implementation of the Belfast Agreement. It is much more fundamental than that – it is about an issue that goes to the very heart of democratic values, the protection of democracy against the threat of violence.

Let me make it clear, Sinn Féin has a conditional right to participate in the government of Northern Ireland at executive level: this automatic inclusiveness is indeed a unique form of government. However, to exercise this right Sinn Féin, and all others, must show responsibility towards democratic values accepted elsewhere.

No other part of the democratic world would accept entry to government by a party which has direct linkages with a paramilitary organisation that has merely declared a ceasefire. A ceasefire alone by the IRA is not enough to demonstrate commitment to peace and democracy. There is an obligation on the republican movement at this time to deliver a clear message that it is committed permanently to peace. The putting of weapons beyond use by the IRA represents a significant step forward in this regard; however, this process must continue.

We wish to see a real and honourable accommodation based on the Belfast Agreement and accepted standards of democracy. For our part, we have been, are, and will remain, committed to universally accepted standards of human rights and democracy. We have no desire to seek to define these in any restrictive manner.

If that willingness from all to continue to deliver balanced commitments is forthcoming, we have the opportunity to put aside old enmities and focus on building a healthy society and a strong economy: a Northern Ireland where human rights of all sections of the community are sacrosanct.

That is the future that the vast majority of unionism wants. The future will show whether or not we can begin finally to put to rest this long outdated quarrel.

**Chapter 5**

# Redefining loyalism

David Ervine

I

Loyalism as we know it in Northern Ireland today was first defined around 1971–2, when the dominant interests within unionism decided that they needed to have a distancing process between themselves and those who, rather than engaging in mere rhetoric, were actually physically prepared to fight. These unionist interests embarked then on a process of developing for themselves a position which separated them from any sense of complicity in the problem that is Northern Ireland. In other words, those relatively comfortable people who live on the 'Gold Coast' – an area outside Belfast where property values are very high, where the quality of life is good and the remuneration is substantial – consciously opted out of involvement in the activities of more militant unionists, allowing them to go their own way.

Of course, paramilitarism is not something to which societies are immune. In real terms the phenomenon of paramilitarism was actually created in the 1970s, and therefore the important question has to do with the circumstances that gave rise to it, and which helped to shape Northern Ireland. What on earth went wrong in the time when there were no paramilitaries? What actually happened when there was no rampant UDA, UVF or IRA? What was so wrong in our society that the circumstances of explosion were created? Could it be that the suppression of a group of people, the denial of political exposure, the denial of any sense of capacity to influence the society in which they lived had some contribution to make, or could act as some kind of cause that led to an explosion of violence?

We have got to remember that 27 years of nationalist opposition in the early years of Northern Ireland brought nationalists to the heady heights where they managed to get one piece of legislation through the Stormont Parliament, a piece of legislation so insignificant that many see it as amusing – an amendment to the Wild Birds Act. That was nationalism's contribution to the legal framework of the Northern Ireland state. This contribution is so insignificant that it is an indictment that puts an onus on the unionist community – even on those who feel themselves not to have been complicit – to begin a digging process and to begin to look at how they might have contributed to the circumstances of this society. The reality is that we had a one-party state; that we *did* discriminate; that we created circumstances where there were 'them' and 'us' – circumstances that undoubtedly create the conditions for bitterness and hatred, because 'them' and 'us' translated into another language implies a zero sum game.

Yet the two communities live and have lived for long often no more than 50 metres apart. If our trajectory was good we could hit each other, and if our voices were loud we could hear each other. But the two communities did not know each other, and indeed, we have never really known each other. We have been born in separate hospitals, go to separate schools, sign on at separate unemployment exchanges, and to add insult to injury we are buried in separate graveyards. Although there are other societies like this, the reality is that Northern Ireland is only 90 miles long by 90 miles wide. The sectarian dichotomy is brutal and vicious. It sees 93 percent of us living in areas that are homogeneously Protestant or Catholic; only seven per cent of our society is mixed. Now I do not for a moment believe that sectarianism does not flourish in the drawing rooms, or that it is absent among the privileged. It flourishes among all classes. Sectarianism can grow among the privileged classes just as easily as in the impoverished areas of cities (which, in other respects, were not greatly different from corresponding districts of Dublin, Newcastle, Manchester, Liverpool or London).

Of course, the growth of sectarianism is fairly understandable when people on one side of the community do not know the other side, and can never appreciate their desires and hopes and dreams – ones that in many ways mirror the hopes and desires and dreams of one's own community. Why is it that such issues as the price of a bag of coal, the price of a loaf, or the pathetic education system at working-class level in Northern Ireland have never drawn the people together? Could it be because of the phenomenon of sectarianism? Could it be the circumstances of division? Could it be the flourishing of elitism? Or could it be that there are those who do well from such division? I contend that the last of these is the case. Why was it that in 1922 the then Unionist government paid – as some are old enough to remember – the small sum of £2 10s. a week to loyalist gunmen (though not so described) to defend the new state, if necessary by shooting Catholics? This arose from the interests of those who believed themselves to be in authority, those who believed themselves to be in control, those who believed that potentially they had something to lose.

## II

The position is different today, but there are still some similarities. It is clear that certain vested interests seek to maintain divisions within unionism; in late 1999 and during 2000 I buried seven of my colleagues, victims of violence perpetrated by other loyalists. Yet it is precisely my party that has stood as effectively the only real bulwark and defence for the Good Friday Agreement on the unionist side for some time. Indeed, in an important sense we have prepared the ground in this respect for the Unionist Party.

But the capacity of my party to follow this independent path depends on the actions of others. When my society is attacked from without, the questions and the challenges enter my community like an Exocet missile and explode inside, causing – or, rather, aggravating – a sense of fear and trepidation. We then do what all tribes do; we weld ourselves into a homogeneous unit to be driven by the lowest common denominator because of the fear of what lies outside the tribe. An important debate about unionism still needs to be fought out within the unionist community. It is a question of defining who we are and what we are, and of overcoming the simple but frightening terms in which we see ourselves, and, indeed, in which others see us. There have to be circumstances within which we have our own security, our own confidence, our own belief. The alternative is that the people of Northern Ireland define that which they do not want rather than embrace that which they do want, and that, surely, leads to a constantly negative form of politics.

Although no conceivable good can come out of a continually negative politics of this kind – other than fear and trepidation – the reality is that unionist leaders have been cultivating precisely such attitudes of fear for the past 30 years. Ordinary unionists have been told: 'you're sold out', 'you're beaten' or 'you've every right to be frightened'; and their sense of insecurity was further exacerbated by use of such phrases as 'the betraying British government' and 'the preying Irish government'. When the violence of the republican movement is added to all of those things, it confirms for the Dr Paisleys of this world that from their own point of view it is better to be defeated than to compromise. We should not forget that his church is called the Martyrs' Memorial Church.

My party is not about martyrdom, but about the construction of a new society, and the pursuit of pluralism, justice and equality. It is indeed an indictment of our society that, at the beginning of the twenty-first century, the struggle for equality is still on the agenda in Northern Ireland – despite the best efforts of British and American politicians. We are not going to wipe away the fears and trauma of generations, passed on and nurtured in this sectarian cauldron, through the medium of the good intentions of outsiders. We have to start almost afresh, and we start on the basis of equality, of our own appreciation of the other community.

When I was a child we used to shout 'we are the people'. Of course, that meant that somebody else was *not* part of the people, but I did not realise that at the time. Now, we would settle for being 'a' people, a consequence of the trauma and suffering through which our community has been. But in addition to this identity, we need to emphasise our common humanity with members of the other community – to promote the issues that unite us rather than those that divide us. We need to address the circumstances that we have to come to terms with, and the promises that we owe to each other: the right to live in peace, free and unmolested in the context of one's political or religious beliefs.

These are true core issues for my community. When the Good Friday Agreement was being negotiated in its draft form we offered the theory of radical change. We argued that we did not want a 'Paddy' bill of rights, we wanted *a* bill of rights. We did not want a bill of rights that just dealt with why Protestants and Catholics, or nationalists, unionists, loyalists or republicans, had found it difficult to live side by side. We just wanted rights for human beings – whether this refers to circumstances that made people homosexuals, to accidents at birth that made people disabled or less able-bodied, to being born a Protestant or born a Catholic, or – the big issue – whether one is born male or female. All of these issues are of central importance in the construction of a modern society.

## III
The main contribution of the Progressive Unionist Party and the so-called new loyalism to the future of our society will be its role in fuelling debate within unionism. Unionism, through that debate, will become stronger. It will be less frightened, and issues such as 'no guns, no government' will become less important. Although politicians may joke among themselves about it, this issue is the most defining and critical circumstance that our society faces, and therefore it is always a 'make or break' one. When an issue acquires a significance of this kind, it becomes dangerous. The successive majorities that Mr Trimble won in his own party in the various votes that have taken place since the agreement was signed required him to keep his supporters happy by imposing some form of sanction against Sinn Féin, culminating in his refusal to authorise their attendance at meetings of the North/South Ministerial Council. We will never know whether or not he would have succeeded without introducing that sanction – this is a judgement call that only he could make.

Developments on the loyalist side depend in large measure on developments on the republican side. My own commitment to the process was based on a belief that Gerry Adams and Martin McGuinness were genuine. This assessment was necessary to sell the Good Friday Agreement – by tramping up and down the whole of the country talking to groups, large and small, trying to explain endlessly what lay in front of us. One of the defining circumstances on which our supporters' acceptance of the Good Friday Agreement depended, and indeed on which acceptance of a loyalist ceasefire had been built in the first instance, was the steady shift in the republican movement.

Few people will have read the 'Green Book', the IRA code. The 'Green Book' is something that most unionists know nothing about, unless they believe it is some kind of set of rules of the road. Notwithstanding the unionist perception that republicans have been killing them for 30 years, unionists never went out of their way to try and understand the mindset of republicanism. But if we make an effort to do this, we will see a seismic shift. We can come to understand how difficult it must have been to turn the juggernaut, and we pay respect to and accept the bona fides of those who did that – not an easy challenge for members of my community. But many unionists do not want to know that Gerry Adams and Martin McGuinness exist; they do not even want decommissioning. The reality is that decommissioning would threaten the political standpoint of the Democratic Unionist Party, by removing the bogeyman on which their political careers have been built. For them, the retention of weapons by republicans is an important political prop.

But retention of weapons is also important to my party. My community in Northern Ireland believes that conflict resolution is a magic formula: that it comes, as it were, in a plastic bottle that is to be found on the shelf in the chemist's shop, and that you apply it like suntan lotion. Or they may believe that it is a particular event. But conflict resolution is not a simple, once-off move; it is a process; and when you are a politician, process protects. Process allows you to manoeuvre and take forward the arguments and the circumstances based upon the protection that process creates. We in the loyalist community have educated our people and worked hard at it, but the larger unionist community has not been educated well enough on the issues of process. There are potential difficulties around the corner for the peace and political processes, but it should be remembered that these are not one and the same thing. It is only when the peace process and the political process converge that perhaps we will come of age.

In the meantime, we watch as the leaders of all of the pro-agreement parties struggle bravely with their constituencies. But the whole structure remains vulnerable to attack, given that the Good Friday Agreement and its parameters prove the interdependency of the relationships between people – not just within Northern Ireland, but between Northern Ireland and the Irish Republic, and indeed between this island and the island of Great Britain. The picture is almost like a set of tent poles or a wigwam; you know that if you take one item away, they will all fall.

## IV

This interdependence shows us that the strength that we should be looking for is from each other. It must be based upon the 'politics of need' rather than the mutually exclusive 'politics of want' about which each side in a divided society keeps megaphoning the other. It is really now high time that loyalism, republicanism, unionism and nationalism began the process of choreography to deliver to the people the benefits of the Good Friday Agreement. If we fail to deliver the benefits, the people will quite reasonably argue that the Good Friday Agreement does not mean a great deal for them. But contained within the Good Friday Agreement, I believe, are substantial benefits for all of our people. It is therefore remiss of us not to get on with the job of delivering benefits as speedily as possible.

I therefore advocate, or indeed demand, that we very soon begin the process of choreography that will on the one hand protect the politicians who have to make the dangerous and risky moves, while on the other hand ensuring that the people begin to recognise the flow of benefit to them, and support the politics of a new dimension rather than the old tired politics of the past. For David Trimble, let's hear Ehud Barak; for Gerry Adams, let's hear Yasser Arafat; for Real IRA, let's hear Hamas. The processes of movement, change and dynamics in any divided society, especially a divided society with violence at its core, are the same. The moralists or the fundamentalists will always bite the ankles of the visionaries. There's nothing new in that, as we should know. We as human beings should have studied that, but of course theories of conflict resolution are so underdeveloped that we have no science of such a thing. It is now in embryonic form, at its very beginning, and we are going to learn more and more about it. We are never going to teach it in our schools because the issue of conflict is one of the things of which we have been victim since man inhabited this earth, and yet is the one science we do not have. We have obstetrics, we have mathematics and all kinds of sciences and yet we do not have a science that stops us killing each other.

Why is that? Why is it that we have not developed as a people enough to encourage each other to have value for all other human beings – that we know each other as people rather than focusing on our perception of an unknown ideology which is different from ours? Why is it that we do not put our children in schools together? What have we to be frightened of when children at four or five years of age begin to know each other as human beings rather than finding out that they do not like someone simply on the basis of their ideology – especially if they have never really met them anyway? Is it not better that we build a society that has people with full educational ability? This should be not just the education of the 'three Rs'; it should be education for life.

I would like to finish with this thought. It is my belief that the conveyor belt which has begun on this island is unstoppable. There are, and have been, and will again be, dark days. But I do not believe that the people can be forever denied the right to peace, justice and pluralism. We must remember that no matter what pain goes on around us, the bigger picture means a lot more in the longer term. There will be peace on this island. Indeed, there will be peace in the British Isles. But we must all realise that no one group, no one person has the capacity to define the price of this peace.

Chapter 6

# Redefining Ireland

Desmond O'Malley

## I

The story is told of an Englishman who sought guidance from an Irishman on the complexities of political attitudes on this island. 'It is very simple', came the answer. 'In the north they love England but hate the English; in the south, they hate England but love the English'. The story may be apocryphal but it highlights the difficulty of defining nationalism, or unionism, or loyalism, or republicanism, or any of the other 'isms' that inhabit the Irish body politic.

My task in this chapter is to examine the process of change in southern nationalism; but before describing southern nationalism as it now is, it may be useful to define it first as it used to be.

## II

For perhaps 40 years after independence southern nationalism was essentially an aggressive and negative political force. It was almost as if the terms 'Irish' and 'anti-British' were synonymous or interchangeable. Effectively, we defined ourselves in terms of our historic conflict with Britain; and that conflict was seen to endure in the struggle to end partition. The Northern Ireland state was viewed as the last British outpost on the island of Ireland, a remnant of the old colonial structure. There was little attempt to understand unionism or to engage with it. There was virtually no acceptance that the Northern majority had any right to determine their own constitutional position.

Economically, southern nationalism adhered to a doctrine of self-reliance. Protectionism was the order of the day. There was a sense of isolationism which allowed us to pursue an 'economic war' with Britain even though the consequences for Ireland were horrendous. The Second World War highlighted some of the inconsistencies in anglophobic nationalism. We were not going to fight on behalf of the old enemy: we would remain neutral instead. Yet, it is widely recognised now that if we were neutral, we were neutral in favour of Britain.

There were inconsistencies also in the economic field. Yes, we had secured our political independence and freedom. But for hundreds of thousands of

Irish people of the 1920s, 1930s, 1940s, and 1950s freedom from England meant little more than the freedom to emigrate to England.

The evolution of southern nationalism was slow, but I think it is fair to say that that evolution began when Sean Lemass became Taoiseach in 1959. Lemass was a veteran of the War of Independence – indeed, he took part in the 1916 rising. But he wanted to face the future rather than be imprisoned by the past. Crucially, he recognised that, in the Irish context, real economic nationalism and independence would require policies which were outward looking, not introspective. Ably assisted by brilliant civil servants such as Kenneth Whitaker and John Leydon, he initiated the internationalisation of the Irish economy which provided the foundation for the economic prosperity which we enjoy today in this country. It was Lemass, too, who finally began to thaw out our frigid relations with unionism. Today, meetings between Bertie Ahern and David Trimble are so commonplace that they hardly make the news any more. Things were very different back in the mid-1960s and the meetings which took place between Lemass and his Northern counterpart, Terence O'Neill, were groundbreaking events by any standards.

W. T. Cosgrave and Eamon de Valera were the dominant political figures of the earlier independent Ireland. Between them, they headed the government of this country for a total of 35 years. Lemass held the position of Taoiseach for just six; but I think the Ireland of the beginning of the twenty-first century is much more the Ireland of Lemass than it is the Ireland of Cosgrave or of de Valera. Lemass sowed the seeds for a new kind of southern nationalism, a positive nationalism that was more extrovert, more confident, less threatening and more vibrant than anything that had gone before.

The process of change was slow, however, and within a few years of Sean Lemass's retirement as Taoiseach the old, negative aspects of Irish nationalism were on view again.

## III

For 30 years the Provisional IRA would wage a cruel and dirty war in pursuit of an atavistic 'Brits Out' strategy. For 30 years they would so besmirch the name of nationalism that many Irish people no longer felt comfortable calling themselves nationalists. It is ironic that the ultimate effect of the Provisional republicans' long war has been to undermine totally the political philosophy upon which their campaign was based.

It is now accepted – even by the Provisional republicans themselves – that the principle of consent applies. It is now accepted that the people of Northern Ireland have the right to determine their own future. Articles 2 and 3 are gone. And it is now accepted that normal, friendly relations should prevail between Ireland and Britain as neighbouring states and as fellow members of the European Union. A lot of what we were told were 'core values' is gone.

Southern nationalism has matured. It is now virtually unrecognisable from the political creed that dominated in the first four decades after independence. It has, in fact, redefined itself.

The pace of change in Ireland just now is quite extraordinary, notwithstanding the recent slowdown in the pace of economic growth. Instead of labour surpluses we now have labour shortages. Instead of emigration we now have immigration. Instead of national poverty we have national prosperity. Essentially, we are making the transition from being one of the developed world's poorer economies to being one of the developed world's wealthier economies. That transition has proven difficult in other countries and it could prove difficult here too. Prosperity, by its nature, produces diversity. There is a drab sameness about poverty. Immigrants arrive with new religions, new cultures and new languages. Former emigrants return with new ideas and new attitudes. Foreign influences become more pervasive through improved access to the media, to overseas contacts and through foreign travel.

The problem is that certain strains of nationalism find it very difficult to cope with diversity: one only has to look at what happened under the Nazis in Europe in the 1930s for proof of this. So how are we in Ireland going to cope with diversity? What political model will we evolve to cope with our rapidly changing situation? What new forms will nationalism take on in the South of Ireland?

According to some media commentators Sinn Féin may offer one such model. In government north and south their political model could come to dominate in both parts of this island, or so we are told. Sinn Féin is certainly nationalist on political matters. But it is decidedly socialist on economic matters. Furthermore, it seems to me that the party can hardly be described as normal and democratic while it retains its own army. They hate those who disagree with them. On reflection I do not think the Sinn Féin model is what either part of this country needs in the years ahead.

## IV

The 1980s did not begin auspiciously in Ireland. In October of 1980 the first hunger strike began. By the following year, against a background of widespread public disorder, ten hunger strikers had died and the whole situation had become hopelessly polarised. Republican terrorism continued. Loyalist groups continued with their campaign of sectarian murder. It was indeed a bleak time.

Charles Haughey had become Taoiseach in December 1979 and immediately threw himself into the search for a new way forward on the Irish problem. He set about engaging Margaret Thatcher in the Irish question at two meetings in 1980 – described as 'summits' in the days before such prime ministerial meetings became commonplace. His thesis was that the Northern Ireland problem was essentially a problem between Britain and Ireland and that it could only be solved by agreement between the governments of Britain and Ireland. Some progress was made, including the establishment of the Anglo-Irish Intergovernmental Council, a new dimension to high-level relations between Dublin and London.

Haughey's approach effectively excluded the views of the people of Northern Ireland from any resolution of the overall problem. I did not agree with this, but it did at least have a certain crude nationalist consistency to it. The problem, however, was that Haughey himself found it difficult to maintain a consistent position on any issue. For his formula to be successful, a close working relationship between the two governments and the two prime ministers was essential. Without such relationships his approach was going nowhere. A major test came with the eruption of the Falklands dispute between Britain and Argentina. Ireland abstained on the vote on European sanctions against Argentina and Haughey authorised his defence minister to describe Britain as the aggressor in the conflict. Haughey lost office some months later. He would spend the next four-and-a-half years in opposition, and his policy on Anglo-Irish relations during that period appeared to be based more on opportunism than conviction.

The new government under Garret FitzGerald set up the New Ireland Forum to examine options for the way forward in Northern Ireland. Haughey participated personally in its deliberations. But he sounded off in outraged tones when the Forum's final report, which he signed, advocated consideration of options other than a unitary state. The following year – 1985 – FitzGerald, building ironically on the progress Haughey had made, persuaded Mrs Thatcher to sign the Hillsborough Agreement. This was a notable achievement in Anglo-Irish relations, giving the Irish government for the first time the formal right to be consulted in relation to the affairs of Northern Ireland.

Most Irish people recognised Hillsborough for the achievement it was. But Haughey led his party in outright opposition to it. He could not bring himself accept the principle of consent which was formally embedded in it, the first time an Irish government had explicitly accepted this principle in its dealings with the British government. Haughey's rejection of the agreement was one of the factors which triggered the foundation of the Progressive Democrats in December of 1985. Again, his position was based more on opportunism than principle: he accepted and worked the Hillsborough Agreement on his return to government early in 1987.

Haughey had a genuine political problem with the hunger strikes in the early 1980s. The election to the Dáil of two hunger-strike candidates in 1981 helped to deprive him of office, and he was looking over his shoulder at Republican threats of varying intensity both inside and outside his own party. Nevertheless, his unwillingness to take a position of leadership on the issue of consent must be considered a failure of leadership on his part. The whole debate about consent seems rather quaint now. Today everybody, even the Provos, accepts the principle of consent; only a few Republican murder-gangs still hold out against it. One might be forgiven for asking what all the fuss was about. But at the time of the formation of the Progressive Democrats it was still a hot issue.

Such is the course of political history. Radical new ideas emerge all the time. But when a radical new idea is accepted it becomes the norm. And so it has turned out with the principle of consent. Looking back now one can see a certain irony in the whole saga of Northern Ireland. For as long as Irish nationalism stuck to its traditionalist line it achieved nothing. Yet, when it abandoned its attachment to the concept of an all-island majority and accepted the concept of consent within Northern Ireland it began to achieve great things, culminating in the Good Friday Agreement. The experience of 'not-an-inch' nationalism may offer important lessons to disciples of 'not-an-inch' unionism. Political engagement will yield them far richer dividends than political isolation.

## V

To return to the larger picture, history shows that the political model best capable of accommodating diversity and promoting prosperity is that of the liberal democratic republic. If Irish nationalism is to redefine itself it could do so by reclaiming for civil society the ownership of the word 'republican'.

To me a republican is someone who believes in the primacy of the people through an exclusively democratic process. To me a republican is someone who believes in promoting opportunity for all and privilege for none. To me a republican is someone who respects the rights of others freely to hold and peacefully to express opposing views. To me a republican is someone who believes in the guiding principle of tolerance as the basis of civilised living in society. Defined in those terms I am proud to call myself a republican.

I got myself into a lot of trouble back in the mid-1980s for saying that I stood by the Republic. Seventeen years on, I still do.

**Part 2**

# Academic perspectives

Chapter 7

# The reorientiation of constitutional nationalism

Jennifer Todd

## Introduction

Irish nationalism in Northern Ireland has been the subject of very little intellectual analysis. If one compares recent writings on unionism, a burgeoning academic field where the character of the movement and distinctions within it are argued out in sophisticated and comparative manner, northern nationalism has had very little attention.

There are exceptions, particularly in the detailed analyses of nationalist attitudes and preferences as given in surveys and opinion polls (see, for example, Rose, 1971; Moxon-Browne, 1983; Breen, 1996; Hayes and McAllister, 1999; Evans and O'Leary, 2000). These works have rightly pointed to the paradoxes associated with northern nationalism. The first paradox is that not all northern nationalist voters want a united Ireland (only two thirds of SDLP supporters in a recent 1998 survey favoured a united Ireland and this figure is consistent with the trend over time; see Hayes and McAllister, 1999). Second, northern nationalist opinion is fluctuating, conditional, varying with the situation and perceived opportunities. Most nationalists favour a united Ireland as a long-term aspiration; the numbers reduce (to about two thirds) when it is posed as a realistic middle- or short-term option, and reduce further (down to a quarter) when it is posed as an immediate possibility (see Ruane and Todd, 1996, 66–7). However, this also varies with the political situation: in an important *Fortnight* poll carried out in 1988, a quarter of Catholics in the sample reported fluctuation in their political views and sympathies after the Gibraltar killings, the Stalker and Sampson reports and the Enniskillen bombing (Fortnight, 1988). Third, strong Irish nationalist identifiers who also want a united Ireland have steadily increased in numbers over the last decade (Hayes and McAllister, 1999).

But there is little or no explanation of the significance of this rich data. Academic writing has fallen short in theorising about the nature of the nationalist/Catholic community in Northern Ireland and of its political options. In effect, we have here a group thrust into existence (as northern Catholics and northern nationalists) by partition, against their will in a situation not of their choosing, whose interests begin to be articulated only as new options are opened and a level of self-determination becomes possible, and whose views are therefore fluid, open-ended, changeable, and hard to catch in surveys. But rather than seeking to develop the implications of this – and there are plenty of comparative examples to explore – the academic literature is silent.

Why is so little academic attention paid to northern nationalism? I can suggest four reasons for this, not all of them convincing. The first reason is that northern nationalists, and leaders such as John Hume in particular, are very articulate: it could be argued that they do not need commentators. But this is unconvincing because it ignores the ambiguities and slippages in northern nationalist discourse which have given rise to radically conflicting interpretations both among the public (peacemaker versus devious nationalist) and among intellectuals (Longley, 1994; Cunningham, 1997; Kearney, 1997).

The second reason is commonly expressed in the Republic. It is said that northern nationalism is now so close to southern nationalism that no analysis of it is needed. But this argument is defective both in its conflation of northern and southern nationalism (as we will see, they are quite distinct in ideological structure) and in its complacency: precisely because the nationalisms are close, people in the South need the sense of distance that intellectual typologies can give.

The third reason, this time rather less unconvincing, is pragmatic. The dramatic success story of the new constitutional nationalism in the North, from the Anglo-Irish Agreement of 1985 to the Good Friday Agreement of 1998, has made intellectual commentary seem superfluous. It was the perceived defeat of unionism in the Anglo-Irish Agreement which prompted the emergence of a new generation of unionist intellectuals: the perceived success of nationalism has prompted intellectuals on the other side to work on other pressing issues. Indeed, the SDLP's impatience with what they call 'theology', i.e. absolute clarity on such issues as sovereignty and the national question, has also encouraged other intellectual priorities. But, now that the Good Friday Agreement is achieved, it may be that this reason has lost its force. I will argue that now, for nationalists in Northern Ireland, the successful ideology promulgated by John Hume no longer gives the necessary direction or guidance about the choices that are generated in the implementation of the Good Friday Agreement. Maybe now theology becomes practically necessary.

The fourth reason for ignoring the intellectual content of northern nation-alism, again an unsatisfactory one, has to do with the cultural limitations of the South (where it is easy to get impatient with it) and of Britain (where it is easy to get bored by it). In neither state is the northern nationalist political agenda *their* agenda, nor are northern nationalist priorities their priorities. In the South, the closeness yet separation in respect of northern nationalists, the commonality yet difference, has led to mutual disappointment and hurt as each learns more about the other and finds their immediate expectations confounded. It should be said, though, that this is an inadequate reason for failing to study northern nationalism. Precisely such cultural tensions are open to intellectual analysis which can throw new light not just on northern nationalism but on aspects of the mainstream Irish–British agenda.

## Traditional nationalism in Northern Ireland

If political scientists and sociologists have been slow to study northern nationalists, historians have begun the task of providing an account of the history of the constitution of the northern Catholic and nationalist community (Phoenix, 1994; Harris, 1993; Purdie, 1986, 1990; Farrell, 1980; most recently Elliott, 2000; Staunton, 2001). This is, first, a story of diversity: Eamonn Phoenix has shown this diversity by locality – Catholics in the border counties were not distinct from their southern neighbours, although the strength of Sinn Féin, and within this of pro- and anti-treaty factions, varied from region to region. Catholics in Belfast were politically distinct, both in the continuing strength of Joe Devlin's Redmondite organisation, and, more profoundly, in their reaction to their situation as a minority in a British provincial industrial city. Even within the Catholic Church, as Mary Harris demonstrates, the whole range of nationalist political attitudes (from old Irish Parliamentary Party to anti-Treaty Sinn Féin) existed in the hierarchy itself in the decades surrounding partition. This diverse population, with little in common other than being the Irish Catholics left over in Northern Ireland after the 1921 settlement, was thrust into community organisation – initially largely church centred – and community identity and ideology.

The nationalist party that emerged by the late 1920s, closely linked to parish organisation, accepted the Irish nationalist ideology of the pre-partition period (Todd, 1990). This classic nationalism took as its premise the primary existence of the Irish nation and its right to self-determination and sovereign statehood. This nation was sundered and mutilated, as Cahir Healy (1945) put it, by partition, which produced an unnatural state – the tearing of a branch off the parent tree (Campbell, 1941). The primary objective was the reunification of Ireland as an independent state. To this, northern nationalists added a righteous anger not just at partition but at the multiple injustices suffered by northern Catholics under unionist rule, from discrimination in work and housing allocation, to intimidation and murder, to cultural humiliation and slights (Healy, 1945; Ultach, 1943). This prioritising of principles of justice was what came to distinguish northern from southern nationalism after 1920. A united Ireland was desired as much as a remedy for injustice as on traditional nationalist grounds, with the injustice of the northern state and the national injustice of partition dovetailing in nationalist rhetoric. The principles of nationalism and justice were not clearly distinguished, nor were the potential tensions between them acknowledged. These did not need to be acknowledged, for there was little prospect of reform of the state, so that criticising injustice was criticising the unionist state. In addition, the content of nationalism was left ambivalent – political nationalism was transmuted into cultural nationalism (a contentment with being Irish) as uniting Ireland faded as a real possibility, only to re-emerge periodically in surges of voting support for republican candidates (Purdie, 1986; Farrell, 1980).

Republican ideology was different from nationalist ideology in that it never forgot the aim of political separatism. But in other respects, the ideologies were formally similar. Belfast republicans in the 1930s were 'militant nationalists' (Munck and Rolston, 1987: 188). Republicans in this period (1920–60) differed from nationalists socially – in mores, family connections, social networks, existential attitudes – but not ideologically. All of this was to change in the decades following the civil rights movement of 1968–9.

## Redefining northern nationalism

Among its many radical effects, the civil rights movement provoked a major ideological crisis in northern nationalism. For the first time since the foundation of the state, the choice between justice and nationalism was starkly posed; the community mobilised for justice (not unity) and in so doing helped bring down the Stormont regime. As an unintended consequence, however, the civil rights movement and the conflict that surrounded it reinvigorated nationalist feeling.

That nationalist feeling required a different ideological form. In the 1970s, real opportunities were opening for northern nationalists to influence policy making, first with some limited offers of input in Faulkner's cabinet, next under direct rule and in the Sunningdale power-sharing executive. The situation was fluid and demanded a new pragmatism and realistic interim goals. The SDLP, formed in August 1970, initially as an alliance of former civil rights politicians, began to work out such an approach – power sharing, Irish dimension, unity by consent. But it was also a situation where the realities of communal power were brutally apparent. When Catholics mobilised, Stormont was eventually brought down four years later; when Protestants mobilised, Sunningdale was brought down in 14 days. The questions which had disabled nationalism from the time of partition were posed and reposed: cooperation with or antagonism towards unionists and the British? A strong nationalism (which would provoke unionists and bring no immediate gains) or a moderate reformism (which was likely to be equally ineffective)?

The answer, brilliantly conceptualised by John Hume, was to change the question and Europeanise the problem. Hume's strategy and ideology crystallised after the fall of Sunningdale. He changed the battlefield, from Northern Ireland and the United Kingdom to the European Union, the island of Ireland and the US connection. He changed the question, from nationalism *or* reform, by formulating principles of legitimacy which demanded nationalism *and* reform. This became the dominant ideology of the SDLP and served as an ideological mode of distinction from the still classic nationalism typical of republicanism in the 1970s, 1980s and much of the 1990s.

The structure of Hume's ideology is two-levelled (see Todd, 1999). The first principles are general contemporary principles of legitimacy, brought from EU and US principles, bypassing the British political tradition. At the second level, in application of these principles to the Northern Irish and broader Irish context, nationalist assumptions re-enter. At the level of first principle, Hume decisively rejected the classic nationalist model of a world of nation states and with it the classic nationalist view that nation and state should coincide. This was irrelevant in an age of European integration and international linkages (Hume, 1996: III, 114–15). Instead he emphasised the multiple and interconnected loci in which interaction takes place (Hume, 1996: 119–24, 130–3, 134–44). He prioritised the principle of agreement: a legitimate political order must be founded on agreement on the mode of government, and self-determination is precisely the process of reaching such agreement (Hume, 1996: 93–5, 138; Hume 1986, 1988). Agreement is reached through dialogue, which in turn requires institutions which ensure equality and protection of basic rights (Hume, 1996: 28, 62). Rights are understood in a broad sense, to include communal and cultural rights, while oppositional notions of identity and culture are rejected: diversity is to be accommodated, and difference is seen as a source of strength, not weakness (Hume, 1996: 59–60, 133, 142).

In applying these principles to the conflict in Northern Ireland, Hume brings back nationalist assumptions. The core – although not the exclusive – identity for one community and tradition in Northern Ireland is an Irish national identity. This national identity requires institutional recognition and respect, entailing a movement beyond Northern Ireland to a strong Irish dimension and role for the Irish state in Northern Ireland (New Ireland Forum, 1984, sections 4.15, 4.16, 5.2; Hume, 1996: 28–9, 43). The British state in the past contributed to the conflict by giving in to Protestant resistance to reform: it must now stand up to this resistance. At the same time, the island of Ireland is prioritised as a locus of democratic agreement. (Hume, 1996: 67–8). Such agreement on the island as a whole, ratified by simultaneous referenda in both parts of Ireland, is what Irish self-determination means today (Hume, 1996: 95, 125). Irish nationalism will be satisfied by this and it is a matter for further generations – once political antagonisms are overcome – to decide for themselves where future political boundaries are to lie. This is a form of nationalism which recognises the equal rights of other nationalisms, which is framed within an overarching liberal-pluralist set of principles, and which – once its minimum conditions are met – sees future change as evolutionary, gradualist and consensual.

Hume's central ideological achievement was to distinguish the two levels of ideology in his political discourse and rhetoric. Hume's nationalism exists only at the second level, and it is a matter of judgement and emphasis – emphasis on the political salience of some (national) aspects of identity over others (regional, local), and of some spatial units (the island of Ireland) over others. The emphasis can shift in the light of dialogue with unionists, of changing attitudes in the population, of emerging political possibilities. It can encompass the variety of views within the SDLP, from regionalists content with a reformed Northern Ireland within the United Kingdom, to strong nationalists. And through its first principles, it can bypass the critiques of nationalism posed within unionism and, until the recent period at least, within British political culture.

This ideology has been immensely flexible and successful politically. It has cohered closely with developments in southern nationalism: the prioritising of agreement on the island, the principle of consent, the retention of national interest in Northern Ireland while rejecting a territorial claim over it, the attempt to attain a level of Irish state influence and all-Ireland integration much less than full state sovereignty and independence. There are also practical parallels: for example the question of the origin of the New Ireland Forum of 1983–4 – whether in Hume's suggestion or in Garret FitzGerald's – can be debated  but not decided. There are, however, differences. Southern nationalism, even in its Fine Gael form, is not two-levelled. Its content is taken for granted; it is made coherent with other nationalisms, opened to world and contemporary trends, but with these provisos it is articulated explicitly. Unlike northern nationalists, the Irish state is not arguing from a position where its right to nationalism is itself challenged. The effect is a quite different structure of ideology North and South, even if it dovetails on policies and practical judgements.

## Comparative categorisation

How is this ideology to be placed in comparative terms? Let me take five possible categorisations:

*Classic nationalism.* This is a principle of political legitimacy which holds that nation and state should coincide and that the nation should determine its form of rule (McGarry and O'Leary, 1995: 13–14).

*Liberal nationalism.* This holds that nations have rights, but these rights can be satisfied by a level of political autonomy and institutionalisation of national culture which falls short of state sovereignty. In the case of conflicting national rights in one territory, they must be so satisfied (Tamir, 1993; Miller, 1995: 81–118).

*Pluralism.* This is a principle which upholds communal and cultural rights and freedoms. It holds that – as a prerequisite of political equality within a state – each relevant group should have the right to some institutionalisation of its culture in the public sphere (Kymlicka, 1995).

*Regionalism.* This involves a principle of political autonomy for regions – including autonomy in some international relations – coexisting with continued state sovereignty. It is sometimes subsumed under the principle of subsidiarity, which involves multiple levels of governance with each set of issues being assigned to the lowest possible level consistent with effective governance (Keating, 1998, points to the interactions of regionalism and nationalism in the 'new regionalism').

*Civic republicanism.* This refers to the formation by agreement of a new political order which defines equality of rights and citizenship and access to the public sphere within that order; it constitutes a civic nationality defined politically rather than ethnically. Once this new political order is constituted, ethnic-national identities become a private cultural rather than a public political matter, and are properly irrelevant to political decisions and organisation.

How should the new northern nationalism be categorised? It is certainly not classic nationalism. There is no assumption that state and nation should coincide; indeed, this premise is denied. National self-determination is redefined and based on agreement. Nor, despite some commonality of premises, is it pluralism, which does not prioritise ethno-national over other groups. Moreover, pluralism takes effect within given state boundaries, rather than between states. In the new nationalism, unlike pluralism, there is a clear territorial dimension whereby the institutionalisation of Irish identity is assumed to require linkages with the southern state.

On the other hand, the new northern nationalism shares many characteristics with liberal nationalism. It argues for institutionalisation of national culture and a level of political autonomy for the nation that falls short of independent statehood, while according equal rights to other nations. It prioritises the rights of the nation as a prerequisite for state legitimacy and nationalist consent. Many within the SDLP are liberal nationalists of this kind. They wish to lessen the significance and substance of British sovereignty in order to increase the linkages with the Irish state, and ease a future transition to Irish sovereignty (in the event of majority wish). In this sense the Good Friday Agreement is taken as initiating a process of change rather than a final settlement.

Equally, however, the new northern nationalism can be interpreted as a regionalism, emphasising the autonomy and multiple linkages of Northern Ireland, and deprioritising the issue of state sovereignty, which, on Hume's account, is becoming decreasingly important in this European and global age. In this interpretation, Northern Ireland can and should retain and expand its linkages with the South, without thus endangering either its own autonomy (expressed through the new Assembly) or lessening its linkages within Great Britain, the British Isles and Europe. Some within the SDLP are regionalists who wish to add a level of political autonomy and linkages to existing British sovereignty. These new levels may develop and expand, but British sovereignty remains unchanged, if in practice inapplicable to the new levels of politics.

It could, on the other hand, be a form of republicanism. Hume has consistently pointed out that once the principle of self-determination by agreement is satisfied by simultaneous referenda in both parts of the island, a legitimate political entity is constituted and the old nationalist territorial claim no longer holds. At this stage the 'healing process', 'shedding sweat rather than blood', begins. Has this stage been reached with the ratification of the Good Friday Agreement in referenda in both parts of Ireland? Has it constituted a new sort of republican political entity (with agreed linkages to Britain and Ireland) within which equality of citizenship prevails, which can become the focus of a civic nationalism? There are those in the SDLP who believe so, seeing the Good Friday Agreement as having replaced British sovereignty with the sovereignty of the people of Ireland, by agreement of its two parts. This is consistent with continuing British rule, with a devolved assembly and North–South and East–West linkages: ultimate authority, however, rests with the agreement of the people of Ireland. As distinct from liberal nationalists, these republicans deem as inappropriate further nationalist assertion within the institutions of the Good Friday Agreement; rather the issue is to work the institutions as agreed, without extraneous nationalist aims.

The answer may be, of course, that the new northern nationalism has combined liberal nationalism, regionalism and republicanism all at once, without distinction or concern for possible tensions between them, just as the old northern nationalism combined classic nationalism with a concern for justice. In the earlier case, the interim goals were the same and no immediate contradictions arose. Similarly, in the recent period, regionalism and liberal nationalism converged, because greater regional autonomy for Northern Ireland within the EU also promised to strengthen the liberal nationalist agenda, loosening the strength of Northern Ireland's integration into Britain and allowing a greater balance between Irish and British linkages. Liberal nationalists and regionalists as well as republicans could emphasise the need for agreement, knowing well that agreement would be possible only with quite radical changes from the status quo and greater North–South linkages.

The immediate goals of regionalists, liberal nationalists and civic republicans in a Northern Irish context therefore converged: they included changing the public culture to allow greater linkages with the South and a real level of political equality within Northern Ireland, in the light of which nationalists and unionists alike could consent to a political settlement. The prioritisation of aims might vary – some prioritised the Northern Ireland Assembly and with it a level of political autonomy for Northern Ireland, some the North–South linkages, some multiple linkages (North–South, East–West and European), and some agreement in a situation of political and cultural equality – but the Good Friday Agreement promised to go some of the way to each of the goals. The new nationalism could, therefore, remain at once liberal nationalist, regionalist and civic republican, without needing to make clear distinctions between these aims and goals. Priorities, direction and long-term future strategy might differ, but for the present there were real rhetorical and political benefits in keeping all options open – this approach maximised both external allies and internal support.

Unionists, however, saw this as a deeply problematic conflation of aims. They might possibly accept the regionalist version of North–South linkages, but not the liberal nationalist version. They might possibly be open to being wooed by the civic republican version of a new Northern Ireland, but not by a liberal nationalist vision of increasing integration with the South up to the point where all-Irish integration was at least as strong as that between Northern Ireland and Great Britain. Once again, they thought, non-nationalist language was being used to cover up nationalist aims. And, as always, this new nationalism was hard to pin down.

## The new political context and the options for nationalists

The new political context after the Good Friday Agreement is no longer so favourable to this dovetailing of distinct political projects. Just as the civil rights movement forced a choice between nationalism and justice, and later a radical redefinition of nationalism, the Good Friday Agreement may force a choice between liberal nationalism, regionalism and civic republicanism and still more redefinitions of northern nationalism. I focus on three aspects of the new political context in order to make my argument.

### The ambiguities of the Good Friday Agreement

The Good Friday Agreement is in many respects the fulfilment of the new nationalism. It also echoes its ambiguities. I will briefly indicate this by looking at the position on sovereignty. The Good Friday Agreement has been hailed by David Trimble and others as a confirmation and strengthening of British sovereignty in Northern Ireland, conditional only on the wish of a majority there. Yet if this is the case formally, substantively it promises to lessen the significance of British sovereignty, disaggregating the functions of the state and dividing them between British, Northern Irish, North–South and British–Irish institutions. Moreover, its reaffirmation of British sovereignty coexists in tension with its rooting of ultimate political authority in the people of Ireland, by agreement between its two parts, and its inclusion of all aspects of the Good Friday Agreement in an international agreement between the British and Irish states.

The text of the agreement is ambiguous on precisely these points (see Ruane and Todd, 2001). The ambiguities about sovereignty in the Good Friday Agreement lay at the root of the controversy which surrounded Peter Mandelson's dissolution of the Assembly in February 2000 against Irish government and northern nationalist advice (O'Leary, 2000). The very crisis over the dissolution of the institutions at that time forced nationalists to choose between these positions: on the liberal nationalist and civic republican views, Mandelson was in breach of the agreement; on a regionalist reading, one could make the argument that he was simply exercising British sovereignty when the lower level of decision making was proving ineffective. Nationalists in the SDLP clearly opted against the regionalist reading. The future implementation of the agreement holds out further tests for new nationalists. For example, civic republicans and liberal nationalists are distinguished by their attitudes to the new system: is it to be worked wholeheartedly, without attempt to increase the significance of Irish linkages, much less to work for a nationalist majority in Northern Ireland? That is the civic republican attitude. Or is it a stepping stone, one which will inevitably develop further and which can and should legitimately be worked to increase the importance of all-Ireland linkages? That is the liberal nationalist attitude. Each SDLP member is implicitly making his or her decisions on this as the implementation process proceeds.

### The dynamics of the new British context

The British context, with assemblies not just in Northern Ireland but also in Scotland and Wales, makes the issue of regionalism versus liberal nationalism all the more pressing. It should be noted that John Hume himself skipped over the British political context, using European and American models and images in fashioning the new nationalist discourse. It is not clear that this is any longer possible.

Today, the Scottish and Welsh Assemblies and the British–Irish Council give the prospect of a regionalism all around within the United Kingdom, albeit with Irish linkages. From this perspective, we have a new constitutional settlement in Britain, with a level of regional political autonomy for many of its constituent parts. In many respects it is analogous to the Spanish case. But in Spain there are tensions between regionalisms and nationalisms in the different autonomous provinces. Andalucian regionalists, for example, may look for as great a degree of political autonomy as Catalonia, but without ambitions of separatism or traditions of nationalism. Catalonian nationalists, in contrast, may use regionalist rhetoric and deny any desire for separatism, while retaining a clear nationalist identity and seeing the Spanish state as the main obstacle to further Catalan prosperity; some foresee a federalist future, while others see a continuing growth of autonomy, albeit without a final breach with the Spanish centre. Basque nationalists, again in contrast, are clearly separatists, using Europeanist regionalist rhetoric only to increase their leverage for separation from Spain. Which of these models is Northern Ireland, or northern nationalists within Northern Ireland, to follow? An Andalucian style regionalism? A Catalan style gradualism where nationalism has accepted for the moment a regionalist mould? A Basque nationalism?

Moreover, a dynamic of regionalisation is emerging within the United Kingdom, where the weak Welsh Assembly looks for powers equivalent to those of the Scottish Parliament, stimulating in turn, perhaps, Scottish demands. One might envisage Northern Ireland increasingly becoming a core part of this new United Kingdom dynamic, rather than a place apart within the old British territorial system. How will northern nationalists feel about this? It is perhaps this prospect that will definitively separate the regionalists in the SDLP from the liberal nationalists, as the latter press for something other and something more than regional autonomy. Of course the closer the Irish state moves to an integrated British Isles area, the more this choice will again be blurred.

## Competition with Sinn Féin

Electoral and ideological competition between the SDLP and Sinn Féin began in earnest in the 1980s at the same time as the social distinction between republicans and nationalists which existed in the Stormont period began to dissolve. From the mid-1980s, the SDLP looked as if it was winning the competition: the effect of the Anglo-Irish agreement was to show the effectiveness and viability of the new nationalism. Since the peace process of the 1990s, the position has changed. The Sinn Féin vote has been steadily increasing since the IRA ceasefire of 1994. Moreover, Sinn Féin has refashioned its own republicanism, borrowing large parts of SDLP discourse, including its flexibility and pragmatism, although offering a more radical egalitarianism, and a sharper nationalist focus. In electoral terms, this has been effective. The demand on the SDLP, therefore, is to refashion its profile so as to win – or not to lose – in the new context. This too forces choices on the SDLP.

The SDLP could opt for a clearer regionalist profile, a clearer liberal nationalist profile or a clearer civic republican profile. There are costs and benefits to each strategy. The first, the regionalist strategy, will pay off only if the electorate is becoming less nationalist; but there is no evidence of this, and indeed the contrary appears to be the case (Hayes and McAllister, 1999). Moreover there is no immediate motivation for such a strategy, as the electoral competition (since the decline of the Alliance Party) comes from the nationalist rather than the regionalist side of the spectrum. The party could emphasise the civic republican aspect of the agreement as SDLP politicians (such as Seamus Mallon) did quite eloquently after the agreement. This provides a clear and, for many, an attractive profile, but is effective only if the agreement is wholeheartedly implemented and worked in this light by unionists and the British, as well as nationalists. The evidence until recently – in such areas as delays in forming the executive, the dissolution of the Assembly in February 2000, and the issue of police reform – was that it was not so being worked. Unless the position changes, this will cut the ground from under the civic republican strategy. Or the SDLP could emphasise the liberal nationalist profile, while emphasising that – unlike Sinn Féin – they provide safe hands. In the long term, this could risk losing voters to a regenerated regionalist party, perhaps a redefined Alliance Party. In the short term it may turn out to be the most effective strategy.

To sum up this section, there is good reason to believe that current political pressures are going to force a further redefinition of the SDLP's variant of nationalism. This could lead to a clearer regionalist focus, or to a stronger liberal nationalist emphasis. For the reasons outlined above, I am inclined to think the latter is the more likely outcome. This will certainly not ease relations with unionism, but it may, perhaps, clarify unionism's options.

## Conclusion

Northern nationalism has certainly been redefined. That redefinition took place in the 1970s, not the 1990s, although in many respects it laid the foundations for the political progress and settlement of the 1990s. I have argued, however, that the very achievements of the 1990s pose new problems and may provoke a further redefinition of northern nationalism. This will involve a choice between the perspectives – regionalist, republican or liberal nationalist – that up to the present were combined in nationalist discourse. That choice will take place with an eye at once to changing attitudes in the nationalist electorate and to the strategies of the other parties and governments in the post-Good Friday political context. In short, the story of northern nationalism is an evolving one, and its probable evolution is closely tied to the development and prospects of the new institutions which have been set up in the context of the Good Friday Agreement, the evolution of governmental policy and the dynamics of British Isles and European level changes.

I pointed out the importance of Europe for John Hume's refashioning of northern nationalism. If European integration is de-emphasised, as is arguably happening in the Republic, it changes the context for northern nationalists. A de-emphasis on Europe, together with increasing British Isles linkages and devolution all around within Britain, could lead to northern nationalism becoming a new form of British regionalism, with republicans alone retaining nationalist aims. On the other hand, a perceived collapse into a British Isles context might provoke in northern nationalists a renewed nationalism and separatism which would lead rather than follow the South. Each option is dangerous in an Irish context. It is not at all clear that the distinctive mixture of reform-orientation, liberal nationalism and open-mindedness about constitutional issues which has characterised northern nationalism at its best is possible in a primarily British Isles context. It needs the EU as a counter-balance and alternative model to the very power of British political culture; without it, there is a danger of schism between British provincial regionalism and a stronger, but also more traditional, Irish nationalism. Perhaps it is here, in working out a new form of liberal nationalism in a European as well as a British–Irish context, that a new redefinition of northern nationalism will lie.

**Chapter 8**

# The transformation of republicanism

Paul Arthur

## Introduction

In this chapter I propose to look at the past before reviewing the future, as is inevitable when we deal with republicanism. I want to set my remarks in the context of several short quotations – but not before I make some comments on an incredible present. When the President of Sinn Féin, Gerry Adams, addressed a gathering of the faithful in Belfast on 22 October 2001 the symbolism of the location and occasion would not have been lost on him. The site was Conway Mill, right at the heart of republican Belfast, an area devastated by loyalist incursions in the summer of 1969. More than 30 years later Adams presented himself as the personification of a people who had endured – indeed had 'overcome'. More than that, his people were not wreckers: 'Our aim has been to save the Good Friday Agreement . . . Sinn Féin's commitment to the process is absolute'. He spoke too as someone who had moved well beyond the mean streets of the ghetto: 'From South Africa to North America there are commitments and promises to support our efforts'. And he succeeded in marrying the local to the global in a classic piece of republican rhetoric: 'We are in a time when world events are dominated by imagery and stories of conflict and violence and terror. At this time these events are replicated locally in provocative and deadly sectarian actions, both in the intimidation of little schoolgirls and in bomb and gun attacks on nationalist families.' The real thrust of the speech manifested itself the following day when General John de Chastelain's International Decommissioning Commission announced that the IRA had finally begun the process of putting its weapons beyond use.

This was a remarkable speech. It represented once again the republican capacity to reinvent itself. It cast republicans in the role of victims *and* as major players on the international stage. The innocent spectator would be forgiven for ignoring the context in which it was being delivered: the arrest of three of their supporters in Colombia in August after they were alleged to have been in contact with the 'narco-terrorist' FARC organisation; and after the profound implications of the 11 September attacks on the United States.

The 'international network of terrorism' was under intense scrutiny and the republican movement had to distance itself rapidly. Adams's speech was choreographed by a visit to the US by Martin McGuinness, who penetrated the heart of corporate Irish-America as well as of the State Department to deliver a similar message. Both of them had 'put the view' to the IRA that movement on arms would 'save the process'. In addition they pressed for further concessions on the issue of demilitarisation. What could have been interpreted as a humiliating climbdown was sold as a piece of magnanimity.

Serendipity, in the form of the FARC connection and the calamitous events of 11 September, forced the hand of the republican political leadership. These events *accelerated* the process. Ever since they signed up to the multiparty agreement in April 1998, Sinn Féin bought into the concept of consent and to recognising the reality of a Northern Ireland political entity, but they resisted the idea of formal decommissioning. With great skill and tenacity, they outmanoeuvred the 'militarists' in their ranks. Insofar as they had bought into decommissioning it was to be on a 'voluntary' basis and it was to be accompanied by the *quid pro quo* of demilitarisation. Essentially it was an act of self-preservation and fulfilled its capability to sustain itself. Above all it was a symbolic act, as symbolic as the decision of the Irish Government to give up Articles 2 and 3 of the 1937 Constitution as one of its contributions to the multiparty agreement. The significance of the decommissioning gesture lay in the fact that it implied that at long last republicans were prepared to play by the democratic rules of the game. And it was truly historic . . . never, ever in the history of republicanism had such a gesture been made.

It is in this context that I want to note the quotations. The first comes from the distinguished French jurist, Roger Errera: 'One of the sound foundations of a political society is a true knowledge of its past . . . But the affirmation of the rights of memory does not mean that the past must become the only, or the main, value' (Errera, 1999). Here we have a warning that in dealing with the past we need to keep it in some kind of perspective. The obverse of that occurs when society looks at its past and engages in erasure, in silence, when there are events it does not wish to confront. In Colm Tóibín's recent work on the Irish famine he quotes the literary critic Terry Eagleton: 'If the Famine stirred some to angry rhetoric, it would seem to have traumatised others into muteness. The event strains at the limits of the articulable, and is truly in this sense an Irish Auschwitz' (Tóibín, 1998). In that respect, the famine fits into the concept that some things are 'unthinkable' in the framework of western thought. In his analysis of the slave-led Haitian revolution (1791–1804) Trouillot states: 'The unthinkable is that which one cannot conceive within the range of possible alternatives, that which perverts all answers because it denies the terms under which the questions were phrased' (Trouillot, 1995: 106). So in looking at the past we need to be aware of how we structure (or ignore) the facts. In the context of Irish history 'memory' has been used as a weapon and republicans have been among its greatest exponents.

So how do we perceive the term 'republican'? In a Dáil debate on proposed family planning legislation the Progressive Democrat leader, Desmond O'Malley, said:

> I am certain of one thing in relation to partition – we will never see a Thirty-Two County Republic on this island until, first of all, we have a Twenty-Six County Republic in this part we have jurisdiction over today, which is really a Republic practising real Republican traditions. Otherwise, we can forget about persuading our fellow Irishmen in the North to join us. 'Republican' is perhaps the most abused word in Ireland today . . . There is an immediate preconceived notion of what it is. It consists principally of Anglophobia. Mentally, at least, it is an aggressive attitude towards those who do not agree with our views on what the future of this island should be. It consists of turning a blind eye to violence, seeing no immorality, often, in the most awful violence, seeing immorality only in one area, the area with which this Bill deals (quoted in Walsh, 1986: 74).

O'Malley was one of those politicians in the Republic in the 1980s and 1990s who began to redefine what 'republican' was supposed to represent in an Irish context. It was a process that began probably with the New Ireland Forum in 1983–4; and his remarks about the awfulness of violence remind us of our capacity for erasure, of our ability to ignore unpalatable facts from our own past.

It is indicative of another trait that much of the thinking and writing on the political nature of republicanism is unreflective. Too much of it is about endurance, victimhood and tales of derring-do. Patterson (1989: 3) lays some of the blame with republicanism itself: 'this is owing to the movement's own pronounced tendency to a monochrome remembrance of itself – as a principled and self-sacrificing minority who have challenged British rule down through the centuries despite and because of the apathy and "materialism" of the majority of the Irish people'. The result has been a 'tendency to decontextualise current Irish terrorism' that limits us 'to a moral outrage which is by now paper-thin and, even more palpably, a diversion from serious thought about contemporary Ireland' (Patterson, 1989: 3–4). But this use of the word 'terrorism' creates its own problems. Apter (1997b: 20), for example, asserts that '[The IRA] rescues itself from "terrorism" by insisting that its armed bands are soldiers and the struggle itself an anti-colonial war'. That enabled them to occupy centre-stage with the likes of the PLO and the ANC.

One of the most prolific writers on the IRA, Bowyer Bell, has set some of his later work (Bell, 2000) in a series on the theme *Terrorism and Political Violence* and an earlier (slighter) book concentrates on tactics and targets rather than ideology and the political context (Bell, 1990). It is as if analysts have allowed themselves to be guided by the *activities* of the IRA. On a slightly broader base, Smith (1995) concerns himself with the military strategy of the Irish Republican Movement, a task befitting someone who at the time of writing the book was a senior lecturer at the Royal Naval College. One good journalistic account (Harnden, 2000) analyses the IRA in one particular locale, that of South Armagh, which may be atypical; whereas an academic sociological approach (Burton, 1978) is an impressive example of observer-participation in the Ardoyne area of Belfast but it is also rooted in a specific period, more like a snapshot than a camcorder.

Part of the problem lies in republican self-perception, some of which is soft-focus. These include Gerry Adams's childhood memoirs (1982) or his autobiography (1996). There is little in the way of a political agenda although, as we shall see, his *The politics of Irish freedom* (1986) is a much more reflective piece. Some such as Sean Mac Stiofáin's *Memoirs of a revolutionary* (1975) are incredibly opaque; and when we look for a critical analysis from within republicanism examples are hard to come by. Maria McGuire's *To take arms* (1973) was written after she had broken with the movement. Mark Ryan's *War and peace in Ireland: Britain and the IRA in the new world order* (1994: viii, ix) detects a 'significant softening of the Irish republican commitment to national self-determination' and a 'relatively unremarked but deep-rooted tendency in Irish republicanism towards compromise and constitutional politics'.

Ryan's work belongs to a new category of analysis that has begun to take republicanism seriously as a *political* phenomenon. To some extent these analyses reflect the distance that Sinn Féin has moved over the past 15 years, from marginalisation to positions in government. Patterson examined the nature of social republicanism that presents a more complex picture of Sinn Féin and the IRA. Arthur (1997) adapted discourse theory to examine the durability and the popularity of republicanism by placing particular emphasis on the mythologics of contemporary republicanism and on the communicative dimension of its violence. Porter (1998) used the two hundredth anniversary of the 1798 rising to bring together politicians and activists to consider republicanism in its current light. All of them have brought a new dimension, but it is fair to say that the definitive book on Irish republicanism has yet to be written.

## The traditional republican position

The Israeli political scientist, Yael Tamir, provided a useful starting point for a discussion of the traditional republican position with her comment that 'inherent in nationalism is a recognition of the existence of others. It is the

way in which the national group treats these others that distinguishes poly-
centric nationalism, which respects the other and sees each nation as enriching
a common civilisation, from ethnocentric nationalism, which sees one's own
nation as superior to all others and seeks domination' (Tamir, 1995: 430). A
number of points arise from this quotation. One is to acknowledge that for far
too long Irish republicanism was essentially ethnocentric. Another is to
recognise the existence of the 'other' and of the need to engage in dialogue.

> Communication entails recognition of the other, and 'the awareness of being
> separate and different from and strange to one another' opens up potentials of
> creative search for dialogue and for understanding of each other. This is also the
> essence of negotiations. Reaching common ground is not necessarily a product of
> similar opinions (Sofer, 1997: 181).

Historically, what republicans failed to do was to make that connection. They
dismissed unionist reaction as a variant of false consciousness. They eschewed
the political. It was as if they occupied a pre-political world where conquest
and dispossession, a loss of patrimony and a historic sense of grievance
dominated. Theirs was not

> a world of choice from which some have been excluded but a universe of meaning
> in which insight is inspired by victimhood and confrontation [where] inversionary
> discourse is a means of altering prevailing boundaries and jurisdictions on the
> ground and in the mind. *If they reject ordinary claims and demands and remain
> aloof from negotiation and the bargaining that accompanies democracy* the intent is
> to create moral and symbolic capital [emphasis added] (Apter, 1992: 23).

The sound of the bomb and the bullet drowned out any prospects of
dialogue. We can suggest why they failed to make connections when we put
it in the context of Ireland's dreadful history.

One of the themes in Joe Lee's magisterial history, *Ireland 1912–1985:
politics and society* was a 'dependency syndrome which had wormed its way
into the Irish psyche during the long centuries of foreign dominance':

> The Irish mind was enveloped in, and to some extent suffocated by, the English
> mental embrace. This was quite natural. A small occupied country, with an alien
> ruling class, culturally penetrated by the language and many of the thought
> processes of the coloniser, was bound in large measure to imitate the example of
> the powerful and the prosperous (Lee, 1989: 627).

The end result was that 'absorption in the British model gravely limited Irish
perspectives. When allied to the elusive but crucial psychological factors that

inspired the instinct of inferiority, it shrivelled Irish perspectives on Irish potential' (Lee, 1989: 629). It led to an attitude based on a reading of history which emphasises victimhood and resistance: 'there is no place in Irish political culture for greatness outside the "heroic" model. Greatness is defined in terms of defiance of the external enemy' (Lee, 1989: 406). Republicanism was an expression of this mentality. So we start with a dependency culture that was long on retrieval but short on projection. As Sean Ó Faoláin put it: 'the policy of Sinn Féin has always been, since its foundation, that simple formula: Freedom first; other things after' (cited in Patterson, 1989: 12). That has been the republican project until fairly recent years.

But we need to broaden that definition of republicanism and to begin to look at it in the context of Plato's *Republic* with its emphasis on justice. We have taken our lead from the past and wrapped ourselves in several layers of ambiguity, so that sometimes the distance between the constitutional and the physical force traditions has not been that far removed. Take, for example, a comparison of the opening words of the 1916 Proclamation with the preamble of the 1937 Constitution. Here we find a political culture laid out in one simple statement: a profound sense of piety, a deep sense of history and of grievance, and an essential sense of the contemporaneousness of the past. It is a narrative of dispossession overlaid by a fundamental religiosity secularised by a doctrine of manifest destiny. It is what has sustained Irish republicanism through centuries of failure. Theirs, they believed, was a search for justice by overcoming the injustice of partition. They could not be held responsible for the relative economic underdevelopment and the perennial problem of emigration that was the lot of the partitioned state. The latter, a major feature of pre-partition Ireland, was malign. Besides denting potential at home, emigration helped to construct a sense of grievance among the Irish diaspora. Miller (1990: 92, 96) asserts that 'as the central experience of post-famine life, emigration demanded interpretation in political and religious contexts'. Central to this interpretation was 'emigration as exile, as *in*voluntary expatriation, which was [made obligatory] by forces beyond individual choice and communal control; sometimes by fate or destiny, but usually by the political and economic consequences of "British misgovernment", "Protestant ascendancy", and "landlord tyranny"'. Much of this historic sense of grievance played itself out in Irish-American ghettos throughout the last century and sustained republican resistance at home.

While there might have been similarities between the 1916 Proclamation and the 1937 constitution, it was in republicans' interest to stress difference. Their monocular reading of history enabled them to work on the assumption of splendid failure within a characteristic Irish time-frame which 'inclines Irishmen to a repetitive view of history and that such a view inclines them – perhaps in defensive wariness and from fear of failure – *to prize the moral as against the actual, and the bearing of witness as against success* [emphasis added]' (MacDonagh, 1983: 13). So it was a long view, and it was a fatalistic view. It enabled them to undertake the hunger strikes in 1980–1 (and at other times in the last century). The hunger strikes allowed the IRA to base its 'claim to a political identity on difference: their distinction from the world of ordinary non-violent politics' (Moss, 1993: 6). Though the republican leadership came reluctantly to the politics of the H-Block they mastered its intricacies and made use of its religious imagery to create a *sacred history*: 'through myth man stands outside (*exstasis*) the futile flow of history which no longer seems to offer any possibility of rational reform or progress. He takes recourse in the mythic law of "eternal recurrence of the same" i.e. the recurrence of the same ancestral heroes, of the same paradigms of destruction and renewal, of the same time of the Holy Beginning' (Kearney, 1976: 136–7). All of these ingredients were in place when the hunger strike began on 1 March 1981, when Bobby Sands, the first volunteer, could expect to be dead by Easter – a time of destruction and of renewal, and of a Holy Beginning – if his demands were not met.

The hunger strikes offered the opportunity to turn the affair into a show of strength for republicans as against every other form of Irish nationalism. It emphasised difference and diminished the role of politics and of politicians 'through the primitive force of a symbolic act' which broke 'the relationship between politics and discourse' (Donoghue, 1981: 227). All of this appeared in the prisoners' post-hunger strike statement in a blanket condemnation of the constitutional nationalist parties and the Catholic Church. The Dublin parties were 'accessories to the legalised murder of 10 true and committed Irishmen who died heroically in the long tradition of Republican resistance to British occupation, oppression and injustice . . . If John Bull doesn't actually rule the 26 counties physically, he still rules in spirit'. The SDLP 'should be recognised for what it is – an amalgamation of middle-class Redmondites, devoid of principle, direction and courage . . . Their whole leadership combined do not possess a fraction of the moral fibre demonstrated so valiantly by our comrades'. And the Catholic hierarchy 'has at all times been established by political considerations rather than Christian values of truth and justice'.

## The evolution of republican ideology

The traditional republican perspective rested, then, on an assumption of failure. This is clear from the manner in which political violence has been used. It might be said that violence in Ireland has sent people out not so much to kill as to die. It is a violence based on martyrology and on the notion of attrition. It is a violence based on a very strong moral dimension – that 'the more of us who die, the more the people will realise that ours is a just cause'. It was at the heart of the hunger strikes in 1980–1.

It is from that time, I believe, that republicanism as an ideology begins to place itself in comparison with its great variants in the French and American models. One of the interesting facts about Irish republicanism is that it has not produced any great narratives or great texts. There is nothing akin to Mao's little red book. There is no equivalent of what Carlos Guzman did with Peru's Shining Path movement. What has been done in Ireland has been to base everything on action, and we struggle to find route maps of what the republican project is about. It is there to some extent in the 1916 Proclamation and in the writings of Wolfe Tone, but we need to make the jump from 1916 to 1986 – in fact to the publication of Gerry Adams's *The politics of Irish freedom* (1986). Here we find the beginning of a route map because Adams is critical of the very organisation that he leads. Adams contends that in the past the republican movement was a separatist movement with a radical tendency; whereas in its current embodiment the radical tendency is in control for the first time. He maintains, too, that since the 1930s there has been no real effort to map out what type of a republic was aimed at.

I am suggesting that from the early 1980s Adams and his associates began to map that route. Unlike the men of 1916 they started with some advantages. In *The politics of Irish freedom* Adams makes the connection between the men of 1916 and the 'barricade days' of the civil rights movement. In other words, the republican movement had moved beyond being a vanguard, a revolutionary elite, to being a popular force. By the 1970s republicanism was sufficiently rooted in the people that it could not succeed without the support of the wider community. Once the northern contingent had taken control, that gave the movement the self-confidence to move along its political project. Adams had written about the three tendencies – militant, conspiratorial and political – within republicanism: now was the time for the last to assert itself. This began particularly after the 1981 hunger strike, itself a classic example of the Pearsean religion of violent nationalism – 'the cults of blood, youth and sacrifice, and the concepts of generational witness, historic roles and the supremacy of the gesture' (MacDonagh, 1983: 89).

It could be said that Sinn Féin moved into politics by accident. The republican leadership outside the prisons had not favoured hunger striking. It put them in contention with the Relatives' Action Committee and it detracted from the war. But it had unforeseen advantages. It demonstrated that there was latent emotional support for their movement. The ten dead hunger strikers forced a change in strategy: the armalite *and* the ballot box came into their own – in another Bobby Sands.

## The dialogue of republicanism and constitutional nationalism

While their politics was still dominated by the politics of community and of territoriality, republicans began to recognise that the 'other' had to be embraced. This began with the dialogue with the SDLP between March and September 1988. But before that occurred they were confronted by an exercise undertaken by the major constitutional nationalist parties in both parts of Ireland to redefine the meaning of Irish nationalism and republicanism for the latter end of the twentieth century. Sinn Féin was excluded and the New Ireland Forum exercise of 1983–4 challenged the conventional wisdom of Irish republicanism. In its final report the Forum noted:

> The negative effect of IRA violence on British and Unionist attitudes [which] cannot be emphasised enough. Their terrorist acts create anger and indignation and a resolve not to give in to violence under any circumstances. They have the effect of stimulating additional security measures which further alienate the nationalist section of the community. They obscure the underlying political problem. They strengthen extremist Unionist resistance to any form of dialogue and accommodation with nationalists (New Ireland Forum, 1984: 14–15).

It was on the back of the revulsion with the Enniskillen bomb that John Hume wrote to Gerry Adams on 17 March 1988 and challenged the fundamental tenets of the IRA and of the place of violence in the republican canon. That led to the SDLP/Sinn Féin dialogue of March–September 1988. Hume came under severe pressure from other nationalists for engaging in this exercise. He was accused of giving succour to the IRA. In fact the concept of self-determination, the disproportionate use of IRA violence and British intentions in Ireland were at the top of the agenda. The SDLP's fundamental challenge to republican methods appeared in its last document where it said that solutions to the problem of division in Ireland 'have been postponed by nationalist/Republican concentration on the language of ideological rectitude rather than trying to face the political reality. The challenge is to change this reality by political dialogue and not to estrange it further by the continued futile and counterproductive use of force against fellow Irish people.' It was at this time that Sinn Féin ceased being a sect full of moral certitude and became a political movement.

The process was interesting for several reasons. To start with, it was the first time that Sinn Féin policies had been scrutinised so closely by a party which sought the same end of Irish unity. The SDLP invoked the ghosts of the republican past to challenge Sinn Féin's claims to be the heirs of non-sectarianism, and to remind them that Tone and Pearse had called off the armed struggle rather than commit their people to further bloodshed.

Secondly, the dialogue had an educative effect. Over the next few years Sinn Féin had more contact with those who did not support the armed struggle. Thirdly, the dialogue rehearsed many of the issues that were to appear in the Downing Street Declaration of the two prime ministers (John Major and Albert Reynolds) of December 1993 by removing the debate about self-determination from its theological plinth and placing it in the harsh political world of the late twentieth century. The result was a move beyond the past and away from insularity. Sinn Féin's earlier decision (at the 1986 ard-fheis) to contest and take their seats in Dáil Éireann had been truly revolutionary in terms of republican evolution. Having made that leap, and brought their people along with them, other things became possible.

Compare, for example, Sinn Féin's 1988 policy document *Towards a strategy for peace* with their 1992 document *Towards a lasting peace In Ireland* – even the titles are revealing. The latter recognised that unionist fears would have to be addressed, and accepted that British withdrawal would only be brought about by a process of cooperation between both governments in consultation with all parties in Northern Ireland. This represented movement because Sinn Féin now recognised the legitimacy and role of the Irish government as well as the rights of Northern Protestants. Finally, the document began to place Irish republicanism in the context of European republicanism and the impact of the French Revolution. Republicans were moving beyond the narrow ground and adapting to a proper sense of time scales.

## Conclusion

We do not do justice to the process if we concentrate too much on the SDLP–Sinn Féin dialogue. Others had played their part. Before his removal from office in February 1992, Charles Haughey had begun to take extensive soundings within the republican movement; this initiative might be seen as the first tentative step (from a southern perspective) in the peace process. His successor, Albert Reynolds, was able to claim the benefits of this policy. It is true that he worked enormously hard to bring about an IRA ceasefire and to establish a strong rapport with John Major (Finlay, 1998: 110–13, 140). It is true, too, that the British government had become more sensitive to nationalist grievances. Contact between an emissary of the British government and an IRA representative between 1990 and 1993 allowed for the beginnings of trust. It was reflected in a speech made by Sir Patrick Mayhew in December 1992 where he acknowledged past British wrongs, paid obeisance to the historic figures of constitutional nationalism, and commented that Sinn Féin had excluded itself from interparty talks: 'if its cause does have a serious political purpose, then let it renounce unequivocally the use and threat of violence, and demonstrate over a sufficient period that its renunciation is for real'. The British government's role was that of a 'facilitator' with no separate political agenda of its own: 'the Government is just as plainly the facilitator of the will of the people in Northern Ireland democratically expressed, as terrorism is its enemy'. The conditions were being laid for the ceasefires of 1994 and, it has to be said, for the IRA breakdown in February 1996. Trust remained a fragile plant and that is why much unfinished business remains in the peace process.

Let us return to the Adams speech at Conway Mill in October 2001. His allusions to South Africa and North America were an acknowledgement that geopolitics had had a role to play in redefining Irish republicanism. The collapse of the Berlin Wall, the end of communism as an aggressive international ideology and the removal of pariahdom from South Africa, all contributed to a redefinition of republicanism. It has to be set alongside the changing domestic dialogue. His references to the continuing sectarianism was to remind his audience where Sinn Féin and the IRA had come from. The presence of such IRA veterans as Joe Cahill symbolised the line of continuity and of resistance that went back to the 1940s. In short it was a typically skilful piece of Sinn Féin choreography that masked the most fundamental decision that republicans had taken in their history, and all without creating a major split. We have noted that they have taken seats in a Stormont government and assembly; that articles 2 and 3 of the Irish constitution have been removed; that the doctrine of consent has been accepted; and that a start on decommissioning has been made. By the end of 2001 republicans were moving into offices at Westminster but refusing to take their seats in the House of Commons. Admittedly, republicans enjoyed the predictable reactions of their political opponents that helped to mask the momentous character of these decisions.

It is too early to ascertain the destination point in this new beginning. What we can say with some certainty is that there is no going back to the armed struggle for this generation of republicans. They have embarked on a journey which is truly momentous. They have made the huge psychological leap away from victimhood and from 'memory'. These will continue to play a bit-role in their narrative, but they have embraced a wider politics of choice with all the responsibilities that that carries with it. They have given up on what Edmund Burke called 'the degenerate fondness for tricking short cuts'. They may be moving us in the direction of new alignments in the politics of Ireland. If I were to judge how far we are moving towards a new republicanism I would refer to the agreement reached in the multi-party negotiations on Good Friday 1998, where the signatories 'recognise the birthright of all people of Northern Ireland to identify themselves and be accepted as Irish or British, *or both*' (italics added). That is what redefining republicanism in the twenty-first century has to be about.

Chapter 9

# The growth of new unionism

Richard English

## Introduction

If one compares unionist responses to the 1998 Belfast Agreement with those to the 1985 Anglo-Irish Agreement, dramatically different pictures emerge. In 1985, the unionist community was almost unanimously hostile to the Thatcher–FitzGerald accord. In the post-1998 period, unionists have been profoundly, and almost evenly, divided as to the proper response to the 1998 Belfast deal. These statements are as true of unionist politicians as of the unionist electorate, and this situation is especially striking because the 1985 Anglo-Irish Agreement began a curve which reached fulfilment in the 1998 agreement. The philosophy embodied in the Anglo-Irish Agreement has run through much governmental thinking (in Dublin as well as London) in the years up to and beyond 1998: parity of esteem for two rival traditions, a structural role for Dublin in the politics of Northern Ireland, and the simultaneous offering of reassurances to unionists and promises to nationalists.

During the same post-1985 period another – less obvious, but arguably important – change has also occurred, this time in terms of analysis surrounding unionism. Most of the books and articles now cited and debated on the subject have been published during the years since the Anglo-Irish Agreement. These include the work of Steve Bruce, Jennifer Todd, Arthur Aughey, Alvin Jackson, Feargal Cochrane, Norman Porter, Dennis Kennedy, Joseph Lee, and numerous others. Remove such works and the shelf of writings addressing Ulster unionism is surprisingly, perhaps embarrassingly, short; the analysis of unionism has, therefore, witnessed a dramatic shift in terms of depth.

In this chapter I want to reflect on these two developments, the political and the analytical, and their implications for our subject: redefining unionism. The two developments clearly have some relevance for one another, which I will discuss towards the end. But – after brief comments on traditional unionism – I shall consider first unionist politics, and then the analysis of unionism.

## The character of traditional unionism

It would be mistaken to assume that there has been any simple, clean break between one (old) form of unionism and a recently emergent (new) one. For one thing, unionist (like other Irish) politics has always been layered and complex rather than uniform and straightforward. Even that supposedly rock-like defender of the union, Edward Carson, emerges from close scrutiny as a profoundly neurotic character (Jackson, 1993). And unionism has always been open to the process of gradual change, to rolling evolution according to the perceived demands of the day. The shift from the Irish, landlord unionism, epitomised by the late-Victorian Edward Saunderson (Jackson, 1995), to an Ulster-centred, more urbanised unionism, more familiar during the twentieth century, provides an important example. But, in a chapter considering recent developments in (and on) unionism, it seems appropriate to mention very briefly at the start some aspects of a unionism once familiar, but now much less so.

The first concerns unionist attitudes towards the neighbouring southern Irish state. In the early decades of Northern Ireland, these amounted to a preoccupation which at times exaggerated quite understandable anxiety into a near-paranoid obsession (Kennedy, 1988). But even into the second half of the twentieth century, there remained not only political fear regarding the intentions of the Republic of Ireland, but also a pervasive image of that state as religiously and economically of a different, and lamentably backward, stamp. A second point about what might be referred to as old unionism was that, until the prorogation of Stormont in 1972, unionists enjoyed a kind of insulatory status: unionist politicians effectively protected London from involvement in the incomprehensible, difficult politics of Northern Ireland and so they had a degree of power and autonomy to which they became at length accustomed. This relates to a third point, that because unionists long held power there was a measure of confidence that their protection and safety lay in their own hands. I remain unpersuaded by the argument that unionism was ever best understood in terms of an inherent sense of superiority (Lee, 1989). But over the 1921–72 period unionists at least had their own regime in Belfast, which offset to some degree the anxieties which they felt on account of southern irredentism, northern nationalist disloyalty and potential British perfidy. In evaluating latter-day changes in unionism, it seems to me that these three points – concerning the southern state, power, and confidence – might helpfully be kept in view.

## The transformation of unionist politics

One significant development within unionist politics during recent years has been the emergence into comparative prominence of paramilitary parties which built on the longstanding (but long unobserved) hostility between the respective cultures of Paisleyism and of paramilitary loyalism. The comparative salience of the Progressive Unionist Party and the Ulster Democratic Party reinforced and highlighted another key development over recent years: the dramatic fracturing of unionist politics in Northern Ireland. Divisions within the Ulster Unionist Party (UUP) have become famous, but they exist along-side the broader, post-1998 divide between pro- and anti-Agreement unionists, and the rancorous divisions variously involving the Democratic Unionist Party, United Kingdom Unionist Party, Northern Ireland Unionist Party, and the aforementioned Progressive Unionist Party and Ulster Democratic Party. If Irish republicans did want to see unionism bitterly and lastingly divided by the peace process, then they have surely got their wish.

But the most important change in unionist politics in recent years has been the emergence of a significant section of the unionist family looking to make a new deal with Irish nationalism. The key figure here is clearly David Trimble. The UUP leader is, as his biographer has put it, 'prepared to give up some ground to his enemies so that the overall siege of his state can be lifted' (McDonald, 2000: 6). In contrast to the stereotypical unionist 'no', this new unionism epitomised by Trimble shows a preparedness to say 'yes' to a series of specific as well as general innovations; this is a process which stretches back beyond Trimble's accession to the leadership of the UUP, but which has been reinforced powerfully since then. In contrast to the frequently crude, inward-looking expression of unionist argument, new unionist politicians have demonstrated sophisticated skills of presentation, and have offered an articulate defence of their views, policies and principles. If for a long time the unionists of Ulster tended to put a reasonable case rather badly, while Irish nationalists put a sometimes exaggerated case rather well, then at least part of that picture has begun to change.[1]

Why is this the case? In part, individual contributions – talents, ambitions, and so on – are essential to any understanding of this development. This is clearly true of the fracturing of unionism to which I have referred – in which clashing personalities have played a significant role – but it is also relevant to the emergence of a new unionism centred on the impressive abilities of Mr Trimble and some of his allies. In part also, there has emerged a sense of the increasingly worsening terms on which unionists are able to make some kind of deal, and of the fact that unionists can neither create nor veto developments indefinitely in Northern Ireland. To govern the place effec-tively, some serious accommodation is required with at least a section of Irish nationalism, and it has been recognised that, for the interests of unionists, this should happen soon.

Indeed, it is the context for change, and the changing contexts, which are vital for an understanding of the true nature of new political unionism. The key changes concern Irish nationalism. The cultural and economic confidence and the profound social changes evident in the Republic of Ireland probably provide surer ground for unionist engagement with Irish nationalism than many unionists yet realise. For the more secure the twenty-six county sense of identity, self and success become, the less relevant to the southern state is that traditional nationalism about which Ulster unionists were so wary. There is much in the new Republic to give unionists ground for confidence, not least the comparative indifference of most of the Republic's population towards Northern Ireland and what they perceive as its peculiar politics. There is, among those in the Republic who do reflect on Northern Ireland, no longer a dismissal of the problem which Ulster unionism poses for Irish nationalism. There is no longer the axiomatic assumption that nation is co-extensive with island, or that separatism, Catholicism or Gaelicism are necessarily indices of authentic Irishness; or, indeed, that progress towards peace in Northern Ireland must be harmonious with progress towards traditional Irish nationalist goals.

Among Irish republicans, of course, the idea remains that there is a natural unity of Ireland, which will encompass unionists (once they effectively cease to be such). But even here, there have been huge changes which both help to explain new unionist politics, and to defend and legitimate its approach. Republican leaders have moved towards the decision that the rewards of paramilitary violence will not include victory, and towards the judgement that indeed they might be outweighed by the rewards offered by alternative methods. This point is so important for understanding where unionism currently stands that it is worth further consideration. The IRA faced serious problems during the late 1980s. It was increasingly vulnerable both to intelligence penetration and to military strikes; it was damaged by publicity disasters involving the IRA killing of civilians, suffering comparative eclipse by constitutional nationalists; and, most crucially, it was lacking the kind of generative, spectacular grievance which had given rise, momentum, and regeneration to Provisional republican culture – rise, with the 1969 attacks on Northern Ireland Catholics; momentum, with internment in the early 1970s and Bloody Sunday; regeneration, with the 1981 hunger strikes. Such episodes, more than anything else, explain the dynamism and energy of Provisional Irish republicanism, and by the late 1980s and early 1990s republicans lacked such stimulating grievances.

Republicans, then, recognised – as had been clear enough to many, for a long time – that, militarily, there existed a three-way stalemate between the respective forces of loyalism, republicanism and the British state. In the early

1970s they had thought that victory was coming, and coming soon; by the late 1980s and early 1990s many of their leaders had realised that it was not coming at all. This sea change has had the most profound implications for unionist politicians, a point sharply identified by Trimble himself (Trimble, 2001); it has helped produce a situation in which a significant section of Ulster unionism believes that a deal can be done which will not be accompanied by republican, oppositional violence. The partial redefinition of unionism which has occurred has also been influenced by the particular combination of political forces triangularly arranged in London, Dublin and Washington. The longer-term development of the British state itself has also had clear implications for a changing unionist politics. In a stimulating article, Tom Bartlett has argued that the decline and fall of the British Empire has left Ulster Protestants feeling 'cast adrift, for that which had given them sustenance and identity has now gone' (Bartlett, 1998: 10). This theme focuses appropriate attention on the complicated inter-relationship between these islands; and, clearly, the decline of empire has had profound significance for Ulster unionists. Yet while it is clearly right to explain the rise of Britishness by reference, in part, to the empire, that was by no means the full story. So, too, the end of empire has not meant that Britishness no longer exists, but rather that adjustments have been made by British people to their changing status in the world. The end of empire has forced the redefinition, rather than the destruction, of Britishness, and I think a similar lesson might be drawn in relation to Ulster unionism. There is, it seems to me, no inevitable disintegration of Ulster unionists' Britishness as a consequence of the end of empire, any more than as a consequence of changes in British attitudes towards religion or towards the monarchy. Indeed, close scrutiny of the debates on British decline tends to imply that the extent and uniformity of that decline have been of a lesser degree than frequently assumed (English and Kenny, 2000). It may, for example, be as important to explain why Britain still possesses a peculiarly prominent role in military and diplomatic events worldwide, as it is to explain the less surprising fact that British world dominance failed to survive indefinitely.

Devolution is another change in British politics with implications for Ulster unionist redefinition. For the devolving of power and consequent reinforcement of regional identity need not be accompanied by the end of the United Kingdom. When examined closely, developments in Scotland and Wales, as well as in Belfast, *might* suggest serious modification rather than abolition of the union. But they surely change the context for unionist argument. To argue, in the mid-1980s, that one wanted to be governed as was the rest of the United Kingdom meant something very different from such an argument now. And this is a point which might suit the instincts not merely of Trimble-style unionists. The Democratic Unionist Party's Sammy Wilson has stated:

I believe that there is wide diversity within the United Kingdom, and I am not just talking about the diversity between Northern Ireland and the rest of the United Kingdom. It is now quite apparent that the Scots feel the same, the Welsh feel the same, even people in the North of England feel the same, and therefore the kind of unionism that I would want to see would allow for an expression of that diversity, and allow for some kind of institutional expression of the diversity as well.[2]

But it is Trimble-style unionism which has most energetically embraced the prospect of newly devolved and newly defined Belfast authority. This occurs against a background of changes which have encouraged, or forced, reappraisal. Alterations in Irish republican politics, in the politics of the Republic of Ireland, in the British political system and in wider historical and political realities have all played their part in suggesting that unionists should engage with London, Dublin and Washington on the basis of seeking a new deal with Irish nationalists; and that they should do so with a grasp of their strengths, their weaknesses, and the need for some change (for example, in the religious inflection of Ulster unionist politics: here, changes in British popular attitudes surely point the way towards a less exclusivist formal politics in Ulster, whatever one's private religious beliefs).

But, as with all such redefinition, successful change requires that much remain the same; and the constants should not be played down. There remains among unionists an understandable hostility to being expelled from the state of their choice, a state to which (for a variety of economic, political, cultural, symbolic, religious and historical reasons) unionists give allegiance. There remains also the economic and security-based reality that a straight-forward united Ireland is not feasible in the immediate future (a fact reinforced rather than undermined by the Republic's economic success as a twenty-six county state).

## The analysis of unionist ideology

If post-1985 unionist politics have changed in complicated ways, then it is also a complex picture which emerges from what might be called the new analysis of unionism. But the weight of scholarly and other analytical judgement certainly now suggests that we should treat the phenomenon with more seriousness than was typically the case in Irish nationalist, and orthodox international, thinking. A former professor of politics in Dublin and Belfast, John Whyte, summarised one aspect of this very well, with his observation of the sturdy, self-reliant quality of unionism: 'On the whole, recent historians have been struck by the depth of Ulster unionist opposition to a united Ireland separate from Britain, and the independence of that opposition from British support' (Whyte, 1990: 125).

A number of points emerging from the new analysis of unionism seem to me particularly important for the question of redefining unionism; I would identify five of them. The first is fluidity. Jennifer Todd's rightly influential 1987 article, 'Two traditions in unionist political culture', provides a useful example here (Todd, 1987). Todd identified Ulster loyalism and Ulster British ideology as two key traditions within Ulster unionism, and speculated upon the possibilities of change in each. This speculation reflected a proper sense of the fluid state of Ulster unionism, as does the fact that her own dichotomous pattern no longer truly holds in some key respects. Her argument that Ulster loyalists see religion and politics as inextricably intertwined is, for example, no longer sustainable, given the clearly secular emphasis of the newly prominent Ulster loyalist parties of recent years. But her focus on fluidity, typical also of much of her later work, remains important. And it is supported by a similar emphasis in the work of other scholars, most engagedly perhaps that of Norman Porter, who has argued strenuously for change in unionist politics – away from cultural and liberal, and towards civic, unionism (Porter, 1996).

Allied to fluidity, analysis over the last 15 years has repeatedly demonstrated the complexity of what for long appeared (and still for many observers seems) a monolithic unionist political community. The annual hit-and-run journalistic summer ritual (fly to Belfast, photograph some incomprehensible Orangemen in baffling outfits, talk – if possible – to a cabaret-performing Ian Paisley, then fly home) consistently ignores or denies the complexity of unionist politics evident in the complicated mosaic painstakingly traced in serious analysis. The pioneering work of Boal, Campbell and Livingstone, for example – examining the actual, rather than the supposed, political attitudes of Belfast Protestants – argued 'how misconceived have been the many previous unquestioning, overhasty monolithic representations of Protestant opinion in Northern Ireland' (Boal, Campbell and Livingstone, 1991: 128). Again, Feargal Cochrane's study of post-Anglo-Irish Agreement unionism argues that the diversity within unionism is both its strength and weakness: a strength in that it encompasses a mass movement which can agree on what it dislikes and which it can therefore resist; but a disadvantage in that unionism 'tends to disintegrate' when unionists have to adopt a more positive course (Cochrane, 1997: viii). While Cochrane's argument was set out before the 1998 Belfast Agreement, it clearly finds some vindication in unionist responses to that deal. Other work, too, such as that by Shirlow and McGovern (1997), has attempted to emphasise the degree to which unionist politics is diverse.

A third, more controversial but potentially more significant, development has been the attempted rehabilitation of the idea of unionism as a rational, defensible ideology. Here academics have provided scholarly (Aughey, 1991) as well as more polemical[3] arguments. They have stressed that there is nothing inherently irrational about preferring membership of the United Kingdom to expulsion from it; that there is nothing necessarily more exclusivist about Ulster unionism than about Irish nationalism; that there are sound economic and other reasons for supporting unionism; and that the partition of Ireland in the 1920s reflected rather than created Irish divisions. This last point has been strongly argued by one of unionism's most striking defenders, Conor Cruise O'Brien: 'nationalists are in the habit of referring to the "artificial partition" of the island. In principle, there is nothing artificial about the partition: it is a result of history, traditions and demography' (O'Brien, 1994: 152).

The fourth point worth emphasising is the long overdue attention now devoted to East–West relations as well as North–South dimensions. The British dimension to the thinking of even the most apparently anglophobic of Irish republicans is a theme on which I have written elsewhere (English, 1998), and I do not want to dwell on that here. But writing the East–West axis into Ireland's story is clearly of vital significance for our understanding of unionism in a number of ways. Unionism, if it is properly to be understood, must be considered in a two-island as well as a purely Irish framework. In particular, the Scottish dimension to unionist identity and experience has now, thankfully, received careful attention (Walker, 1995).

Fifth, there emerges from the new analysis of unionism the vital question of confidence, or, more specifically, the lack of confidence now so typical of unionist culture. Arguably, the problems of the North of Ireland during the last 30 years might have been significantly reduced had unionist confidence – and therefore unionist flexibility and preparedness to move – been greater. The work of scholars such as Graham Walker and Steve Bruce epitomises much of what analysts have had to say on this subject, the latter referring to a Northern Ireland Protestant 'sense of inadequacy' (Bruce, 1994: 62) – a far more persuasive explanation of phenomena such as Orange marches than the more common belief that such events reflect a deep-seated unionist sense of superiority. Vulnerability and insecurity are key themes which recur in closely focused studies of Ulster unionism.

I am not attempting to suggest that an agreed picture can be drawn about unionism from the materials which scholars have amassed over the last 15 years. Academics rarely agree on anything too comfortably. But I think it is possible to claim that serious students of Ulster unionism in recent years have tended to stress that unionism is not properly understood if it is read as being static, homogeneous, necessarily irrational, superior in its self-image, or adequately understood in a one-island framework. It is none of these things.

## Conclusion

There are clearly a number of links between my two preceding sections (unionist politics, and the analysis of unionism). The most facile and deceptive of these is that certain scholars and commentators have had some input into the political new unionism which I addressed. But what I want to do here is consider the connection rather differently, and more subtly. If we read unionist political change in the light of analytical developments such as those I have discussed, then I believe we can redefine our response to unionism and to Northern Ireland politics as they have developed over the last 15 years. This will produce a perhaps heretical argument, and one which will serve, I hope, to stimulate some discussion and reflection. My argument is this. The last decade and a half has witnessed some changes in unionist politics which are encouraging (an articulate, sophisticated section of the family, keen to engage with nationalism in new ways), and some which are deeply discouraging (profound divisions and bitterness, and among many unionists a depressing lack of confidence and security). Both the positive and negative developments are, in part, responses to the kind of politics practised by London and Dublin in the Anglo-Irish Agreement–Belfast Agreement period.

If scholars are to be believed, then the fluidity and schism here identified should come as no surprise, and the absence of confidence should cause us some considerable alarm. Put bluntly, if one wants a community traditionally accustomed to advantage to yield some of that advantage lastingly, smoothly and peacefully, then the worst context in which to do it is one where that community is fractured, internally embittered, and substantially lacking in confidence in itself, its government and its neighbours. That is the situation we have faced, and continue to face.

It could have been different. The positive aspects of new unionism could have been nurtured and sustained, and accompanied by unity and confidence, if a different route had been followed over the post-1985 period. Here the problems began with the era of Margaret Thatcher. Mrs Thatcher's crude inflexibility produced the pyrrhic victory of the 1981 hunger strikes, which could have been avoided, and which gave the republican movement an avoidable energy injection. Fear that this republican energy would exceed that of the Social Democratic and Labour Party (SDLP) encouraged London and Dublin to engage in a process which was embodied in the Anglo-Irish Agreement, and which intended to work towards an overall constitutional settlement at the same time as addressing what in the eighteenth century might have been called Catholic reform.

But the pursuit of a constitutional settlement which unionists held to be a political defeat, and the tying of that pursuit to the question of quotidian reform, made the achievement of that reform much more difficult. If you weave together questions of jobs, policing and parades, to the structural involvement of Dublin in what Ian Paisley calls 'in embryo a condominium',[4] then the achievement of extensive, smooth reform at the expense of Paisley's community will be more difficult to obtain. It is far more difficult to adjust an unequal set of societal arrangements between two divided communities if the community which is expected to yield constantly feels that every concession is tied to the broader political goals of securing its defeat, and of driving it out of existence. This is especially true if the government cannot be trusted, and if there is a neighbouring enemy with a foothold inside one's state. Catholic grievances were (and are) more likely to be satisfactorily addressed if the majority community did (and does) not believe every concession to be part of a wider defeat.

Arguably, had there been a separation of the pursuit of a still elusive, agreed constitutional settlement from the question of Catholic reform, then unionism could indeed have been redefined, in ways more fruitful and positive perhaps than those which have ambiguously occurred to date. The unity and self-belief sustained by confidence in their government and in their sure place within the United Kingdom could have provided the foundation on which to build more extensive reform on questions affecting Catholic life in Northern Ireland, much earlier and more effectively than we have even yet seen. The most significant part of this picture is the question of loyalist violence – easily the most appalling thing experienced by Northern Ireland Catholics. It is important to point out that loyalist violence had substantially ended before the Anglo-Irish Agreement and the beginning of the long peace process. If the post-1994 period has witnessed a partial taming of the beast of paramilitary violence then, on the loyalist side at least, this was a beast stirred into life by the philosophy of the peace process itself. Between 1985 and 1994 the number of loyalist killings in Northern Ireland increased dramatically. This development was, to a significant degree, due to the Anglo-Irish Agreement and the politics which it initiated. Over the 1985–2001 period, the genuine nurturing of unionist confidence (through trustworthy government, and the absence of any grand neo-constitutional settlement plans) could have ensured the effective removal of loyalist violence from Northern Ireland.

There are, of course, no such alternatives today. As a consequence, many people might feel, despite scepticism about aspects of the partially implemented Belfast Agreement, that the 1998 deal still outlines the best route currently on offer. They might similarly believe that the more positive wing of unionism has grounds for its case. But it is possible that surer, better government – and possibly less overall violence too – was perhaps available through a different route from that down which we have travelled. There was an alternative in the mid-1980s which would have allowed for a road to peace at least as quick as this one, and which was much more just and more soundly based on principles of democracy and good government. Most crucially, this alternative route would have involved far more substantial gains, and far less awful suffering, for northern Catholics than they have experienced under the long peace process.

A major ingredient in the emergence of a redefined unionist politics has been the view, held by some, that republicans have shifted ground, having recognised the futility of their violence. Had republican vibrancy in the mid-1980s been recognised for what it truly was – substantially a function of the 1981 hunger strikes, and not necessarily a lasting threat to the SDLP – then a redefined unionism could have been built earlier and more securely. If from 1985 there had been virtually no loyalist violence, no catastrophic stimuli for Provisional republicanism, and had there been significant progress regarding policing, parades and jobs, then we might have seen a redefined, united and confident unionism as the condition for a redefined Northern Ireland.

Chapter 10

# The emergence of new loyalism

James W. McAuley

## Introduction

The contemporary politics of Northern Ireland remains dominated by the search for a stable political settlement. Graham has succinctly put the dilemma:

> Conflict in Ireland often seems so deeply entrenched as to be beyond solution. In part, this reflects the immensely powerful trope of nationalist Catholic identity which gave unionists nowhere to go. In turn, they have responded only with a conditional, ambiguous and ill-justified notion of Britishness which can never accommodate the nationalist population of Ulster. The deconstruction of monolithic representations of nationalist Irishness and unionist Britishness . . . is a necessary precursor of political change (Graham, 1997: 13).

One of the more important outcomes of this dilemma has been the increased fragmentation within the politics and social relations of unionism. In this chapter, I want to consider how sections of Ulster unionism and loyalism have responded to contemporary events in Northern Ireland and to outline and analyse the emergence of that political grouping which has become known as 'new loyalism'.

The response from unionism in the current phase has been segmented and at times revealed many of the internal contradictions between unionists. In party political terms, the Democratic Unionist Party (DUP) has consistently stated its mistrust of, and has organised against, the 'peace process'. Furthermore, notwithstanding its formal endorsement of the new institutions in Northern Ireland, the largest unionist grouping, the Ulster Unionist Party (UUP), is clearly still deeply divided on the issue, with many of its supporters engaged in the new regime only extremely reluctantly. Beyond that, there are important consequences for any reconstruction of loyalism, some of which I highlight below.

Within unionism, it is only those political groupings originating in the loyalist paramilitaries – the Progressive Unionist Party (PUP) and while it existed in a coherent form, the Ulster Democratic Party (UDP) – that have been prepared to promote positive involvement in the search for a negotiated settlement. Central to this has been the surfacing, from deep within working-class loyalism, of those openly challenging many of the values and structures of traditional unionism. In particular I wish to discuss and analyse the attempts in the contemporary period to redefine loyalism.[1] Central to this will be an outline of the contours of contemporary loyalism and the development of a newly articulated social democratic politics from some sections of Protestant working-class communities.

Indeed, the current period has witnessed a growing recognition from within key sections of loyalism that unionist politicians have largely absolved themselves of many social and economic responsibilities, by giving primacy to the constitutional issues. This has led not just to a reassessment of the unionist leadership and the Stormont system, but in some cases an attempt to redefine what loyalism means and its relationship to the British state. This reflects a developing sense of awareness that the system in which they saw their unionism as playing a central role has failed for the loyalist community. Moreover, there is a growing sense that many unionist politicians are more concerned with restating their position on the constitution than they are in addressing the realities of everyday life in working-class loyalist areas.

Hence, the views being expressed by the political leadership of the PUP offer a clear attempt to dispute and to reassess traditional unionist discourses. Central to this has been the challenge offered by new loyalism to the authority of the established unionist political leadership and to some of the core organising discourses within unionism.

## The nature of new loyalism

So what is new loyalism? One way of characterising it is through those key figures, such as David Ervine and Billy Hutchinson, who have emerged to the foreground. Even so, this needs to be set in context. Both Ervine and Hutchinson are ex-members of the loyalist paramilitary grouping, the Ulster Volunteer Force (UVF). Indeed, they were both arrested within days of each other in late 1974, for paramilitary activities. In turn, along with many others, they were highly politicised during their period in jail and greatly influenced by Gusty Spence (initially, in his position as commanding officer of the UVF in Long Kesh). Indeed, as the journalist, Peter Taylor, put it:

> Spence more than any other single person sowed in the hard soil of Long Kesh the political ideas that were to flourish many years later in the form of the UVF's new political party, the Progressive Unionist Party (Taylor, 2000: 141).

The real genesis of new loyalism is thus much earlier than many believe. Its conception lies in the recognition by some of the inability of the established political parties of Ulster unionism to represent their views, and the growing political and economic marginalisation of many within Protestant working-class communities. That is not to say that those expressing such new views were in any way dominant, or to ignore the importance of sectarianism as an organisational feature of these communities. However, in 1977, when still UVF commander in Long Kesh, Spence issued a statement claiming that violence was counterproductive and promoting reconciliation, claiming, 'Let us reconcile and permit the grass and flowers to grow over the battlefields just as they have at the Somme and Passchendaele' (cited in *The Irish Times*, 12 December 1984). Spence resigned as UVF commander in March 1978 and was eventually released from prison in 1985.

While the inception of the contemporary PUP can be found in the UVF's attempt to organise in a party political way in 1974 (see McAuley and Hislop, 2000), its real momentum came with the release from prison of certain figures, including David Ervine and later Billy Hutchinson, who began openly and coherently to articulate criticisms of unionism and the British state. This was particularly pertinent since it came from those loyalists who had served time for what they regarded as defending the state. The process was slow. It should be noted that even as recently as 1995 the PUP was described by one leading journalist as a lone voice sounding in the loyalist wilderness (Brown, *Financial Times*, 8 February 1995).

Under the influence of its current leadership, however, the PUP has grown from a single branch of around 30 members located in the Shankill Road in Belfast to a structured party with a claimed membership of around 600. It has also had representative success, with seven councillors returned in the local elections of 1997 and four in 2001, and representatives at the Forum Talks and in the Northern Ireland Assembly. Billy Hutchinson explains the party's development as follows:

> I think that . . . the reason why the fringe parties have come out [is] because there has been a war going on here for 25 years that has been fought by working-class people. The establishment parties have kept clear of it. They've never, ever got involved in it. They've always made sure that they've stayed out of jail. Whenever it came to actually trying to resolve the problem, nothing happened (*An Phoblacht/Republican News*, 10, 2 February 1995).

Partly because of such awareness the PUP has often sought to fix ideological and social distance between itself and mainstream political unionism.

## The nature of the Progressive Unionist Party

The party that has emerged proclaims itself as 'intensely Unionist, but avowedly socialist in its ideology'. Furthermore, the party has consistently continued to air the view that it is working-class people who have suffered most from the conflict. As Ervine has expressed it:

> There can never, ever, be a return to the awful political and social abuses of the past and Stormont as we knew it is dead and gone, never to be resurrected. Granted there are those political dinosaurs who would opt for the 'good old' sectarian and strata system of the past where everybody knew their place and forelock touching was the norm. We have had enough of that obnoxious trio . . . bigotry, sectarianism and hypocrisy. We would oppose as vehemently and strenuously as anyone else a return to such a divisive and partisan system of government (Progressive Unionist Party, 2000).

One central feature of the PUP project has been its attempt to reconstruct and reinterpret loyalism's past. From this beginning the PUP has sought to locate its politics directly in the claim that this group was not being properly represented by the traditional unionist leadership and to provide a different understanding of the past from within unionism. As this statement explains, 'For too long politics have been pronounced by those who have failed to consult and therefore misrepresent the views of the Unionist people especially in working class areas' (Progressive Unionist Party, 1998). Likewise, the PUP has continued to articulate a coherent analysis of the class structure of traditional unionism. Take the following, for example:

> We, too, the working class Protestants have felt the slow-burning agony of powerlessness and ineffectuality. Sir Edward Carson warned the majority to treat the minority magnanimously. That advice from one of the Fathers of Unionism was not heeded and we have paid a heavy price. There are still those fools in Unionism who long for the heady Stormont days of privilege and patronage (Spence, 1995: 4).

The party constitution, for example, includes the British Labour Party's old Clause Four, with its commitment to state-owned industry and Keynesian economic interventionism. The PUP has also claimed the need for direct state intervention in key areas of the economy. It has emphasised the need for strong state support for the health and social security services and in particular higher education, where it advocates a full return to state subsidised funding to the equivalent levels of 1979 (see Progressive Unionist Party, 1996a, 1996b, 1996c).

Much of what the PUP currently promotes continues to suggest a distinct fracture with what has gone before. Thus, the PUP, through its discrete policies

and willingness to engage in debate, has been an important element in a
process that has nurtured an increased introspection and discussion amongst
key elements of the Protestant working class. This has been reflected in some
of the materials produced from within Protestant working-class communities,
often guided by community workers and/or ex-paramilitary members
(see Hall, 1994, 1995, 1996; Ballymacarret Think Tank, 1999a, 1999b;
Ballymacarret Arts and Cultural Society, 1999; Seeds of Hope, 2000; Shankill
Think Tank, 1995, 1998).

In recent times the PUP has also argued (echoing Spence, some 25 years
before; see Garland, 2001) that the increasingly weakened social and economic position in which many working-class Protestants now find themselves
is largely a result of the same pattern of social deprivation that affects their
counterparts in nationalist areas. Another result of this process has been the
reassessment by some of the core values and beliefs that have guided unionism,
and their relationship to the state of Northern Ireland since its formation. As
part of the party's official literature says:

> Fifteen years ago, Republican leaders spoke of the fifty years of hard bitter
> experience when referring to the old Stormont government. Unfortunately, they
> did not include the Protestant or Unionist community in that experience. For
> fifty years there had existed the hard line two party state. Uncompromising
> Unionism faced uncompromising Nationalism. The politics of the mind was
> substituted by the politics of emotion maintaining the survival of these two
> extreme power blocs. The seriousness of the matter emerged even before the
> violent events of the late sixties. Some Unionists opposed reasonable legislation
> simply because it emanated from 'Republicans' and the Nationalists opposed
> reasonable legislation simply because it was put forward by Unionists. Extremist
> politicians came to power, not because of any votes cast for them, but for votes
> cast against the other side (Progressive Unionist Party, 1999).

Perhaps one of the most striking developments surrounding the PUP is not
what they are saying (this has been reasonably consistent since around the
mid-1980s), but, rather, the ideological space which has been created within
unionism and loyalism to allow the PUP to openly express and find support
for such notions. The importance for the future direction of unionism of the
ability of the PUP to gain and maintain populist support cannot be overstated.
Although it is of no little significance that the PUP has successfully presented
its arguments to an extremely wide audience, it is its ability to convince its
more immediate constituency that will ultimately prove of most importance.

In the past, many in the Protestant working class have steadfastly refused
to engage with any thought of possible political accommodation with their
nationalist and republican counterparts. Furthermore, any left of centre

articulation of social and economic issues from within unionism was liable to be seen as a direct challenge to unionist control, and sometimes to the very legitimacy and existence of the Northern Irish state itself. Hence, such views found little favour within working-class loyalist communities. Despite this deep-rooted oppositional culture an important stated goal for the leadership of the PUP remains:

> an injection of working class politics to get people to rally around social and economic issues. That won't make the constitutional problem disappear, but at least it will show that there is a common ground on which we can agree and then maybe we can find a way forward on the constitution (Cusack and McDonald, 1997: 117).

Furthermore, the PUP argues that it is the intransigence of sections of political unionism (particularly the DUP and at times the UUP), throughout the peace process, which has been mostly detrimental to the aspirations of the broader unionist community. Rather, the PUP promote and support the idea of power sharing, arguing for a 'shared responsibility' between the 'two traditions' and the diminishing of sectarian social relations as the basis for a solution. As David Ervine has explained:

> The only vehicle which I think will destroy . . . sectarianism is class politics and we've got to replace that sectarianism with something. . . . I advocate that the only thing that I think can put it right is class politics. . . . We've got to be forging circumstances here that at some future date actually create real alignment in politics on economic and social issues, as opposed to the divisive religious and constitutional ones.[2]

The PUP has also increasingly expressed views on a wide range of other social issues, which sets it apart from other unionist parties. The party, for example, directly promotes women's issues on its agenda. Indeed, almost half of the PUP executive committee is made up of women. The PUP is also one of the few political organisations in Northern Ireland (and certainly amongst unionism), which has been openly supportive of gay and lesbian rights (see Purvis, 1998) and which is candidly pro-choice on the abortion issue (see Ward, 1998). It has also given serious consideration to wider ranging policies, such as those on urban regeneration, the environment and energy. Such views are far from primary to traditional expressions of unionist ideology.

The party has also sought tentatively to establish cross-community dialogue and to support members who have become involved in such cross-community projects. Hence, another important aspect of PUP ideology is that which justifies its willingness to enter into debate with the traditional 'enemies of

Ulster'. In part, this has meant recognition that they will have to negotiate and form a working relationship with other groupings, including Sinn Féin. In part also, it has given rise to the promotion of a series of policies suggesting the need for a bill of rights and the introduction of a written constitution in Northern Ireland, which are seen as essential in safeguarding minorities in Northern Ireland. Indeed, upon winning his Belfast city council seat, Billy Hutchinson returned to a theme he had raised previously, when he said:

> Why shouldn't we work with Sinn Féin in the council? The other Unionists do it at the moment. If Sinn Féin or anyone else has decent arguments to put forward we will listen to them, as long as they are for the benefit of all the people of Belfast (*Andersonstown News* 10, 26 June 1996).

David Ervine is clear on the importance of achieving these goals. He has highlighted this in the following statement when talking about possible political realignments in the Northern Ireland Assembly:

> We can't live in isolation from the economic constraints that are happening in a global context, but I think there is a social dimension to all of the parties in Northern Ireland and I think that, in a collective sense that will come out, of that I have no doubt, that it will come out. . . . But it won't only be the PUP and Sinn Féin in agreement, although that will happen. I think it will be the PUP, it will be elements of the Ulster Unionist Party, elements of the SDLP and Sinn Féin, and it may even be part of the DUP. The gas pipeline to the North has absolute cross-community and cross-party support and that's evidence of just one issue where for the needs and for the good, you see the floor being crossed, no physical crossing on the floor of course, but you know what I mean by that. It's already begun.[3]

This willingness to engage with the political opposition, even with those constructed as traditional enemies (and in some cases literally so), clearly marks out the PUP from other strands within unionism. Until very recently the open expression of such a political stance would have been untenable from a representative of working-class loyalism. It is little wonder that such views from the PUP have raised much concern from within unionism itself, and drawn such a harsh retort from that section of it, notably the DUP, which locate their reading within unionism's traditional analysis. The PUP has been relatively successful in drawing support for its position. Recent research in which I have been involved indicates that over 80 per cent of PUP members have never previously been a member of any political party in Northern Ireland (McAuley and Tonge, 2001). By and large they have been supportive of that broad spectrum of unionism which since the mid-1990s has given credence to those political discourses supporting the Good Friday Agreement.

Needless to say, such views are far from universally accepted within unionism. Here it is useful to understand discourse as that which refers to systems of meaningful practices that form the identities of subjects and objects, that help construct frontiers between 'insiders' and 'outsiders' and between that which is seen as 'legitimate' and 'illegitimate' political aspiration (see Laclau and Mouffe, 1985; Howarth, Norval and Stavrakakis, 2000). Moreover, such discourses are historical constructs always vulnerable to shifting political forces. One way of understanding the ruptures within loyalism, therefore, is to comprehend the differing frames of reference and discourses being used to construct conflicting understandings of contemporary events.

Here I shall identify two of these: a 'discourse of perpetuity', emphasising the need to maintain perpetual vigilance in defence of the Ulster Protestant identity and interests, and a 'discourse of transformation', stressing the need for loyalism to adapt to the changed political environment in which it now exists (see also McAuley, 2002).

## Unionist discourses of perpetuity

One key discourse unifying contemporary unionists against the development of the peace process is that of betrayal by 'Britain'. There remains a deeply held unionist belief that the contemporary political settlement marks huge concessions to republicanism and the methods of terrorism, and a commitment to a form of unification by stealth involving the denigration of a distinct 'unionist culture'. In fact, many unionists perceive the entire 'peace process' as a direct reply by the British government to a nationalist set agenda in an attempt to 'buy off terrorism'. Hence, for many unionists, the latest initiatives surrounding the closer workings of the British and Irish governments and even the introduction of the Northern Ireland Assembly mark political defeat.

Many of those who seek to reproduce this discourse do so in terms of the securing of traditional values and react to what they see as a recent history of unionist demise. This is given credence through direct reference to a continuity of events that includes the Sunningdale and Anglo-Irish agreements, the Downing Street declaration (1993), the Framework document (1995) and the contemporary Good Friday Agreement. All these attempts at a political settlement are seen as instalments of a longer process involving steps on a slippery slope to a united Ireland.[4]

Sections of unionism continue to construct this powerful all-embracing discourse capable of forming a coherent social and political identity. Importantly, it is this that binds together a multiplicity of other potential identities involving, among others, class, nation, gender, sexual orientation, race, ethnicity, language, regional identity, lifestyle, religion and workplace.

So while unionism is an identity that is capable of superimposing itself on these, it is neither fixed nor constant. It is socially constructed as a call for individuals to constitute their 'self' around a particular identity.

Unionism is capable of mobilising those who have been successfully summoned by motivating them to engage in particular forms of action and experience. Furthermore, in Northern Ireland, unionism also often demands a public statement from its supporters. Unionism, hence, is not only important in identity formation but also in engaging its followers in activism, whether this be in voting behaviour, public meetings, rallies or other forms of public events. To be successful, unionism in all its contemporary forms must draw on the above in some recognisable way. Furthermore, it must do so in a way that is capable of confirming these core principles and solidifying together the identity of its supporters into a coherent politics.

In response to these competing discourses unionism has responded to contemporary events in a fragmented manner. Some sections of unionism have simply drawn directly on long standing discourses and sought to return unionism to the fundamentals of its doctrine and oppose what they see as a dilution of the unionist position. This can be seen, for example, within the political discourse of the DUP, within which the very future existence of Northern Ireland is always at stake. Take, for example, the following from Peter Robinson, the deputy leader of the party:

> Unionists now have notice of the scope and scale of the intended betrayal. Modern-day governments seek to avoid any single change so grievous as to occasion mass resistance. So there will be no big surrender, just dozens of little ones. No event so momentous in itself as to provoke community unrest. One thing is certain – once the line of all-Ireland executive authority has been crossed (in whatever form and to whatever extent) it is only the slipperiness of the slope that will determine when we arrive in an united Ireland, as the destination will have been irreversibly set on that fateful day (Robinson, 1996).

In recent times the DUP has consistently repeated its claim that the foundations of the union have been made insecure by the implementation of the 'treacherous Framework Document' (see Ulster Democratic Unionist Party, 1996a, 1996b, 1996c, 1996d). Central to this framing is the DUP's self image as unwavering sentinels against Ulster's enemies (see, for example, Ulster Democratic Unionist Party, 1997a, 1997b, 1998, 1999; Paisley, 1998). It positions its followers around a discourse of fear with only the DUP in a position to reveal the 'truth'. Ian Paisley's statement just before the last UK general election illustrates this well:

Ulster's future within the Union cannot be secured under the terms of the Belfast Agreement. The Agreement is the drip feed of IRA/Sinn Féin to take us into a fascist Irish Republic where the Protestant population has already been decimated. This election week is to be followed by the presentation to the new Parliament, legislation agreed in the dirty deal brokered by Mr Trimble, Mr Blair and IRA/Sinn Fein, which will remove from the Law Courts of Northern Ireland all symbols of Britishness and the Monarchy. The Royal Coat of Arms is to be ditched, and buildings which have it incorporated in their architecture will have it covered over until it can be demolished. . . . Ulster is to be made a prey to Republican domination. It is vital that a body blow is struck now against the conspiracy and treachery afoot. Our destiny is in the hands of the Unionist voters, and I would appeal to them all to close ranks and give to Unionist politicians who can be trusted the mandate to resist and destroy this programme of betrayal (Paisley, 2001).

Such 'traditional' unionist values have been increasingly expressed by widening factions of unionism. Another clear example can be found in the writings and speeches of Robert McCartney. I have argued elsewhere (McAuley 1997a, 1999) that for some time McCartney has promoted a central duality in his politics. On the one hand he has offered important criticisms of traditional unionism, particularly in its more sectarian manifestations. On the other, however, he has consistently utilised and drawn upon traditional unionist discourses and conservative interpretative frames for the basis of his politics. Hence, he has regularly articulated the view that the peace process is part of an orchestrated conspiracy against unionists and the Union. It is a process the implementation of which 'ultimately threatens the very existence of democracy itself', no institution of government can be properly termed as democratic if it includes political representatives linked to a terrorist organisation (see for example, the collection of works in McCartney, 2001b).

One of the main overall themes within McCartney's writings suggests that the central task of the British government has been to promote a settlement that persuades unionists to sacrifice their British identity, modifying and diluting it to the point where it will not prove a viable obstacle to the unification of Ireland. The overall policy of recent British governments is to disengage from Northern Ireland by creating and putting in place institutions agreed jointly with the Irish government. These institutions will gradually evolve into a factually and economically united Ireland that will render the final consent to the transfer of legal constitutional sovereignty a mere formality. Eventually, at the end of this process, an acquiescent unionism will agree to the end of the Union.

For McCartney too, the current political settlement is merely part of a broader strategy. Both governments, albeit for differing reasons, are engaged in a slowly evolving scheme in which British identity in Northern Ireland will gradually be replaced by an Irish one. The political strategies of the British and Irish governments dovetail. Both seek to bring about Irish unity, although economic, social, and political restraints and opposition will mean that its final accomplishment will take some time. Nevertheless, the overall direction and motivation for the peace process is clear. For these plans to be realised, however, the continued suspension of violence is a necessary condition. Hence the argument that the major dynamic of the peace process is to appease the republican movement, and to offer concessions in return for the halting of its paramilitary campaign. McCartney again made this point when he drew the following analogy following the events of 11 September 2002 in New York:

> Nor has the bitter irony of Foreign Secretary Jack Straw's advice to the United States that it should remember the failure of a British policy of appeasing Hitler, escaped those British citizens who have watched his government endorse and pursue a similar policy in Northern Ireland – the same government which has treated the pro-Union people with similar expediency in the face of terror as Neville Chamberlain afforded to the Czechs in 1938 (McCartney, 2001a).

This reading of contemporary events is supported by others whose central belief is that their British identity, expressed either as unionism or Protestantism, is under attack. Unionists are to be persuaded to accept an inevitable greening of their cultural and political identity. This has been partly reflected across the wider unionist community, the clearest example of which surrounds the contested 'rights' of Orange lodges to march their 'traditional routes', by far the best-known example of which surrounds events at Drumcree (see Bryan, Fraser and Dunn, 1995; Jarman, 1997; Jarman and Bryan, 1996). While for many nationalists such parades are triumphalist and offensive (see Garvaghy Residents, 1999; Ryder and Kearney, 2001), many Protestants see them as an essential part of 'their' culture and claim that all they want to do is to uphold long standing customs. It is now a common view, for example, among unionists that if they lose the Garvaghy Road in Portadown today, they may lose Northern Ireland tomorrow.

The reactions of many unionists on this issue can be understood only in the context of broader fears that what the community is witnessing is yet another example of a Protestant unionist culture under direct and continuous threat. This notion is increasingly reproduced in a variety of forums. Sometimes it is even presented as a deliberate project to 'ethnically cleanse' Northern Ireland of its Protestant population. Consider the following example from a recent edition of the official newspaper of the Orange Order:

> There has been a sustained and orchestrated attack on Protestant areas along the many peace lines in North Belfast. There is a real feeling in Protestant areas that

this is the latest and most sustained bid by republicans to ethnically cleanse even more areas of North Belfast and 'green' this strategic part of the city to an even greater extent. . . . It is important that this nefarious plan to take over North Belfast is recognised by the authorities, and by the liberals and well-meaning 'moderates' who can speak from the safety of tree-lined suburbs in the east and south of the city, or in North Down. . . . This is a struggle for territory, and on the republican-nationalist side it is very much a bid for further expansion (*Orange Standard*, October 2001, p. 6).

The same theme is taken up in a second example:

The extent of the exodus of Protestants from places like Londonderry cityside, Newry, and parts of North and West Belfast has been documented, but recent statistics show that the situation is even more serious than was thought. . . . As in Londonderry, the ethnic cleansing of the Protestant population has almost gone unnoticed and unreported. . . . The ethnic cleansing of townlands along the border, especially in Co. Fermanagh and South Armagh is another well-known fact of history. . . . The constant intimidation of Protestants in parts of Belfast like the Ardoyne, Suffolk, Oldpark and Whitewell is but a continuation of a process which has transformed large tracts of territory in the capital city . . . Protestants are not going to move out of Northern Ireland to suit the plans and ambitions of extreme republicans (*Orange Standard*, November 2001, p. 2).

From such a perspective, the main dynamics of the peace process and the wider political settlement are seen as being directly aimed at undermining the British presence in Northern Ireland, and at subverting Protestants from their traditional British allegiance in an attempt to transfer this to Irish nationalism.

The challenges to Orangeism's 'right to march' and to unionist physical space are thus seen as the manifestation of key political policies implemented by enemies, and of the 'greening' of Ulster. This perceived drive towards 'Irishness' is seen everywhere and rests on that construction of the current peace process as involving all sorts of hidden dangers to Ulster Protestants, who are engaged in 'a last battle for Ulster'. Unionists generally must guard unceasingly against the insidious propaganda and attempts to subvert their British allegiance.

This discourse emphasises a particular set of understood realities within unionism. It highlights a constructed political identity within a particular form of constitutional arrangement. In political issues the concern that these arrangements are under threat has most straightforwardly been uttered by the DUP in its representation of the situation. This is that the unionist people of Northern Ireland are being subject to a process driven by an untrustworthy British government, the dynamic for which comes from the combined forces of Irish nationalism and republicanism, supported by the Irish government and the Irish lobby in the USA.

The inevitable outcome, this line of reasoning goes, will be a united Ireland, unless unionists can be awoken to the dangers and organised against them. The core of the DUP project continues to frame the conflict in this way and to construct discourses that re-emphasise and reinforce the central fears of many unionists. The broad perspective of those promoting perpetuity within unionism can thus be set out as follows. The grand strategy behind the peace process is to bring about a functionally united Ireland that will ultimately render a transfer of sovereignty inevitable, through a concealed process of unification and a conceding of executive political power to Irish nationalism and republicanism.

Importantly this discourse of fear is non-party specific in its appeal to unionists. It is capable of arousing and mobilising across several of the factions of the unionist party political bloc and from within other sections of non-aligned unionists. The discourse and politics of perpetuity is now firmly established across the DUP, the Orange Order, the UK Unionist Party, that section of the Ulster Unionist Party led by Donaldson, and other sections of unionism and loyalism. It was given a cutting edge in *Realpolitik* by Reverend William McCrea's victory in the South Antrim by-election in September 2000, by the repositioning of much of the UUP around the anti-agreement bloc, and the increased support for the DUP in the 2001 UK general election. Such recent events highlight the increasing lack of enthusiasm in the loyalist community for the Good Friday Agreement and the politics of the broader peace process.

## Unionist discourses of transformation

While the strength and breadth of the discourse of perpetuity should not be underestimated, it is important to note that not all unionists have adopted this as their key frame of reference. Sections of working-class loyalism in particular have begun to critically examine their historical and cultural identity in a meaningful way. This experience needs to be understood in the changing context of dramatic economic decline, political disarticulation and ideological disintegration within unionism. The period of the peace process has opened up much deliberation within loyalist working-class communities, one possible reading of which suggests a marginalisation of sectarianism as a fundamental organising principle.

This has been reflected in the new politics of loyalism and the continued criticism of the traditional leadership of unionism. The PUP has been to the fore in this attempt to restructure unionism. In recent times, the PUP leadership has stated its commitment to maintaining and strengthening Northern Ireland's constitutional position within the United Kingdom. It has repeatedly claimed that it will actively work by all democratic means to ensure that there will be no constitutional changes that either diminish the constitutional position of Northern Ireland as an integral part of the United Kingdom or dilute democratic structures and procedures within Northern Ireland. The party's recent manifestos have also supported the right of any individual or group to seek constitutional change by 'democratic, legitimate and peaceful means' and spoken of the rights and aspirations of all those who abide by the law regardless of religious, cultural, national or political inclinations. They have also declared that there can never, ever, be a return to 'the awful political and social abuses of the past and Stormont'.

Factors such as these have served to expose inconsistencies in the relationships between key sections of the Protestant working class and the British state. Importantly, from this section of unionism there has been a growing awareness of the consequences of the rapidly changing historical, social and economic context within which contemporary unionism exists. The loyalist parties have effectively begun to harness views such as those expressed above. In this sense the parties have provided focal points for increasingly coherent social, economic and political challenges within unionism. They have also begun to confront some of the dominant discourses with unionism.

These processes have loosened the bonds and shifted the interpretative frames within loyalism; but these developments have not meant that such groupings have weakened their commitment to the Union. The position of the loyalist working class should be seen in the context of the renegotiations of the ideological boundaries within which they seek to express their identity. These shifting contours of unionist identity are extremely important. As several commentators (such as Dunn and Morgan, 1994; Shirlow and McGovern, 1997) and unionist politicians have noted, there are widespread feelings from within the Protestant working class that they are in decline, increasingly subject to forces of rapid economic, political, cultural and psychological retreat.

The hegemonic construction of a 'British' identity by Ulster loyalism has not only traditionally included but also absorbed a multitude of other key identities, such as geographical location, sexual preference, class identity, and gender. These have been organised into a collective political will through an all-embracing discourse. Thus, Jacobson (2000: 191) rightly identifies how gendered constructions of the public and private in Northern Ireland have led to a 'startling absence of women from all forms of political representation'. This has been particularly true of unionist politics. New loyalism has partially created ideological space for some women within the loyalist community to demand the right to have their politics included within a redefinition of unionist politics and identity.[5] If such trends continue, new loyalism may thus provide the further dynamic to begin to separate key identities, and to reformulate the central components of unionism. In time, this may form the basis for the creation of a coherent set of alternative discourses and locations of identity within unionism.

## Contesting loyalism's future

The contemporary period has often revealed overt antagonism between the PUP and other sections of the unionist political leadership, notably of the UUP and the DUP, many of whom see the current political settlement as merely part of a broader strategy whereby unionists are to be persuaded to accept the inevitable greening of their cultural and political identity. Here the main dynamic of the peace process and the political settlement is perceived as undermining the British ethos in Northern Ireland, and as subverting Protestants from their traditional British allegiance in an attempt to transfer this to Irish nationalism. Whether tangible or not, there is strong historical evidence to suggest that whenever this discourse has become dominant, unionists have traditionally returned to an entrenched political position.

The prominence of the PUP clearly has not gone uncontested from within these sections of unionism. Another focus of hostility towards the forms of new loyalism expressed by the PUP comes from those forces coalescing around sections of the loyalist paramilitaries, particularly the Loyalist Volunteer Force (LVF) and parts of the Ulster Defence Association (UDA). The LVF, led until his murder by the late Billy Wright, was formed by disillusioned paramilitaries from within the UVF and UDA. It broke with the leadership, claiming that the UDP and PUP were selling out the 'loyalist people' through an uncritical acceptance of the peace process.

This grouping openly seeks to oppose what they call the 'peace (surrender) deal' and to undermine the PUP leadership. A special loathing appears to be reserved for Ervine, who has been accused in pamphlets and graffiti of treachery, of being an MI5 agent, of working 'hand-in hand with the enemies of Ulster' and of having lost contact with his loyalist roots.[6] They have also claimed that 'Billy Hutchinson and Davy Ervine are more than willing to sit around a table with the enemies of our country' (*Leading the Way*, no date). Such views played a central role in the loyalist feud that occurred during much of 2000, resulting in deaths of seven people. The tensions are far from resolved and it is conceivable that the section of the loyalist paramilitaries who seek to reaffirm the conflict or break with the political settlement may yet undermine the political, organisational and electoral position of the PUP.

## Conclusion

The possibility of an agreed settlement in Ireland can only be fully assessed if the shifting contours of unionist politics and identity are traced in detail. The hegemonic construction of identity by Ulster loyalism has traditionally absorbed a multitude of other key identities, organised into a collective political will through an all-embracing discourse of 'Britishness'. New loyalism may provide a dynamic to begin to separate out the key component of this identity, and to reformulate its central components. This may form the basis for the creation of alternative discourses and locations of identity within unionism. Such processes are, however, highly contentious.

It is possible to suggest two major discourses around which unionism is currently mobilising politically. The first appeals to unionists to reinforce its traditional form; the second, that to continue, unionism must change to adopt a more pluralist and liberal form. The manifestation of these discourses can be broadly understood as the differences between those groupings which seek to reinforce traditional unionist positions and those promoting some form of political change. Fragmenting as it has along these fault lines, unionism as an ideology and as a political force is in no small state of upheaval.

In the period directly following the ceasefires and the Good Friday Agreement, 'traditional unionism' found it increasingly difficult to dominate the discourses of identity. Unionist hegemony was increasingly challenged from within by those with alternative notions of the nature of unionism. New loyalism set about articulating a class and sometimes a gender perspective challenging unionism's traditional construction.

The most recent period, however, has witnessed a strong restatement of unionism's previously dominant values. The DUP remains foremost in its organisation and in promoting the continued criticism of those loyalists engaged in the search for an inclusive settlement. Furthermore, the DUP no longer appears marginalised in this stance. The broad restatement of the discourse of perpetuity is capable of rallying significant sections of unionism against any continued settlement.

When considering the possibilities for a discourse of transformation within unionism it is important to recognise that the society in which the PUP exists remains structured and determined by sectarian social relations. Given its origins and the still close relationship with a particular paramilitary organisation, one of the indisputable tests for the PUP is whether it can develop any genuine cross community recognition for the merit of its position. In this context, therefore, there are serious and difficult questions to be asked about the representative character of the PUP, and how far the leadership's thinking may be ahead of the ordinary working-class Protestants it seeks to represent. It is also clear that because of its origins the PUP may only be able to draw upon a limited, if possibly still growing, constituency. Such a task is not made easier in the wake of a bloody feud between the major loyalist paramilitary groups.

The first task for the PUP, therefore, remains that of convincing broader sections of unionism of the validity and substance of its position and that it can create a creditable electoral base. Certainly in the period immediately following the ceasefires and the signing of the Good Friday Agreement, the PUP harnessed a new political dynamic from within the Protestant working class and provided an increasingly coherent challenge from within unionism. This saw the partial renegotiations of the ideological boundaries within which many sought to express their identity. These processes have loosened some of the political and ideological bonds within unionism, and shifted some of the interpretative frames within loyalism.

Should the PUP project succeed further, then what we may well witness is a permanent breach within established unionist politics and ideology. This might offer at least some possibility of the development of a lasting political settlement in Northern Ireland. Whether or not the final outcome of the contemporary period is that new loyalism becomes a substantive political force is, however, still some way from being determined.

Chapter 11

# The fading of traditional nationalism in the Republic of Ireland

Tom Garvin

## Introduction

Nationalism is the leading political ideology of the early twenty-first century, and has outstripped its main ideological and philosophical competitors (such as communism, fascism, nazism and racism) as the most common organising principle of large numbers of ordinary people across the world. Nationalism comes in many forms, often disguised as liberalism, conservatism, religious enthusiasm or other political systems of ideas. It is only rivalled by various religious fundamentalisms, which usually need a nationalism on which to piggyback. The cases of Iran, Taliban Afghanistan or Pakistan in Asia or the Polish, Greek and Irish cases in Europe spring to mind as examples of such alliances in the past or the present.

The Irish are not peculiar in their adherence to popular nationalism, although they have been commonly berated for it; in fact the Irish are clearly far more aware of their nationalism than the English, for example, an extremely nationalist people who are frequently unaware of their own ideological condition. Commonly the English suffer from a rather fraught and uncertain Anglocentrism that is long outdated. Unlike the English, the Irish know they are not at the centre of the world, and behave accordingly. The English, rather like the French attempt in the 1950s to piggyback on renascent Germany, attempt to piggyback on the only world superpower, the United States. Stratagems of this kind fool no one.

One of the reasons for nationalism's political success in the modern, post-Soviet world is that it offers a simple principle of collective solidarity, collective self-protectiveness or whatever one might like to call it, to communities in a world that is commonly less than friendly and sometimes frightening, bullying, menacing or even genocidal. Nationalism is intellectually opportunistic, redefines itself constantly and commonly does so without ever admitting that that is what it is up to. As *1066 and all that* put it a generation ago, the 'Irish question' was always and automatically problematic in British politics because, whenever the English thought they had figured out an answer to the Irish question, the Irish changed the question. The Irish, of course, were simply demanding a redress of what they perceived as monstrous historical grievances on what amounted to the instalment system, and were not fully aware that each assurance that they gave the English that this recent demand for reform would 'settle Ireland' was really just such an instalment: freedom by the drip method, perhaps.

I have just suggested that the phenomenon of nationalism is intellectually opportunist and therefore 'revisionist' and I believe that we Irish, North and South, afford no exception to this generalisation; both nationalists and unionists on the island of Ireland have been forced repeatedly to revise their self-definitions because of political and historical circumstance. This condition of being willing to change one's collective mind is one that is best seen as being essentially healthy, and not deserving of the intellectual opprobrium heaped on it by fundamentalist republicans.

Furthermore, nationalist 'revisionism' in Ireland is not new; it is actually very traditional. 'Revisionism' as a term of abuse is usually directed by the unschooled at writers who are re-examining an older revisionism. The 'Story of Ireland' has been repeatedly reinvented at intervals over the last three hundred years, starting with Geoffrey Keating's seventeenth-century plea for a unification of the Gaels and Old English in Ireland into one united Catholic nation, a nation which would eventually assist in the defeat of Protestantism in Ireland and, by implication, Britain (Keating, 1723). Eoin MacNeill was essentially doing a similar ideological job two centuries later when he published his *Phases of Irish history* in the middle of the Anglo-Irish war in 1919. MacNeill, a noted scholar of Gaelic Ireland, reinvented Ireland by linking up Celtic Ireland and modern Anglo-Ireland as one, continuous and indivisible entity (MacNeill, 1919), an idea taken up by, and popularised by, Eamon de Valera among many others.

Again, Sean Ó Faoláin, in two masterly biographies, *King of the beggars* and *The great O'Neill,* reasserted the constitutional tradition of Irish nationalism and the validity of a non neo-Gaelic version of that national identity (Ó Faoláin, 1938, 1942). By so doing, he was facing down the reigning historicist orthodoxy formulated by MacNeill and others. Michael Sheehy, writing his *Divided we stand* in the mid-1950s, questioned the realism of Irish official posturings on the issue of partition (Sheehy, 1955). Yet again, Conor Cruise O'Brien, in his *States of Ireland* (O'Brien, 1972) supplied the nation with a devastating analysis of the insincerity and unreality of official attitudes toward the problem of Northern Ireland.

O'Brien's book was a crucial cultural event, and marked a turning point of sorts. The academic debate on revisionism achieved a culmination of sorts with Ciaran Brady's collection of articles by historians of 1994, *Interpreting*

*Irish history* (Brady, 1994). However, no recent work appears to have touched the popular imagination as much as the earlier books cited did in their day. It may be that a nationalistically impelled fascination with historical argument, as distinct from a relatively detached interest in history, is weakening. The nearest parallel I can find in recent years is Neil Jordan's film *Michael Collins* (1996) which had an ideological popular impact similar to that of O'Brien's 1972 book.

## Traditional nationalism in the Republic

Events such as the publication of books or even films affect relatively few people directly, but commonly a successful book touches a cultural nerve, much as the books I have instanced certainly did in their day, in their very different ways. As most of us – certainly the older cohort of Irish people in the Republic and even in Northern Ireland – are aware, the political culture in the twenty-six counties has been undergoing a profound change over the past generation. I would personally date this change back to the 'Mother and child' scheme of 1951, when, as most Irish people know, a welfare and health scheme which was perceived to be contrary to Catholic principles was struck down by the Catholic hierarchy. In fact, it was covertly seen as contrary to the monetary interests of the medical profession and sympathetic to a series of principles then labelled 'communist', 'British', or worse than either, 'secularist'. This condemnation went against the advice of many intellectually independent priests.

Despite the fact that much of the substance of the proposals was enacted two years later by Eamon de Valera, Taoiseach 1951–4, the Catholic Church in Ireland never recovered from this denunciation. George Bernard Shaw had prophesied long before Irish independence that a native Irish government would immediately dismantle the extraordinary apparatus of political, cultural and social power that the Catholic Church had amassed in the nineteenth century. He was wrong, but not completely wrong; it took two generations for the decay of Catholic power in independent Ireland to become evident, and for the first 40 years after independence, an alliance which I have elsewhere termed the alliance of 'priests and patriots', an alliance of Irish nationalism and Catholic triumphalism, dominated the politics of independent Ireland (Garvin, 2000). 'Physical force' republicans, often anti-clerical, found themselves, politically speaking, in bed with nationalist and anti-Protestant clerics. This alliance slowly disintegrated in the generation after 1951.

## The politics of retarded development

I would argue that the inevitable split between priests and patriots after 1922 was delayed until the 1950s by several factors: first, by the continuing and unresolved political, economic and cultural tensions between Ireland and Britain after 1922, partly due to 'dependency', whether cultural, economic or political, and partly due to partition; second, by the coming of the great depression in 1929, which froze political thinking and behaviour in a 1920s mode and ensured the survival in office of an increasingly gerontocratic political elite right through to the 1960s; third, the isolation of most of the island during the neutrality period of the Second World War, which aggravated the cultural and psychological effects of the depression; and fourth, misguided government policies concerning economics, education and foreign affairs during the period 1945–60. I would like to deal briefly with each of these propositions in turn.

First, British–Irish tensions: the Anglo-Irish Treaty of 1921–2 reflected within itself this set of problems; it resulted in the 1922 constitution of the Irish Free State, which the German scholar, Leo Kohn, in a classic work published in German in 1928 and in English in 1932 (*Die Verfassung des Irischen Freistaats/The Constitution of the Irish Free State*), described as a republican and democratic document pretending to be a monarchic document (Kohn, 1928, 1932). All sovereignty was derived from the Irish people, but the king was in the document essentially as the agent of the Irish people; it took 30 years to get rid of poor old George V and his heirs and successors. Northern Ireland and the Free State were to be linked by a Council of Ireland. It was hoped that it might be – or sceptically or even cynically declared to be – a vehicle by which both parts of Ireland could reconcile their differences in some kind of confederal all-Ireland polity. As we know, this was very certainly not to be, and two of the causes of this political failure and copperfastening of partition were Orange intransigence in the North and republican intransigence in the South. Arguably, the republicans were as responsible for the partition of Ireland as were the unionists. Neither side wished to negotiate, and both sides got short-changed. The civil war in the south, provoked by six months of republican impossibilism, combined with the death of Collins at republican hands, was exactly what Orange supremacists in the North yearned for and got. From their point of view, a successful and peaceable Free State, high in the councils of Empire and the League of Nations, allied with Canada and Australia, was a true menace. The IRA campaign against the new Irish government failed, but exhausted the Free State to the point at which it effectively abandoned Northern Ireland. Green and Orange bullies between them conspired, in effect, to defy the will of the Irish people.

Northern Ireland became a Protestant state for a Protestant people, despite genuine preliminary concessions toward the Catholic minority, and the Free State became studiously and monistically Catholic, despite a similarly genuine streak of liberalism and tolerance toward minorities that was never quite snuffed out by fundamentalists. Each Irish state, absurdly, rebuked the other for not living up to English liberal orthodoxies.

Second, the great depression of 1929–31 had huge political consequences all over the planet. In the United States and Sweden, leftist and welfarist governments were swept into power, mainly in reaction to the perceived failures of capitalism and acceptance of the claims by various ideologues of the time that government intervention in the form of state enterprise and tariff control would bring about a new era. In the US, they merely got Franklin Delano Roosevelt, the Tennessee Valley Authority, the Blue Eagle and a general attempt to use state resources to assuage the consequences of what was often described as unbridled capitalism. In Sweden they got a generation of statist but popular social democracy, following emotionally on the Adalen Incident, where strikers were machine-gunned by the military. In Ireland we got Eamon de Valera's mixture of cultural apartheid, statism and protectionism, in part fuelled by emotionalism following on the conflicts of 1916, 1919–21 and 1922–3. In Germany, of course, they got Hitler, fuelled by the great collective disaster of the First World War and a collective despair which was far greater than the similar moods or misfortunes of the United States, Sweden or Ireland. Incidentally, Hitler was elected by a minority vote of 33.3 per cent in 1932, being given the premiership mainly because of the cowardice of the Catholic and nationalist opposition and the historicist idiocy of the Stalinist communists of the period.

Third, in Ireland, the Second World War, neutrality, isolation and stagnation had a consequence of reinforcing, to an abnormal extent, the cultural and intellectual conservatism of the depression period. Mancur Olson, the American economist and political scientist, in a famous argument, has argued that, in essence, defeat is good for you economically speaking. Twenty years ago, in 1982, he pointed out that the real victors of the post-1945 peace had been the defeated Axis powers: western Germany, Austria, Japan and Italy. To these defeated powers could be joined defeated France, Finland and Spain (defeated in a sense by itself in its Civil War of 1936–9). Ireland and Portugal slumbered on, the argument went, because older elites with older ideas stayed in power. Ireland was held back by perhaps 15 years after 1945, Portugal by 30. Interestingly, the argument is a mixture of political determinism and idealism: younger and outsider elites tended to be more flexible, adventurous and creative (Olson, 1982).

Fourth, Irish economic and educational policies after 1945 remained misguided and even perverse for far too long. Children learned Irish at school, commonly being taught the grammar of what was effectively a foreign language in that language. Science and nature study were abolished in primary schools to make room for 'double Irish' in the 1920s by the Cosgrave government. In the 1930s the pressure to use the educational system primarily for linguistic transformation intensified, despite many enlightened educationalists pointing out that the educational system was being bent, essentially, to a profoundly non-educational purpose.

Middle-class children got the same treatment, but Latin, and, sometimes, Greek were added to this academicist educational fare; obviously, the primary purpose of the system was to turn out clerics, which it undoubtedly did. The idea that children should be taught how to earn their living and given an education that was applied as well as one that was literary and linguistic was ignored as far as the key emergent middle-class groups were concerned. The predictable and wholly understandable reaction against exaggerated academicism, itself exaggerated and intellectually destructive, is still with us. Higher education remained the prerogative of a privileged few right into the late 1960s.

## Nationalism and Irish society

Olson's arguments amount to an appealing thesis and seem to fit the Irish facts. Irish nationalism was indeed extraordinarily backward looking in the years after 1945, years that were at once dull, uneventful and absolutely crucial in Ireland and pretty well nowhere else; Ireland slept while the rest of the world was turned upside down. Ageing men remained in power and, unlike most other European countries, no generational shift occurred in the aftermath of the world war. An attempt at such a shift did happen in the shape of younger people in Clann na Poblachta, but it failed. Ironically, the emergence of the Clann enabled a mainly conservative Fine Gael-led government to come into power in 1948, and essentially spancelled Sean Lemass and his drive for modernisation for 10 years. The ultimately inevitable shift had to wait until the 1960s, when the old men retired or died off.

The late 1940s were the years of the Marshall Plan and the beginning of the greatest 30-year economic boom in human history, and Ireland missed out on the first 15 years of it because of pre-War or even pre-1914 political and economic ideas. In 1949, the secretary of the Department of Posts and Telegraphs, the distinguished historian Leon Ó Broin, denounced the offer through US aid of 100,000 phone lines on the grounds that it would only encourage suburban housewives to gossip. That the telephone and its derivatives were essentially a convenience rather than a necessity was still being asserted by some civil servants as late as 1958, while others were driven to defend the instrument as an essential tool of commercial and industrial development. A modern telephone system was eventually put into service in the 1980s, just before such systems became obsolescent in the era of the mobile phone.

Nationalism prompted a persistence with high tariff walls, and an insistence on the Irish language revival programme, right into the 1960s. In 1948 an ambitious road-building programme was cancelled in favour of a massive programme of social housing; only rich people owned motor cars, and, as Taoiseach Costello put it privately, there would be 'no racetracks for plutocrats' in Ireland. The emergent transatlantic airline was similarly closed down at the beginning of the great post-war boom in air travel, the argument being that only rich people would use it. Nobody had the idea that today's toys of the rich might be everybody's toys in a few years' time. In the minds of populist policy makers, Ireland had no need for aircraft, telephones or roads. Essentially, they thought in static, redistributivist and non-developmentalist terms and were possessed of a mentality which was rural, pastoral and sometimes extraordinarily complacent.

The idea that the educational system might be a mechanism by which young people could learn a way of earning their living was unfashionable or even denounced as antinational and barbarous. It took a mixture of academics, civil servants and politicians, including Kenneth Whitaker, Patrick Lynch, Sean O'Connor, Patrick Hillery and Donough O'Malley to break through this particular cultural and political logjam in the mid-1960s. In so doing they had to defy the rules of the game and by-pass powerful interest groups: the Catholic Church, the teachers' unions and the quiet apathy or even active resistance of the ensconced and rather small middle class of the time. The rest is history, and we are now living in the world created, possibly unknowingly, by the policy-makers of a generation ago.

## The birth of the new nationalism

This all does come back to defining nationalism in independent Ireland. A paradigm of nationalist ideology which proposed that Ireland could be free, Irish-speaking, frugal, quasi-rural and somehow more virtuous than anywhere else came gradually to be seen as betraying the real interests of the Irish people. It was replaced by an equally nationalist paradigm which was entrepreneurial, open to the outside world, agnostic on cultural matters and eventually on religious matters as well. Irish nationalists in power had to make their mistakes and acquire a certain hard-earned wisdom in the same expensive way. Protectionism went first, but a lingering statism has been far slower to die. Survey evidence clearly points to an ideological shift in the general population of independent Ireland dating from the cohort born around 1940, a shift in the direction of religious and political pluralism, an increasing amnesia about what once was 'British Ireland' and an increasing sense of difference from the Northern Irish, whether unionist or nationalist in political persuasion.

With some exaggeration, it could be similarly argued that the generation of the 1970s (those born after about 1970) is the generation about to take over political and social power as adults, and is the generation of Donough O'Malley as educational revolutionary and putative father. The grandfather is, of course, Sean Lemass, who recognised the bankruptcy of the de Valeran statist system, a system which he himself had done so much to construct, and later so much to deconstruct in the sad but hard-eyed awareness that it no longer worked. A similar and less philosophically interesting pilgrimage to Canossa was to be made a generation later by Charles Haughey and Ray MacSharry in 1987. In the latter case, it was the etatist ideas of Lemass and Garret FitzGerald which were being jettisoned against a background of economic crisis in some ways rather similar to the far greater crisis of the 1950s. Perhaps it was not so much that the crisis of the 1980s was serious as that it actually *looked* like a rerun of the 1950s that really put the wind up Irish policy makers like Charles Haughey and Ray McSharry. No one in the Republic of Ireland wanted ever to relive the terrifying year of 1956, when it appeared that the country would never recover. This was a year after which, as a famous cartoon in *Dublin Opinion* had it, Ireland, as a saddened and frightened young woman, could be visualised as plaintively asking a fortune teller, 'have I a future?' The Irish have never quite forgotten that sense of hopelessness and complacent regression into isolationism and rural obscurantism that briefly overtook the country in the mid-1950s. They were given another look in that particular rear mirror in the 1980s and simply accelerated away from the view of the past that it offered.

The extraordinary economic transformation of the 1990s is, to this writer's mind, irreversible. Hundreds of thousands of newcomers have entered the workforce, and Ireland has had, for the first time in centuries, to accept the condition of being an immigrant rather than an emigrant country. A seemingly endless stream of scandals and instances of bizarre public behaviour on the part of leading clerics betokened a major collective nervous breakdown on the part of the once all-powerful Catholic Church. The death of the Soviet Union meant an end to communist support for Irish nationalist insurrectionism. The IRA campaign ended in quiet disgrace in the mid-1990s, and the Good Friday Agreement of 1998 recognised the interdependence of the two parts of Ireland and the necessity of their living in peace with each other. Above all, the presence of the new Europe reminded the Irish that they were not an island any more.

## Conclusion

Today's Irish nationalism, because of this rather strange series of evolutions, has gone far beyond the 'priests and patriots' alliance of 50 or 100 years ago, but this is not to say that that nationalism no longer exists. My own belief is that the extraordinary changes of the last quarter century are such that the ordinary people are miles ahead of the intellectuals, the journalists, the academics, the economists and even, dare I say it, the politicians who are supposed to manage cultural changes of this kind. The deep realism of Lemass, O'Malley, Whitaker and others in the 1950s and the often forgotten William Cosgrave, Richard Mulcahy, Kevin O'Higgins and their colleagues in the 1920s won out over the fantasies of the various Sinn Féins which this country, North and South, has had to endure since 1905.

Generational change, the impact of the outside world, particularly in the shape of the European experiment and the radically different collective experiences which the peoples of Ireland have had in both parts of this island have forced an increasing awareness, and acceptance, of each other's differences on all fronts (Garvin, 2000). Things as mundane as successful soccer teams, successful economic developments, universal education to relatively high levels and a general relative secularism have widened the cultural gap between North and South. The armed struggle in Northern Ireland orchestrated by the Provisional Irish Republican Army from 1971 to 1994 has had the ironic effect of increasing southern mental distance from the North while intensifying southern awareness of northern hatreds. Ironically, such developments have also encouraged a better and cooler understanding between the two parts of Ireland, as each finds it increasingly difficult to fantasise about the other in either a sentimental or a paranoid manner.

The older monist definition of Irishness has had to be modified or even dropped, and it is clear that a rapprochement with the peoples of Britain is also going on; the new Institute for British–Irish Studies, founded in 1999 at University College Dublin's Department of Politics, is only one small symptom of a wide cultural and ideological sea-change in our collective self-understanding. We are not simply an island people, but are peoples of this island; we are all also peoples of the islands, and we are European peoples who are learning to celebrate our diversity and also our underlying deep cultural kinship with one another. Furthermore, we have the advantage also of being peoples of the Anglo-American world and partakers in, and contributors toward, the American experiment. Ireland may look back to her often sorrowful past, but the Irish know that the world is their oyster, if they have the wit to see it that way. The evidence is that they do.

Chapter 12

# Conclusion: new strains of unionism and nationalism

John Coakley

## Introduction

The perspectives on political change presented in this book need, at this point, to be assessed collectively. A central issue is the pace of change within the major political traditions; it is worth considering the extent to which ideological shift, or at least policy repositioning, may have permitted the emergence of a common ground on the basis of which parties were able to negotiate. This question – the degree of change within the major political traditions – is addressed in the second part of this chapter, separately for the main northern and southern parties.

But before reviewing developments within the political traditions that have been covered in this book, it is important to note the significance of the traditions that have been omitted. First, it is salutary to take stock of two groups that claim to have remained faithful to the old values, and between which only a relationship of conflict is likely: traditional republicanism and what may, for want of a better phrase, be labelled fundamentalist unionism. Second, it is important to note that not all change has taken place *within* particular political traditions: new political forces laying claim to the ideological middle ground have also appeared, and are considered below.

In reviewing these patterns of stability and change, this chapter takes account of the analyses presented by the authors whose contributions constitute the core of this book. But information from other sources may also be considered. The major parties to the conflict have themselves sought to define their positions in highly formal statements of aims, of the kind to be found in party constitutions. A selection of such statements is reproduced in appendix 1, pp. 155–68. It should not, of course, be assumed that constitutions of parties – any more than those of states – include crystal-clear summaries of contemporary priorities. Rather, they are programmatic in a long-term sense, seeking to embody the ethos of the party. As such, they are likely to be shaped as much by the ghosts of the past as by the spirit of the present, to be relatively conservative and slow to respond to sudden shifts in opinion, and quite possibly to clash with election manifestos prepared by the party leadership at particular points in time. They thus tend to reflect the values to which party ideologues wish to be seen as subscribing, rather than the pragmatic policies that party leaders actually pursue. But this makes them more – rather than less – valuable as insights into the inner value core of any party.

Quite apart from their constitutions, a number of parties have also produced carefully considered, detailed analyses of the nature of the conflict on the island and prescriptions for its resolution. Some of these documents are discussed below; but, in addition, appendix 2, pp. 168–83 presents extracts from three documents (from 1949, 1984 and 1996) that were based on efforts to pursue a pan-nationalist consensus, and that show a fascinating evolution in nationalist (or at least southern nationalist) thinking. It is more difficult to find corresponding documents that seek to summarise the broad unionist perspective in an authoritative way, but extracts from two documents that come close to this model (from 1975 and 1987) are reproduced in appendix 3, pp. 183–95.

## Old certainties: poles of nationalism and unionism

The distance that has been travelled by the parties that assented to the Good Friday Agreement emerges with striking force if we remind ourselves of the roots from which they have sprung. As indicated in chapter 1, much of Irish political history in the twentieth century was conditioned by the evolution of Sinn Féin and by the succession of divisions within the movement that were occasioned, in the eyes of the radical side, by the fact that a section of the party leadership was engaging in unprincipled compromise for short-term political gains. Denunciation of compromise and allegations of 'sell-out' and surrender were also a central part of the vocabulary of a certain strand of unionism, represented most obviously by Ian Paisley and the Democratic Unionist Party (DUP). Since these two positions represent in an important sense the poles of a continuum along which other parties have been moving (in different directions and at difference paces, of course), it is worth considering them in turn.

### Traditional republicanism
On each occasion that Sinn Féin has undergone a major fracture, those who claimed to remain true to the old political faith accused their opponents of being prepared to sell out the republic by contemplating recognition of 'British-imposed' institutions – in particular, those that came into existence in Ireland in 1921–2. Not only the concepts, but the very language in which they were expressed, have tended to remain substantially unaltered. Charges

along these lines were made against the moderate side in 1922 when the original split over the 1921 treaty took place, in 1926 when de Valera's supporters seceded from the parent movement, in 1970 when 'Provisional' Sinn Féin broke away, in 1986 when Republican Sinn Féin was created, and again in 1997 when a new wave of Sinn Féin dissidents formed the Thirty Two County Sovereignty Movement.

The essence of the fundamentalist position had already become clear immediately after the first of these developments. A formulation that has persisted to the present was articulated in a resolution approved by the anti-Treaty Sinn Féin Dáil deputies on 17 November 1922. According to this, the treaty had been approved under duress, and threat of renewed war; as a surrender of sovereignty, this could not be binding on the 'Republic of Ireland' proclaimed in 1916 and ratified in 1919; and the government of the Irish Free State was deemed an illegal body, guilty of rebellion against the republic (O'Higgins, 1932: 7). This interpretation survived with remarkable tenacity through the decades that followed. Election results showed its adherents becoming increasingly marginalised, but this did nothing to undermine their faith. Following the split in 1970, Provisional Sinn Féin echoed this view. As its president put it on the occasion of the 60th anniversary of the 1916 rising, the 'republic' of 1916 was endowed with an eternal significance, but

> that Republic proclaimed in 1916 and set functioning in all 32 counties from 1919 to 1921, was overthrown by force and suppressed by a British Dominion for 26 counties and a Crown Colony for Six Counties. . . . While that British Dominion, known as the Irish Free State, changed its name and its constitution, over the years, it remains manifestly what it was designed to be by the English government which created it 55 years ago – a colonial state destined to rule the greatest part of Ireland in the interests of Britain (Ó Brádaigh, 1976: 2).

This perspective was articulated once more when Republican Sinn Féin broke away in 1986. As a party statement put it,

> Whereas no group, minority or majority, claiming to serve the historic cause of national freedom and sovereignty, can grant recognition to the British-created institutions of Leinster House, Stormont and Westminster, . . . we renew our allegiance to the sovereign Irish Republic proclaimed in 1916 and which was endorsed by the majority of the people of Ireland, acting as a unit, in 1918 . . . we uphold the historic right of the Irish people to use whatever degree of controlled and disciplined force is necessary in resisting English aggression and bringing about an English withdrawal from our country for ever (*Republican bulletin: Iris na poblachta*, Nov. 1986).

From this perspective, the referenda of 1998 could be interpreted as out-standing instances of political manipulation rather than as legitimate exercises in democracy, and republican dissidents continued to insist on the irreversible character of the declaration of independence of 1919. Thus the Thirty Two County Sovereignty Movement, in its constitution ratified on 24 June 2000, declared the following to be its 'fundamental democratic principles':

(a) That the sovereignty and unity of Ireland are inalienable and indefeasible.

(b) That the organisation solely stands to uphold the Declaration of Independence as established by the Irish people in 1918 and ratified by Dáil Éireann on January 21st 1919.

(c) That only the Irish people as a whole acting freely and without external impediment can mandate government for the Irish people.

(d) That the Irish people have a right to national self-determination.

(e) That partition is illegal.

(f) That recognising the denial of national sovereignty to the Irish people through British occupation of part of the national territory, we hold that all adminis-trations and assemblies purporting to act as lawful government for the Irish people, or otherwise functioning as partitionist entities, to be illegal under international law as they usurp Irish sovereignty.

(g) We hold that it is both a right and a duty of all Irish people to uphold Irish sovereignty.

(h) We reaffirm the right of the Irish people to use all legitimate means necessary to restore National Sovereignty as declared in the Declaration of Independence 1919 (Thirty Two County Sovereignty Movement, 2002)

Notwithstanding the small numbers who hold this view and the increasing difficulty they face in interpreting contemporary political realities in terms of the nationalist values of the 1920s, it would be dangerous to underestimate the potential of this strand of republicanism to destabilise current constitutional and institutional arrangements. Insistence on the 'inalienability' of Irish independence and unity sets absolute parameters on the domain of legitimate decision making: in this view, the people have no right to do wrong (as, for example, by voting to accept partition or to approve of restrictions on Irish sovereignty), and it is the responsibility of the republican vanguard to defend national integrity against internal and external enemies. This perspective is a compelling yardstick against which to measure the distance that the current leadership of Sinn Féin has travelled down the path of conventional politics. Not long ago, after all, this very leadership was itself articulating precisely this point of view, and as recently as the late 1980s Sinn Féin publications continued to express hostility to the Republic of Ireland and to its institutions, which they purported to see as 'British-imposed' (for example, the Taoiseach was consistently referred to in the party newspaper *An Phoblacht* as 'the Free State premier').[1]

## Fundamentalist unionism

Much of the resilience of traditional republican ideology can be explained by the fact that it is embedded in a distinctive world view, one commonly to be found in nationalist movements, and that rests ultimately on the quasi-spiritual notion of a 'national soul' (even if such metaphysical roots are now rarely acknowledged). Its unionist counterpart is quite different and lacks this ideological resource, typically rejecting (at least overtly) conventional nationalist-type rhetoric. Instead, the purest and most uncompromising form of fundamentalist unionism has a religious basis: the other community is not merely economically menacing, culturally distasteful and politically threatening; it adheres to a belief system that is evil – in the fullest biblical sense of the word. The strand of opinion represented by Ian Paisley and the Free Presbyterian Church, among others, illustrates this viewpoint clearly. As an illustration of the potent marriage of politically loaded theology and historiography, one may cite Paisley's 1969 description of the roots of the conflict, with an implied clash between civilisation and barbarism:

> So these people [seventeenth-century Protestant settlers] brought to Ulster the grand message of evangelical Protestantism and of liberty. Of course, the Romanist population withdrew. Ulster at that time was a wilderness, and these colonizers came and carved out of the Ulster wilderness a fair and lovely and prosperous land. Everybody knows that Ulster is entirely different from the South of Ireland. Whenever you cross the Border from Northern Ireland to the South you can almost smell popery. Certainly you can breathe its atmosphere and know that you are in a different type of country. The Roman Catholics do not give in easily; neither does the devil (Paisley 1970: 7–8).

This represents more than a mere interpretation of history that is biased in favour of one community and against another; the conflict between the two is seen as fundamental, enduring and divinely ordained – a struggle that can be won by the righteous only by means of eternal vigilance and refusal to compromise. This perspective has been summarised as follows by the authors of one highly perceptive study of Paisley and his movement:

> Between Catholicism and Protestantism there could never be compromise, only conflict. In Ireland, as elsewhere, Catholicism straddled the spiritual and political worlds, constantly seeking new ways to achieve its ambitions. Sometimes it sought to weaken Protestantism in subtle fashions, undermining it from within, as with ecumenism. At other times, it made open alliances with political movements, like

the nationalist struggle for political independence, the civil rights movement or the IRA, in an effort to erode and destroy Protestantism's defences (Moloney and Pollak, 1986: 434).

Paisley's success, they concluded, depended on 'a deep and immutable anti-Catholicism among a large section of Northern Ireland's Protestant population' (Moloney and Pollak, 1986: 433). The Catholic Church, in this line of thinking, falls outside the Christian community and is, in scriptural language, 'mother of harlots and abominations of the earth'; and it is seen as being behind the civil unrest in Northern Ireland (Cooke, 1996: 41). There is no space for negotiation or even dialogue with such an entity – outright confrontation is the only appropriate response. In this particular strand of Ulster Protestantism, dubbed a 'covenantal' one, Protestants resemble the chosen people of the Bible and have a compact or covenant with God; Catholics, adhering to a form of 'baptised paganism' and worshipping 'wafers, idols and pre-Christian deities', have rejected God and fall outside the covenant, thus inviting divine wrath and the committed opposition of true Protestants (see Brewer and Higgins, 1998: 135–46). The political implications of this world view are not surprising. Union with Great Britain is central to the interests of the community: 'without Union Protestants would be aligned to a nation dominated by Popery and would thus lose their covenant with God and sacrifice all the blessings it brings in politics, economics, culture and theology' (Brewer and Higgins, 1998: 143).

It would, of course, be wrong to attribute this perspective to Ulster Protestants collectively; as with all such belief systems, it is likely to be adhered to strictly by only a portion of the community, while for others its elements may be present in the background. Many, indeed, especially within the major Protestant churches, would entirely reject this interpretation, and see Catholics as part of the Christian community; even the great figures of the past in the Protestant tradition would have stopped well short of the Paisleyite extreme.[2] It would also be an oversimplification to depict Protestant opinion as lying on a continuum between fundamentalist belief and secular agnosticism. This dimension is no doubt present; but there are other dimensions, such as intensity of commitment to the ethnic community, level of attachment to traditional geopolitical arrangements, and degree of willingness to move outside the armoury of conventional politics in advancing one's objectives. There may be relationships between such dimensions as these, but they are notionally separate. There is thus more than one way to be an 'extremist', a concept that will depend on the dimension in question. Indeed, it would also be wrong to discount altogether the appeal of explicitly nationalist rhetoric for certain strands of Protestant activism (this has been obvious since the days of the Vanguard movement in the early 1970s, and has achieved both political and cultural articulation since then).[3]

On the other hand, notwithstanding its firm statement of aims (see appendix 1.8, p. 166), there is some evidence of flexibility in the approach to political change of the DUP and even of its leader, Ian Paisley. Thus, for a brief period in late 1971, Paisley hinted at a willingness to contemplate Irish unity; the DUP response to the New Ireland Forum report, though robust in its defence of traditional unionist priorities, was measured and comprehensive (Ulster Democratic Unionist Party, 1984a); its own proposals for the government of Northern Ireland, though remaining close to the traditional unionist position, hinted at the degree of adaptability that the party was later to display (Ulster Democratic Unionist Party, 1984b); in 1991 it looked briefly as if the party would be prepared to enter a power sharing arrangement that would include nationalists (Bloomfield, 1998: 123); and the party has worked effectively within the new institutions at Stormont since 1999 – protected, admittedly, by the fig leaves of non-attendance at executive meetings, non-participation in north–south bodies and periodic efforts to bring about the collapse of the settlement. Yet these apparent inconsistencies may be explained by the very strength of one underlying principle: the fact that priority is given to the defence of Protestant Ulster even over maintenance of the union with Great Britain (Smyth, 1987: 130). The 'covenant', in any case, is at least implicitly with a community that has one essential but not necessarily permanent feature: a Protestant monarch as head of state.

It would be dangerous to ignore the profound significance of this belief system, with its implications for the need to remain steadfast against compromise with what is seen as intrinsically evil. Although the Free Presbyterian Church has relatively few members (a little over 12,000 in 1991), these are very active within the DUP. Analysis of some 400 DUP activists between 1972 and 1980 showed that 64 per cent were Free Presbyterians (Bruce, 1994: 22–3).[4] Furthermore, Ian Paisley is personally able to win huge numbers of first preference votes in European elections (193,000 in 1999). The reality is that by the end of the twentieth century the Paisleyite position continued to be a vibrant force, its message still widely shared: 'Paisleyism regards the Roman Catholic Church and Republicanism as part of a world strategy – devised within "the kingdom of the beast" – to overthrow Protestantism' (Cooke, 1996: 221). It is thus likely that fundamentalist Protestantism, resting on deep theological and sociocultural roots, will continue to constitute a steady bulwark for traditional values in the face of rapid contemporary social, political and ideological change, and, notwithstanding the extent to which this world view deviates from that which is taken as the norm in western Europe, it is a force not to be underestimated.

# New politics: rediscovering the centre

The faithful adherents of the diametrically opposite points represented by old-style republicanism and fundamentalist unionism have not been the only stable political perspectives in the turmoil of ideological shift that has been discussed in this book. There has also been a stable, if usually weak, 'centre'. This has tended to take two historically different forms: parties and other groups that have defined themselves self-consciously as occupying the middle ground, and parties and groups that have sought to supplant the dominant dimension – the constitutional one – by arguing the importance of other dimensions, and which, by virtue of this, find themselves in the 'centre' on the constitutional question. The Liberal Party in the past, and now the Alliance Party, are representative of the former type; and the Northern Ireland Labour Party in the past (with its emphasis on the centrality of class-based politics) and the Northern Ireland Women's Coalition in the present (with its stress on the importance of the gender dimension) are representative of the latter.

### The struggle for the middle ground

Although the Alliance Party was founded only in 1970, it was not an entirely unprecedented force in the politics of Northern Ireland. There was an important respect in which it was heir to the old Liberal tradition. The Liberal Party had been a great if amorphous force in Ireland in the middle decades of the nineteenth century, associated with policies of reform, and with a substantially Catholic support base; it was from its midst that more radical parties, such as the Repeal Party in the 1830s and 1840s and the Home Rule Party in the 1870s and 1880s had arisen. But the 1885 election had seen the complete elimination of the Liberals in the south. Thereafter, the party was able to maintain an electoral presence – and a tenuous one at that – only in Ulster, but even there the secession in 1886 of the 'Liberal Unionists', who were ultimately absorbed by the Ulster Unionist Party (UUP), reduced the party to marginal status. Nevertheless, it was represented by a single MP (in North Tyrone) from 1895 to 1918, the election that all but wiped it off the electoral map.[5] Thereafter, it remained on the margins, apart from flickers of life in 1929 and in the 1960s.[6] By 1970, this self-consciously centrist tradition was weak, but not quite dead.[7]

Although the Ulster Liberal Party had a vigorous leader in the Rev. Albert McElroy, and an active Stormont representative in Sheelagh Murnaghan (MP for Queen's University, 1961–9), it was not this party that was to become the vehicle for the new drive to reinforce the middle ground. Instead, a new party appeared in 1970 – the Alliance Party, which included former nationalist, unionist and independent activists, but which also introduced to political life large numbers of people who had previously remained aloof. Many of the last group had been involved in the New Ulster Movement, founded in 1969 with the object of reforming politics and society along non-sectarian lines. The Alliance Party's initial statement of principles (see appendix 1.10, pp. 167–8) sought to position it decisively in the middle of the political spectrum, appealing to both blocs for support and offering assurances to each – for nationalists, the pursuit of an equality agenda; for unionists, maintenance of the link with Great Britain. The main evolution in the party's policy since its foundation took place in the early 1970s, as it moved beyond the principle of individual equality to that of equality between communities, a principle implicit in its consistent support for power sharing in the executive branch of government. Indeed, the party successfully carved out for itself a clearly defined ideological niche in the centre, rather than merely amounting to a marriage of convenience between otherwise divergent groups (McAllister and Wilson, 1978). It later elaborated a carefully considered scheme for a new constitutional structure, with power sharing within Northern Ireland as its central feature (Alliance Party of Northern Ireland, 1988).

The Alliance Party, then, has remained consistently committed to a policy of bridge building in tackling the problems of governing a divided society. But its location in the middle of the political spectrum has, ironically, undermined its centrality to the process of constitutional negotiation. The reality is that when tough bargaining takes place, it is normally the extremes that are called on to make concessions; it is therefore these extremes that are the main actors in the negotiating process (this need not, of course, always be the case, but this is the shape that recent negotiations in Northern Ireland have taken). In addition, if a party defines itself as representing a 'third tradition' – neither unionist nor nationalist – its strategic interests are imperilled in any constitutional arrangement that places a premium on membership of one of the two major blocs. Ironically, then, Alliance may well have become the victim of its own success, as the form of segmental institutionalisation provided for in the Belfast agreement tends to marginalise those not aligned to either bloc (see Leonard, 1999: 63–72). This was to be seen most clearly in the pressure on the party's Assembly members to redesignate as nationalist or unionist in November 2001, rather than adhering to the 'other' category preferred by the party and compatible with its refusal to identify with either bloc.[8]

### Sidelining the constitutional question

As it happens, many would see the Alliance Party as heir not so much to the Ulster Liberal Party as to the Northern Ireland Labour Party (NILP). The Irish labour movement of the early twentieth century sought, with only partial success, to redefine the fault-lines of Irish politics: to assert the primacy of class interests over religious or ethnic ones. Partition resulted in the appearance of separate labour parties in the two parts of the island, but the NILP found itself squeezed between pro- and anti-union positions. In its early years, it managed to reconcile formal if unenthusiastic opposition to partition with considerable electoral success in Belfast. But the tension between the issue of Irish unity and the instincts of the Protestant working class surfaced in the 1940s and culminated in 1949 in the party's reversing its position and formally endorsing a pro-union stance.[9] This cost the party such support as it had had in Belfast's Catholic constituencies; although it performed well in the elections of 1958 and 1962, its support base was now confined substantially to Protestant constituencies, and it collapsed altogether in the course of the 1970s as intercommunal tensions grew, especially in the party's Belfast heartlands.[10] In general policy terms, its position has resembled that of the British Labour Party, but on the question of partition it continued to be implicitly pro-union.[11]

If the NILP was, from a comparative perspective, unusually unsuccessful, the second significant attempt to impose an alternative political dimension was quite the opposite. The presence of a labour or socialist party as a well-established member of the party system is the norm in western Europe; so, too, is the *absence* of a women's party.[12] Nevertheless, remarkably, a tradition of women's activism in Northern Ireland was built on in 1996 with the formation of the Northern Ireland Women's Coalition to fight the Forum election in that year, and the party was able to go on to secure representation also in the 1998 election to the Assembly (see Hinds, 1999; Fearon, 1999). The party fought a difficult battle on two fronts: against the more misogynistic elements in Northern Ireland who felt that politics was a man's job, and against those who felt that women, like men, must first and foremost be either nationalist or unionist (both strands were particularly pronounced in the DUP). Nevertheless, the party was able to build up a distinctive agenda, based on the principles of inclusiveness (implying a greater openness to the participation of parties with paramilitary links), equality (with its implications for the status of women, as well as of other categories), and human rights (including the rights of prisoners; see Fearon and McWilliams, 2000; and see appendix 1.11, p. 168, for the party's statement of objectives as defined in its constitution).

There have been some striking similarities between these two attempts to redefine Northern Irish politics along a dimension other than the 'national question'. First, both tapped into a reservoir of resentment at the domination of the political agenda by constitutional issues at the expense of politically marginalised groups such as workers and women (Mitchell, 1974: 220–2; Wilford and Galligan, 1999: 181). Second, notwithstanding some striking successes, both fell well short of mobilising their full potential constituencies (respectively, the working class and the female half of the population), though, from a comparative, cross-national perspective, the Women's Coalition was much more successful than the Northern Ireland Labour Party. Third, however, to the extent that they were able to mobilise electoral support, the evidence suggests that they did so remarkably evenly from the two communities. Finally, as with all such challenging parties, both were viewed in varying degrees as a potential threat by the older established parties. Even in its early years, the Unionist Party sought to forestall the challenge from socialists and suffragettes, or at least to extend its own communal hegemony, by establishing separate workers' and women's sections within its own ranks. Thus, there appeared in 1911 the Ulster Women's Unionist Association, a body that was soon able to enrol close to 50,000 members; its more prominent leaders were the Duchess of Abercorn and the Marchioness of Londonderry, figures unlikely to embrace radical causes, though this would in any case have been an improbable departure in a body whose primary object was to maintain the union, 'on the unimpaired integrity of which we believe our civil and religious liberties depend' (Harbinson, 1973: 62).[13] As the association resolved in 1912, and in sharp contrast to the self-definition and rhetoric of the Women's Coalition many decades later, the role of women was supportive, not autonomous: 'we will stand by our husbands, our brothers, and our sons, in whatever steps they may be forced to take in defending our liberties against the tyranny of Home Rule' (Harbinson, 1973: 62). The other main Unionist support body, the Ulster Unionist Labour Association, founded in 1918, has been described as a form of 'social toryism' and as 'designed to counter working-class independence of a secular kind', while maximising support for the Union (Morgan, 1991: 215).

## Paths towards compromise: policy shift in Northern Ireland

The pattern of ideological shift in Northern Ireland has been much more complex than may have been implied in the last two sections. It is possible to create images of ideologically frozen positions that could be described as traditional republicanism, fundamentalist unionism and radical biconfessionalism, but these should be seen as ideal types. Their capacity to describe actual political reality is limited. No party is entirely monolithic: diverse ideological tendencies, crystallised in varying degrees, exist within all of them; the relative strength of such tendencies varies over time; and even individuals prominently associated with a particular position may change over their own life spans in terms of their personal political belief systems. Nevertheless, it is useful to draw a distinction between those parties whose positions have remained relatively stable and those where ideological evolution is more obvious. In turning now to this latter group, we may consider the evolution of unionism and nationalism separately.

## The unionist bloc

The long-term, explicit domination of unionism by a single issue ('to maintain Northern Ireland as an integral part of the United Kingdom', as the party constitution put it; see appendix 1.7, pp. 165–6) left the Ulster Unionist Party with little room for ideological manoeuvre, and its secure political position left it under little pressure to engage in such manoeuvre. But the fall of Stormont in 1972 brought to a head many of the tensions between reformers and conservatives in the party that had been highly visible since 1968, and the trauma of the 1970s accentuated divisions within the unionist bloc as a whole. Nevertheless, as election results of this period showed, there was a clear majority within the bloc for a form of modified traditional unionism. As the report of the Constitutional Convention of 1975 illustrates, the preferred unionist blueprint was for a return to devolved government for Northern Ireland on the old model, based on majority rule and without an Irish dimension (though the opposition would have a place in a reinforced committee system, there would be a bill of rights, and a policy of 'good neighbourly relations' with the Republic of Ireland would be followed; see appendix 3.1, pp. 183–9).

From a strategic point of view, this was not an unreasonable negotiating position for a community determined to protect its status – provided the most likely alternative was simply direct rule from London. Indeed, for many unionists there was another desirable alternative: complete integration with the rest of the United Kingdom. This project was pursued with some vigour by a number of prominent unionists, and eventually led to the Campaign for Equal Citizenship (1986).[14] Moves in Dublin to redefine the nationalist position, especially through the New Ireland Forum, provoked further reconsideration within unionism, and resulted in a document representing a significant shift in emphasis in the main unionist party (Ulster Unionist Council, 1984). This paid obeisance to the Convention report of 1975, but it displayed a much greater sensitivity to the nationalist position. In concrete terms, it sought to break the devolution log-jam by opting for a form of administrative devolution: Stormont would have fewer powers, but reliance on a network of committees to administer these would in effect give a significant administrative role to nationalists (the full implications of this were not spelt out; indeed, the report rejected power sharing in a formal sense).

The Anglo-Irish Agreement of 1985, however, showed that direct rule and devolved government were not the only options for Northern Ireland: British rule modified by Irish influence, symbolised by the presence of Irish officials in Belfast, was the central ingredient in the agreement. Given the agreement's exceptionally distasteful character in unionist eyes, the search for alternatives was vigorously pursued. These ranged from renewed arguments in favour of devolution to demands for full integration within the United Kingdom, but one of the more concrete outcomes was the creation of a joint UUP–DUP task force, charged with consulting widely with unionist opinion and devising a new approach.[15] The report of this group, *An end to drift*, showed an open-ended attitude to negotiation and a willingness to place all issues on the table (see Joint Unionist Task Force, 1987, and appendix 3.2, pp. 189–95). As Dermot Nesbitt points out (chapter 4 above), this was a marker of an important evolution in unionist thinking. Although the release of the report itself had few immediate consequences, it signalled a level of strategic and policy flexibility that was a prerequisite to the negotiation process that resulted in agreement in 1998.

One of the more unexpected impediments to ideological change on the unionist side has been not so much deep conviction as to the unanswerable character of the unionist case, but rather the opposite – a sense of suspicion of the intentions of those in power, and an absence of communal self-confidence. Richard English (chapter 9 above) comments on this sense of insecurity, and on its consequences. Vigorous efforts have been made by unionist intellectuals to provide a rationally argued, unapologetic case for the pro-union position (Foster, 1995), and the point has been made convincingly that internal intellectual coherence is not more obviously integral to the nationalist case than to the unionist one (English, 1996). In addition to efforts to rework long-established unionist positions, a more inclusive alternative to the two main existing alternatives – dubbed 'civic unionism' – has also been elaborated (Porter, 1996). Such efforts have won uneven acceptance from the broad unionist support base, within which, as Richard English has pointed out in chapter 9, a complex set of ideological strands continues to be intertwined: unionist political culture, he argues, is complex rather than monolithic, and it is also fluid rather than static.

Striking though these reconsiderations within what may be labelled mainstream unionism are, they are overshadowed by yet more dramatic transformations in one of unionism's more militant tendencies. The distinctiveness of this tendency was as yet unclear in the 1960s, when unionist opposition to the liberalising path of O'Neill and to the perceived subversion of the civil rights movement seemed to be concentrated in an umbrella grouping whose most visible and most vocal representative was Rev. Ian Paisley. Although Paisley flirted then and subsequently with the idea of heading a militia-type force (such as the Ulster Protestant Volunteers in 1966 or Ulster Resistance 20 years later), tensions between him and militant loyalism, as represented at the time by the Ulster Volunteer Force (UVF, founded 1966) were already present, and these were later to expand to become a recurring feature of loyalism (see Nelson, 1984: 54-66).

The ideological trajectory of an influential component of the UVF leadership was remarkable. As David Ervine points out (chapter 5), early loyalist paramilitaries were sectarian in outlook and unsophisticated in their analysis of the unionist political mission. Yet, the UVF gave birth to a political party that was eventually to combine a capacity for critical analysis of the unionist case with an imaginative approach to the design of new political institutions, one that was ultimately to become a key support for the Good Friday Agreement. This took shape initially as the Volunteer Political Party (founded 1974; see Nelson, 1984: 181–92), and was replaced in more permanent form by the Progressive Unionist Party (PUP) in 1979. In chapter 10 above, James McAuley draws attention to the capacity for original thinking and the strong socialist commitment of this new party; a challenge to sectarianism and hostility to the past manipulation of Protestant workers by the unionist middle classes also runs through David Ervine's contribution (chapter 5; see appendix 1.9, pp. 166–7, for the party's constitution). This leftward evolution of a strand of loyalism had inevitable consequences for the constitutional question: class consciousness contributed to a new perception of a line of division that cuts across the sectarian divide, and that is compatible with the pursuit of a political settlement with the other national community.

But the PUP was not the only loyalist political party with paramilitary origins. The Ulster Defence Association (UDA, founded 1970), though primarily a paramilitary organisation, also took some tentative initiatives in the world of politics. One of the most significant of these was the New Ulster Political Research Group (1978), made up of UDA activists and responsible for the publication of a highly original document, *Beyond the religious divide* (New Ulster Political Research Group, 1979). This proposed an independent Northern Ireland with a presidential-style constitution that would nevertheless incorporate powerful minority safeguards. The group was replaced in 1981 by the Ulster Loyalist Democratic Party (ULDP, UDP; it dropped the word 'loyalist' from its title in 1989), but continued with its efforts to stimulate debate on constitutional options. Its next political initiative was a new constitutional model that intriguingly anticipated certain of the provisions of the Good Friday Agreement: it proposed an autonomous Northern Ireland within the United Kingdom, with an assembly elected by proportional representation and an executive whose members would reflect precisely the political balance in the assembly (Ulster Political Research Group, 1987). The sophisticated originality, self-confidence and capacity for political compromise displayed by the PUP and UDP leaderships were central ingredients in putting the Good Friday Agreement in place. These also represented a major shift in orientation on the part of former paramilitaries. But electoral support for the PUP and the UDP was limited, and the extent to which their new thinking had a political impact has been questioned (Bruce, 1994: 98–107). Furthermore, there were obvious strains between the political leadership and worried supporters. Especially in rural areas, many UVF supporters voted not for the PUP but for Paisley's DUP (Cusack and McDonald, 1997: 350–1), and internal tensions finally surfaced with the secession of more militant elements, who formed the Loyalist Volunteer Force in 1996. The difficulties faced by the PUP leadership in holding the line of support for the Good Friday Agreement were even more intense among their UDP counterparts. The UDA was a more decentralised body than the UVF, and a majority of local UDA organisations eventually came to oppose the agreement. Finally, in November 2001, following a period of bitter divisions within loyalism, the UDP dissolved itself.

While the significance of the new loyalist rationalism should not, then, be underestimated, neither should it be exaggerated. For more than two centuries, optimists and idealists have been hoping for a class-based alliance that would transcend confessional divisions and promote a more 'normal' kind of politics in Ireland. But, from the United Irishmen to the NILP, such efforts have eventually foundered, and those episodes where Protestant radicalism has gone down the path of pursuing class rather than ethnic allies (such as Independent Orangeism in the early years of the twentieth century) appear not to have had a lasting impact. Especially in the face of resurgent nationalism, the pressure on Protestant radicals to play down their socialist beliefs has tended to become irresistible (Bruce, 1992: 243).

### The nationalist bloc

The pattern of ideological change within 'mainstream' nationalism in Northern Ireland has been either more dramatic or less dramatic than within other traditions, depending on time perspective. It has been more dramatic in that the replacement of the Nationalist Party by the Social Democratic and Labour Party (SDLP) in 1970 represented a change not just in the nature of party activists (in terms of characteristic occupation, education and age) or in level of party organisation, but also in ideological articulation. Focusing on the single issue of Irish unity, the Nationalist Party had been largely an organic outgrowth of the Catholic community rather than an autonomous political party. The SDLP, by contrast, began life as a political party in the classical sense, with a formal constitution and structures, professional staff and a relatively disciplined group of elected representatives; and it developed carefully considered policies on a whole range of issues.

If the time frame is shortened to the three-decade history of the SDLP, change has been less dramatic. The founding principles of the party have stood the test of time. The party constitution originally specified as an aim 'to promote the cause of Irish unity based on the consent of the majority of people in Northern Ireland', and this has survived intact; the condition of consent was later redefined so that unity would be 'freely negotiated and agreed to by the people of the North and by the people of the South' (see appendix 1.6, pp. 164–5). In effect, this amounted to putting unity on the long finger; but the party also proposed a more specific blueprint that was to anticipate later developments. This provided for a Northern Ireland administration headed by two commissioners, one appointed by each of the two sovereign governments, and an executive reflecting party strengths in an assembly elected by proportional representation. There would also be an all-Ireland senate drawn equally from the Northern Ireland assembly and the Irish parliament, charged with planning integration of the island and harmonisation of structures, laws and services (Social Democratic and Labour Party, 1972). Although the notion of joint Dublin–London rule was later to be revived by the party, in the short term it focused on diluted versions of the two main planks in this policy, which depended on reform within existing constitutional arrangements: the pursuit of a power-sharing administration within Northern Ireland, and of an institutionalised Irish dimension. When the first experiment at implementing these principles collapsed in 1974, the party was forced to reconsider its strategy. The outcome was an attempt to redefine the geopolitical parameters of a settlement. As Jennifer Todd shows in chapter 7, the party, especially under John Hume's influence, began to present the problem in a European context and to pay particular attention to the potential of the American connection (see also Todd, 1990).

But John Hume and the SDLP have been effective not only in bringing about a shift in mainstream nationalist thinking; they have, as Alban Maginness argues in chapter 2, also had a significant impact on the evolution of republican thought. Much of this influence was indirect, but direct talks between the two party leaders, John Hume and Gerry Adams, in 1988 and in 1993 played a considerable role in this, with Hume's persuasive powers and the prospect that Sinn Féin could be a player in negotiating a settlement as the main pressures on republicans (see Farren and Mulvihill, 2000: 141–4, 157–62). In this, Hume was no doubt assisted by the fact that the Sinn Féin leadership was now firmly located within Northern Ireland, and would have to live on a daily basis with the consequences of any settlement. Paul Arthur (chapter 8 above) points to the centrality of these talks in marking a transition on the part of Sinn Féin towards a new interpretation of the national question, one with radical implications for the legitimacy of existing political institutions and for the use of violence. He points to the policy document *Towards a lasting peace in Ireland* (Sinn Féin, 1992), with its recognition of the need to address unionist fears and of the need for a broad, intergovernmental approach to a solution, as evidence of significant evolution since a comparable policy document had been issued in 1988.

The tone of the 1992 document indeed reflects such a transition; but the distance travelled *since* 1992 has been even more striking. The central points of *Towards a lasting peace in Ireland*, notwithstanding their more restrained tone and emphasis, are clearly compatible with the uncompromising republican past. But they hint only in the most general way at the changes that were to come, and that were embedded, with Sinn Féin's assent, in the 1998 agreement. The gap between the central provisions of this document and of those agreed six years later are a measure of Sinn Féin's capacity to adapt. Thus, the document insisted on the sovereignty of the Irish people and its right to self-determination, while offering to engage in dialogue with unionists; it accepted armed struggle as 'an option of last resort', though it considered this to be applicable 'when all other avenues to pursue freedom have been attempted and suppressed'; and it dismissed the whole three-stranded approach central to the Good Friday Agreement as a distraction from the fundamental cause of the conflict, the British presence (Sinn Féin, 1992). Sinn Féin had, of course, laid the armed struggle option aside even before the agreement, and on Good Friday 1998 it accepted a principle to which up to then the movement had been fundamentally opposed: the right of Northern Ireland to self-determination, with its implications for partition, for north–south relations and for the administration of Northern Ireland. Mitchel McLaughlin's contribution in this volume (chapter 3) indicates the extent to which new thinking has permeated Sinn Féin.

The path down which Sinn Féin has travelled since 1994 has far-reaching implications for other components of the northern nationalist tradition. In important respects, its route resembles the path that the main anti-Treaty party followed in the south in 1922–7: a steady process of movement away from the armed struggle and a decision to work within the existing constitutional order, while retaining radical long-term objectives. To the extent that a single moment can be identified as symbolising acceptance of a new reality, it was 11 August 1927 (when Fianna Fáil took its seats in the Dáil) in the one case and 10 April 1998 (when Sinn Féin accepted the agreement) in the other. In the former case, Fianna Fáil had been formed by the group which had *lost* in the battle within Sinn Féin in 1926, but it was able to reverse this setback electorally, entirely sidelining fundamentalist republicans and going on to defeat its pro-Treaty constitutional nationalist opponent. In the latter case, the Sinn Féin leadership was able to bring its supporters along, so that it was the fundamentalists who dropped out; and, having moved onto the same ideological terrain as the SDLP, it may well be able to mount a challenge to that party similar to that which Fianna Fáil offered to Cumann na nGaedheal and Fine Gael decades earlier in the south.

There is, of course, an important difference between the two contexts. In the south, the electoral struggle took place at the centre of an autonomous party system. In Northern Ireland, it is taking place within one community only, and it is influenced by (and in turn influences) developments within the other community. This poses a singular challenge to a party like Sinn Féin as it seeks to bury its paramilitary past. When bitter intercommunal tensions spill over into violence that the security forces are unable to control, pressure on the movement that has presented itself as defender of the Catholic ghettos to revert to its traditional role grows. On the other hand, as unionist opponents of the agreement seek to embarrass its supporters by alleging that they are sharing power with gunmen, Sinn Féin comes under pressure to engage in essentially symbolic acts that undermine the party's carefully cultivated image of keeping faith with the values of the past while embarking on a new, radically different political strategy. Calling this image into question in turn offers space for a new generation of dissident republicans to take up the armed struggle, and local sectarian violence extends this space further. The evidence to date suggests, however, that Sinn Féin has been remarkably successful in holding this difficult line and in managing the delicate balance between accepting a new political reality and reassuring supporters that the old principles remain valid.[16]

## Adapting to partition: neo-nationalism in the South

It would be all too easy, in examining the forces whose ideological evolution has been associated with change in Northern Ireland, to be blinded to the extent of similar movement in the other part of the island. The 'constitutional' approach to political change has been securely established in the south for several decades, in the sense that there has been little support for the pursuit of political goals by military means. But it is also possible to identify a significant ideological shift, one which was a prerequisite to the Good Friday Agreement. It seems that there have been two strands to this shift: on the one hand, a steady diminution in the intensity of traditional nationalism, or a redefinition of traditional nationalist objectives; on the other, the appearance of a new, geographically narrower form of nationalism in place of the traditional variety.

### Redefining traditional nationalism

Uncomfortable though the point may be to many, it should be recalled that change in attitudes towards Irish unity that were dominant in the Republic over the last three decades of the twentieth century followed a path similar to that of Sinn Féin. The main differences between the two routes lay in the fact that southern nationalism had for long rejected the use of force as an instrument for bringing unity about, that it accepted the need for 'consent' two decades or so before Sinn Féin, and that its willingness to accept partition has been more complete. Furthermore, as Desmond O'Malley and Tom Garvin point out (in chapters 6 and 11, respectively), the older form of insular, economically cautious and clerical nationalism was being gradually (but not necessarily completely) replaced by a more outward-looking, dynamic and pluralist perspective, one that was more conducive to economic growth and less inimical to ethnic inclusion.

To the extent that a southern consensus existed on the issue of Irish unity before the 1970s, it is summarised in the statement of the All-Party Anti-Partition Conference of 1949, reproduced in appendix 2.1 (p. 169). In tone and content, in its analysis of the problem and in its prescription for a solution, this converged entirely with the traditional Sinn Féin position (the latter would have diverged from the nationalist consensus only in its willingness to endorse the use of force to bring unity about). But the early years of the Northern Ireland troubles, and especially the activities of the IRA, provoked a fundamental reconsideration of the position. First, the use of force for the attainment of political objectives was increasingly vehemently rejected; in the early 1970s official commemorations of the 1916 rising were discontinued, the broadcasting of 'rebel' songs on state radio and television ceased, and efforts were made to change the manner in which history was taught in schools to ensure that violence would not be presented in a favourable light. Second, the rhetoric surrounding the attainment of unity increasingly emphasised not just peaceful methods, but the principle of free consent to unity on the part of Northern Ireland.

Arguably the most solemn stage down this path was reached with the publication of the New Ireland Forum Report in 1984. Though strongly nationalist in its conclusions, the report emphasised that 'the political arrangements for a new and sovereign Ireland would have to be freely negotiated and agreed to by the people of the North and by the people of the South' (see appendix 2.2, pp. 169–74). A further stage was reached in the discussions of the Forum for Peace and Reconciliation. Although it did not issue an agreed report, its final draft statement summarised the position of parties other than Sinn Féin. This was open-ended in terms of the kind of settlement considered acceptable, but one of its central principles was that 'it is for the people of Ireland alone, North and South, to determine their own future by agreement and consent'; furthermore, it was made clear that a settlement would have to be reached 'with and subject to the agreement and consent of a majority of the people of Northern Ireland' (see appendix 2.3, pp. 174–83).

This change in the political priorities of mainstream southern nationalism was reflected in parallel changes within the political parties (see appendix 1). In the case of Fianna Fáil, the traditional aim 'to secure the unity and independence of Ireland as a Republic' was changed in 1995 to read 'to secure in peace and agreement the unity of Ireland and its people'. As Desmond O'Malley points out in chapter 6 above, the Progressive Democrats endorsed the principle of unity by consent from the outset, and emphasised the strategy of peace, one of its objectives being 'to promote unity among all Irish people by peaceful means based on pluralist principles'. In the case of Labour, a new party constitution adopted in 1991 focused on a denunciation of politically motivated violence rather than on endorsement of unity. Fine Gael had traditionally not defined its objectives in its constitution, but, especially under the leadership of Garret FitzGerald, the party undertook a root-and-branch reconsideration of the issue of Irish unity, and published a detailed and thoughtful pamphlet outlining its conclusions, and making a considered case for unification (Fine Gael, 1979).

### Rejecting traditional nationalism

The tendency for traditional nationalism as articulated in the south to be redefined along more moderate lines (with a more vocal denunciation of violence, a more committed endorsement of the principle of consent and a more muted emphasis on the desirability of unity) might be seen as a pragmatic response to current political realities, and as reflecting a diminished appetite for the problems for the south that unity would bring in its wake (Girvin, 1999). But it can also be seen as part of another quite different process: a steady ethnic differentiation of the two parts of the island. Increasingly, the word 'Ireland' is used in the south in a narrow sense, to refer to the territory of the state, and, for many, 'Irish' identity seems to be based on a perception of the community as extending over 26 rather than 32 counties.[17] This perspective also seems to be reflected in an increasing acceptance of partition as permanent rather than transitional, and in an anxiety to quarantine civil unrest within the borders of Northern Ireland.[18]

This strand in ideological evolution is to be seen in certain aspects of public policy. Although this point has attracted little attention, a clause of the Downing Street Declaration of 1993 made a settlement dependent on endorsement by referendum not only in the north but also in the south. This southern veto on change (including a veto on unity) was carried over into the Good Friday Agreement, and it was written into the Irish constitution, which now requires a united Ireland to have 'the consent of a majority of the people, democratically expressed' in the Republic as well as in Northern Ireland. Although those who drafted this wording may have taken it for granted that southern endorsement of unity would be automatic, opinion poll evidence suggests that a pro-unity majority in the south cannot be taken for granted; much would depend on the wording of the question and on the context within which it was put.

This perspective on partition is not merely a recent and largely intangible development; it has its own intellectual roots. Although isolated earlier examples could be cited,[19] one of the more important, but infrequently acknowledged, sources for this ideological strand was the Irish Communist Organisation in the late 1960s and early 1970s. In a number of highly original but rarely cited studies, this body explored the nature of the relationship between north and south and popularised a 'two nations' interpretation of the problem.[20] Rather more prominent was the similar position adopted by leading public figures such as Conor Cruise O'Brien (see O'Brien, 1972). As the 'two nations' analysis was developed, its political implications were extended; for many, it implied not just an acceptance of the right of unionists to remain outside the Republic of Ireland but also a rejection of the right of northern nationalists to join it. This interpretation was expressed in a most forthright manner by Democratic Left, whose leading members had themselves made a long transition from Sinn Féin through the Workers' Party (see Rooney, 1984). As the party's policy statement on Northern Ireland put it,

> The 70 years of separation from the South, the development of the welfare state, divergent social development North and South, and 25 years of terrorism have made Northern nationalists a people apart. They have potentially more in common with their fellow Northern Irish people than with their southern neighbours. The primary objective of an Agreement should be to unite the people of Northern Ireland on the basis of peaceful co-existence by putting in place structures which will help develop a pluralist democracy (Democratic Left, 1994).

It would be a mistake to see this new phenomenon merely as a diluted version of traditional Irish nationalism. It may indeed appear to have been watered down from the perspective of Irish nationalists of an older generation, but it can more appropriately be seen simply as a new form of nationalism, one whose 'imagined community' corresponds broadly with the population of the state. In this sense, it is not an anti-nationalist or a non-nationalist alternative to the traditional ideology; it shares the classic characteristics of nationalism, unfamiliar though many of these may be in their transmuted shape. It thus resembles the form of European nationalism to which many supporters of European integration adhere, however strongly it may proclaim its own 'non-nationalist' character.

## Conclusion: prospects for the future

The very considerable ideological shifts that have been reviewed in this book and that have facilitated the Good Friday Agreement and its implementation have contributed to the resolution of certain tensions, but they have inevitably given rise to others. These may be summarised in terms of the perspectives of the three main domestic sets of actors (once again, leaving aside the perspective of the important fourth actor, the British). In each case, what is at stake is the interplay between ideology and the range of strategic choices open to the actor.

First, from the viewpoint of northern unionists, while 'Britishness' may be emphasised in an effort to retain the support of allies in Great Britain, the shaky character of this alliance suggests that other alternatives need also to be considered. Since the prospect of a tactical alliance with the south has never been particularly attractive, two principal domestic options remain. The first is self-reliance, a resort to loyalist 'Sinn Féin'-type policies – an exceptionally hazardous option, given the demographic strength of the Catholic population, but one that nonetheless appears attractive to many. The alternative is an alliance with moderate nationalism; the object of this strategy would be to prevent the alienation of pro-union Catholics and to ensure their continued acquiescence in the constitutional status quo, even, in the longer term, in the event of a Catholic majority in Northern Ireland.

Second, northern nationalists are faced with a similar range of options. Notwithstanding big differences, there are similarities between their dependence on the south and unionists' dependence on Great Britain, including the risks of depending on such external allies. Nevertheless, the baggage of history probably provides a more secure basis for a North–South nationalist alliance than for an East–West unionist one. The option of an alliance with Dublin is thus not unrealistic – and it is ironically more manageable for the SDLP (a purely northern party) than for Sinn Féin (a 32-county party, which therefore finds itself on an electoral collision course with the main parties in the south). Within the northern nationalist community, the SDLP also has a wider range of options than Sinn Féin. The latter has no immediate potential allies other than the SDLP; but the SDLP has the option of exploring with moderate unionism the possibility of a distinct 'Northern Irish' political and ideological agenda. In this, its choice is likely to be conditioned not only by the nature of any implicit bid from unionism but also by consciousness of the growing demographic strength of the community from which it draws its own support.

Third, the South's options are more constrained. As an actor in the international field, it has a vested and mutual interest in maintaining good relations with both the British and the European Union. When it looks northwards, it sees three options, between which it appears not yet to have finally chosen. It can pursue the difficult challenge of reaching out to both communities, notwithstanding the hostility of one of them, in line with traditional republican ideology. It can present itself as ally and 'guarantor' of one community, a role in which it has found itself in recent decades. Or it can distance itself from both communities, and seek to limit its involvement, by pursuit of an internal settlement in Northern Ireland and institutionalisation of modest North–South co-operation.

In addition to the complex web of options open to the various parties (oversimplified above, by assuming that each bloc is a monolith), further issues of fundamental importance arise. Of these, the most central are the related concepts of 'consent' and 'self-determination'. A century ago, self-determination referred to the question whether the Irish had a right to determine their own future. This could then give rise to a second question: whether Ulster Protestants had a similar right, the right to opt out of a decision by the 'Irish people' (see Gallagher, 1990). The matter appeared to have been 'resolved', at least to the satisfaction of the British, in 1921, by concession of the collective (but not individual) right of six northern counties to opt out of the new state. In subsequent debate, and especially since 1949, it is the right of 'Northern Ireland', rather than of Ulster unionists, to self-determination that has dominated the agenda. The profound significance of this is that Northern Ireland was never more than two-thirds unionist; and as the green–orange balance changes, so too does the divergence between 'Northern Ireland' and 'the unionist community'. It may well be the case that the failure to assert coherently the unionist right to self-determination *as such* in 1921 has fatally undermined any attempt to assert this right now (and, indeed, strong and explicit demands for such assertion are rarely to be heard). On the issue of constitutional change within the island of Ireland, then, the decision-making unit in the north is the people of Northern Ireland, not the unionist community, whose consent for new constitutional structures linking north and south is not required. On the other hand, within Northern Ireland each of the two communities has a veto, and its consent is required if current structures are to survive.

Constitutionally and politically, then, the range of options and possibilities continues to be wide. Nevertheless, it appears that ideological evolution has been sufficient to permit the emergence of a common ground between the communities, and that this has so far been sufficient to sustain the new, post-1998 institutions. For supporters of the agreement, the road ahead is likely to continue to be rocky. This book began with an optimistic quotation from *The Irish Times* front-page editorial the day after the Good Friday Agreement that hailed the enormous political achievement that had taken place the day before. But it is appropriate to end with another extract from the same editorial, one that introduced a prescient note of caution, modified by hope:

> What has been achieved over these days is a beginning. It marks but the start of the challenging experiment, so often and so painstakingly prescribed over the years by John Hume; the bringing together of the representatives of the people of all of Ireland to agree how they might share this space of land upon which they have been cast by the tide of history. They have set out a structure. Will it be sturdy enough to endure the strains and stresses which will bear upon it? Other, earlier agreements – Sunningdale and Hillsborough – were unable to withstand the destructive forces which flow from our tribal polarities. But this time it will hopefully be different (*The Irish Times*, 11 April 1998).

**Appendix**

# Perspectives on the future of Northern Ireland

Selected political documents

## 1 Fundamental aims of the parties

The formally defined aims of political parties, typically written into their constitutions, normally provide a valuable historical recording of the original purpose for which the party was founded, or at least outline a vision of society with which it would like to be associated (these formal aims frequently clash with the current de facto or even explicit programmes of the parties in question). The extracts below reproduce either the full text of such formal statements (where this is necessary to appreciate the context of any implications for policy on Northern Ireland) or the portions that have a bearing on Northern Ireland policy.

### 1.1 Fianna Fáil

The first six of the party's fundamental aims were incorporated in its constitution in 1926 and remained unchanged for 69 years; the seventh was approved in principle at the same time, and the actual wording had been incorporated by 1929.[1]

> The aims of Fianna Fáil shall be:
> 1   To secure the unity and independence of Ireland as a Republic
> 2   To restore the Irish language as the spoken language of the people, and to develop a distinctive national life in accordance with Irish traditions and ideals
> 3   To make the resources and wealth of Ireland subservient to the needs and welfare of all the people of Ireland

---

Extracts from key documents have been selected with a view to capturing expressions of political positions at particular points in time. Capitalisation has been standardised (except where it appeared that the use of capitals might have had a particular political significance), but punctuation and spelling remain as in the original documents.

4   To make Ireland, as far as possible, economically self-contained and self-sufficing
5   To establish as many families as practicable on the land
6   By suitable distribution of power to promote the ruralisation of industries essential to the lives of the people as opposed to their concentration in cities
7   To carry out the Democratic Programme of the First Dáil.

At the party's 1995 ard-fheis, these basic aims were revised, and are now as follows (Fianna Fáil, 1996)

Fianna Fáil is a national movement. Its aims are:

(i)    To secure in peace and agreement the unity of Ireland and its people
(ii)   To develop a distinctive national life in accordance with the diverse traditions and ideals of the Irish people as part of a broader European culture, and to restore and promote the Irish language as a living language of the people
(iii)  To guarantee religious and civil liberty, and equal rights, equal treatment and equal opportunities for all the people of Ireland
(iv)   To develop the resources and wealth of Ireland to their full potential, while making them subservient to the needs and welfare of all the people of Ireland, so as to provide the maximum sustainable employment, based on fostering a spirit of enterprise and self-reliance and on social partnership
(v)    To protect the natural environment and heritage of Ireland and to ensure a balance between town and country and between the regions, and to maintain as many families as practicable on the land
(vi)   To promote the family, and a wider sense of social responsibility, and to uphold the rule of law in the interests of the welfare and safety of the public
(vii)  To maintain the status of Ireland as a sovereign state, as a full member of the European Union and the United Nations, contributing to peace, disarmament and development on the basis of Ireland's independent foreign policy tradition
(viii) To reform the laws and institutions of State, to make them efficient, humane, caring and responsive to the needs of the citizens.

## 1.2 Fine Gael

Fine Gael's predecessor, Cumann na nGaedheal, defined its objectives as follows in its constitution (Moss, 1933: 205).

OBJECTS

To carry on the national tradition, *and*

To utilise the powers of Government in the hands of the Irish people, as well as other forms of public activity, for the fullest development of the Nation's heritage – political, cultural and economic.

PROGRAM

1    To secure the unity of Ireland and to combine the divergent elements of the nation in a common bond of citizenship in harmony with national security

2    To preserve and foster the national language, literature, games and arts, and every element of national culture and custom which tends to give Ireland distinction as a nation

3    To promote the development of agriculture, fisheries and other natural resources

4    To stimulate and safeguard the development of suitable manufacturing industries by all means at our disposal

5    To make the whole soil of Ireland available for the use of the people by completing land purchase and by utilising the de-populated grass-lands in accordance with a broad national plan

6    To obtain the provision of adequate financial assistance for a national scheme of housing, urban and rural

7    To substitute, as far as possible, for the unemployment dole, national schemes of useful work, including arterial drainage, reafforestation, improvement of roads and waterways

8    To encourage the proper physical development of the children of Ireland

9    To secure the fullest opportunities of educational advancement for every section of the community.

The Fine Gael party constitution has always focused on organisation rather than on a statement of basic aims. However, early editions of the Fine Gael constitution began with the following statement of aims (Fine Gael, 1963).

**What Fine Gael stands for:** To secure for all our people in a united Ireland a decent standard of living with equal opportunity for all – whether they live in town, city or country – to earn a secure livelihood in their own land and to use their talents for the betterment of themselves and our common country.

### 1.3 Labour Party

The Irish Trade Union Congress and Labour Party (renamed the Irish Labour Party and Trade Union Congress in 1918) had the following aims from 1921.[2]

(a)   To recover for the nation complete possession of all the material physical sources of wealth of the country

(b)   To win for the workers of Ireland, collectively, the ownership and control of the whole produce of their labour

(c)   To secure the democratic management and control of all industries and services by the whole body of workers, manual and mental, engaged therein, in the interest of the nation and subject to the supreme authority of the national government

(d)   To obtain for all adults who give allegiance and service to the commonwealth, irrespective of sex, race or religious belief, equality of political and social rights and opportunities

(e)   To abolish all powers and privileges, social and political, of institutions or persons, based upon property or ancestry, or not granted or confirmed by the freely expressed will of the Irish people; and to insist that in the making and administering of the laws, in the pursuit of industry and commerce, and in the education of the young, property must always be subordinate to humanity, and private gain must ever give place to the welfare of the people

(f)   With the foregoing objects in view, to promote the organisation of the working class industrially, socially and politically, e.g. in trade unions, in cooperative societies (both of producers and consumers) and in a political labour party

(g)   To secure labour representation on all national and local legislative and administrative bodies

(h)   To coordinate the work of the several sections of the working class movements

(i)   To promote fraternal relations between the workers of Ireland and of other countries through affiliation with the international labour movement

(j)   To cooperate with that movement in promoting the establishment of democratic machinery for the settlement of disputes between nations; and in raising the standard of social legislation in all countries to the level of the highest; and

(k)   Generally to assist in the efforts of the working class of all nations in their struggle for emancipation.

When the party and the trade union movement separated in 1930, the party adopted the following statement of objectives.[3]

(a)   To stimulate and assist the exploitation of the natural resources of the country and the organisation on cooperative lines of agriculture, fisheries and industry and the transference of banking, transport and sources of power to public control, so as to secure more tillage, an increased industrial output, more systematic and economical marketing, less waste in distribution and better credit facilities

(b) To maintain, extend and improve the social services organised by the state and public authorities

(c) To establish the rights and accept the obligations of Ireland as a sovereign state in relation to the other states of the world, to increase its activity and influence in international affairs, and to cultivate friendly relations with other states;

(d) To secure the political union, by mutual agreement, of Northern Ireland with the Saorstát, with such degree and form of autonomy for Northern Ireland as may be found desirable, and meanwhile to foster friendly cooperation between the two parts of the country;

(e) To cooperate with the Irish Trade Union Congress in matters of common concern

(f) Generally to secure that the legislative, financial and administrative powers of the State shall be used to the fullest extent for the benefit of the whole community.

In 1934, the party redefined its fundamental aims in a more left leaning and a more explicitly nationalist direction by inserting two new clauses at the beginning and making certain other changes. These were as follows.[4]

(a) To establish in Ireland a workers' republic founded on principles of social justice, sustained by democratic institutions and guaranteeing civil and religious liberty and equal opportunities to achieve happiness to all citizens who render service to the community;

(b) To win for the people of Ireland, collectively, the ownership and control of the whole produce of their labour; to secure the democratic management of all industries and all services by the whole body of citizens.

The party adopted a new constitution in 1952, and the statement of aims survived with few changes until the 1980s. The new text is reproduced below.[5]

(a) To establish in the entire national territory a republican form of government founded on the principles of social justice, sustained by democratic institutions and guaranteeing civil and religious liberty and equal opportunities to achieve happiness to all citizens

(b) To secure the political union of Ireland in conformity with the principles set out above in paragraph a and pending the realisation of this objective to foster friendly cooperation between the two parts of the country

(c)   To provide the widest possible measure of social security for all classes in the community

(d)   To provide on an insurance basis and without any means test, a comprehensive scheme of medical services for all citizens so as to make available to them the best possible services in all branches

(e)   To ensure the fullest utilisation of the natural resources of the country so as to provide greater wealth for the nation and a rising standard of living for the people

(f)   To bring under public ownership such industries and services, including banking, as will promote the common good by the provision of better services for the community

(g)   To provide the best possible conditions of employment with special regard to wages, hours of work, annual holidays and factory and office accommodation in conformity with modern standards

(h)   To secure for organised workers the right of participation in the management of industries and public services

(i)   To expand agricultural production by providing credit facilities to farmers to purchase stock, equipment, fertilisers, to protect the home market for Irish agricultural produce, to guarantee fair prices for main agricultural commodities and by breaking up ranch lands, to settle as many persons as possible on adequate holdings with facilities for stocking and working the land

(j)   To establish the rights and accept the obligations of Ireland as a sovereign state in relation to the other states of the world, to increase its activity and influence in international affairs and to cultivate friendly relations with other states

(k)   To cooperate with the Irish trade union movement in matters of common concern

(l)   Generally, to secure that the legislative, financial and administrative powers of the state shall be used to the fullest extent for the benefit of the whole community

(m)  To encourage and foster the national language by all reasonable means and by the provision of schemes designed to inculcate a love of the language in people, to induce them to speak their native tongue.

A radical overhaul of the constitution in 1991 relocated the party's statement of 'Principles and objects' to a very long schedule of about 2,000 words. The sections with implications for Northern Ireland policy came under the heading 'Freedom', of which the first and seventh points were as follows (Labour Party, 1991).

• Freedom and the unity of Ireland are major, long-standing questions on the political agenda. The unity for which James Connolly died was the same unity promoted by Wolfe Tone – a unity of Protestant, Catholic and Dissenter, living and working together in harmony. This unity, captured in James Connolly's phrase 'Ireland without her people is nothing to me' is the same unity to which the Labour party aspires – a coming together of people from different cultures and traditions – a mutual acceptance of and respect for differences and a willingness to work together in a spirit of harmony, trust and goodwill. We reject absolutely the use of force and violence in the otherwise legitimate cause of a united Ireland. Terrorism and violence kill not only people, but trust, dialogue, and the very concept of unity itself, together with the willingness to understand the alternative view and the very concept of unity itself. Only death and terror grow from the barrel of a gun – never true unity. . . .

- The Irish republic is a free, sovereign state. But it is also a willing member of the European and global community. Any diminution or dilution of this sovereignty arising from that membership can only take place with the consent of the Irish people as a whole.

## 1.4 Progressive Democrats

The constitution approved at the party's national conference on 25 September 1996 defined its aims as follows (Progressive Democrats, 1996).

The aims of the party are:

1 To build in Ireland a democratic society organised on republican principles
2 To encourage greater economic and political participation by all its citizens
3 To protect and help the weak and deprived members of society
4 To establish and maintain laws which safeguard the rights of the individual
5 To establish a fair and just system of taxation which fosters and encourages the work ethic
6 To ensure that the legislative, judicial and administrative arms of government function effectively and serve the purpose for which they were established
7 To reduce the role of the state in the affairs of the citizens
8 To improve the social environment by dealing determinedly with unemployment, poverty and crime and by promoting community spirit
9 To conserve and protect the natural, physical and built environment of Ireland through appropriate legislation and by fostering civic awareness in this regard
10 To promote unity among all Irish people by peaceful means based on pluralist principles
11 To promote and maintain laws which reflect the independence of church and state
12 To safeguard and develop all strands of Irish culture and heritage and to promote the use of the Irish language
13 To support the participation of Ireland in the building of a united Europe.

### 1.5 Sinn Féin

The constitution of the 'first' Sinn Féin, whose formal name was the National Council until 1908, defined the following objectives.[6]

The object of the National Council is the re-establishment of the independence of Ireland.

The aim of the Sinn Féin policy is to unite Ireland on this broad national platform:

1st.  That we are a distinct nation

2nd.  That we will not make any voluntary agreement with Great Britain until Great Britain keeps her own compact which she made by the Renunciation Act of 1783, which enacted 'that the right claimed by the people of Ireland to be bound only by laws enacted by His Majesty and the Parliament of that Kingdom is hereby declared to be established, and ascertained for ever and shall, at no time hereafter, be questioned or questionable'.

3rd.  That we are determined to make use of any powers we have, or may have at any time in the future, to work for our own advancement and for the creation of a prosperous, virile, and independent nation.

That the people of Ireland are a free people and that no law made without their authority or consent is, or ever can be, binding on their conscience. . . .

The 'second' Sinn Féin, said to date from the party's 1917 ard-fheis (convention), amended this statement of objectives, which now read as follows (Sinn Féin, 1917).

2  Sinn Fein aims at securing the international recognition of Ireland as an independent Irish republic. Having achieved that status the Irish people may by referendum freely choose their own form of government

3  This object shall be attained through the Sinn Fein organisation, which shall, in the name of the sovereign Irish people:-

(a)  Deny the right and oppose the will of the British Parliament and British Crown or any other foreign government to legislate for Ireland

(b)  Make use of any and every means available to render impotent the power of England to hold Ireland in subjection by military force or otherwise.

The 'third' Sinn Féin (which appeared following the split in 1922) adopted a similar statement of objectives when it approved its constitution at its 1924 ard-fheis.[7]

2  Sinn Fein aims at securing the international recognition of Ireland as an independent Irish republic. Having achieved that status the Irish people may by referendum freely choose their own form of government

3    This object shall be attained through the Sinn Fein organisation, which shall, in the name of the sovereign Irish people:

(a)    Deny the right and oppose the will of the British Parliament and British Crown or any other foreign government to legislate for Ireland

(b)    Make use of any and every means available to render impotent the power of England to hold Ireland in subjection by military force or otherwise

(c)    Give its undivided allegiance and entire support to Dáil Éireann, the duly elected parliament of Ireland, in the exercise of all its legitimate functions and in all the steps it legitimately takes to maintain public order, to provide for national defence, to secure good government, and to promote the general welfare of the whole people of Ireland.

This statement of aims was retained by the 'fourth' Sinn Féin after the split of 1926, though there were further amendments in the 1950s. Following the split of 1970, the 'fifth' ('official') Sinn Féin moved in an increasingly socialist and non-nationalist direction. By 1983 its aims were defined as follows (Chubb, 1983: 147).

(a)    The complete overthrow of Anglo American imperialism in Ireland, in all its manifestations (economic, political, social and cultural), by the establishment of a united Democratic Socialist Republic of Ireland, in which state power will lie in the hands of the working people of Ireland, and the means of production, distribution and exchange will be controlled democratically by the working people through public ownership;

(b)    To defend the existence of the Irish nation against the influences and effects of foreign imperialists and native collaborators, to promote the native Irish language and culture both externally among the people and internally in our own organisation.

The party dropped 'Sinn Féin' from its title in 1982, and by 1991 its aims had been revised:[8]

(a)    To change the political , economic and social structure of both States of Ireland to establish a democratic, secular, socialist Republic; a unitary state on the island of Ireland

(b)    To enrich the life of all citizens by enabling and encouraging them to develop their talents and their cultural interests to their fullest extent, to strengthen our indigenous cultural heritage and to increase the use of the Irish language so that bi-lingualism in Irish and English will become the norm.

The 'sixth' ('provisional') Sinn Féin re-adopted a version of the old constitution at its ard-fheis in 1970.[9]

The objects of Sinn Féin are:
(a)  The complete overthrow of English rule in Ireland, and the establishment of a democratic socialist republic based on the proclamation of 1916
(b)  To bring the proclamation of the Republic, Easter 1916, into effective operation and to maintain and consolidate the Government of the Republic, representative of the people of all Ireland, based on that proclamation
(c)  To establish in the Republic a reign of social justice based on Christian principles, by a just distribution and effective control of the nation's wealth and resources, and to institute a system of government suited to the particular needs of the people.

### 1.6 Social Democratic and Labour Party

The initial constitution of 1970 defined the party's objectives as follows (only minor changes were made to these until the 1990s; McAllister, 1977: 168).

1  To organise and maintain in Northern Ireland a socialist party
2  To promote the policies decided by the party conference
3  To cooperate with the Irish Congress of Trade Unions in joint political or other action
4  To promote the cause of Irish unity based on the consent of the majority of people in Northern Ireland
5  To cooperate with other Labour parties through the Council of Labour and to cooperate with other Social Democratic parties at an international level
6  To contest elections in Northern Ireland with a view to forming a government which will implement the following principles:
   (a)  the abolition of all forms of religious, political, class or sex discrimination; the promotion of culture and the arts with a special responsibility to cherish and develop all aspects of our native culture
   (b)  the public ownership and democratic control of such essential industries and services as the common good requires
   (c)  The utilisation of its powers by the state, when and where necessary, to provide employment, by the establishment of publicly owned industries.

By 1995, these had been redefined as follows (Social Democratic and Labour Party, 1995).

1  To organise and maintain in Northern Ireland a socialist party
2  To promote the policies decided by the party conference

3    To cooperate with the Irish Congress of Trade Unions in joint political or other action

4    To promote the cause of Irish unity freely negotiated and agreed to by the people of the North and by the people of the South

5    To cooperate with other Labour Parties and Social Democratic parties through the Party of European Socialists and the Socialist International

6    To work for the full participation of women in social, economic and public life on the basis of full equality

7    To promote unity and harmony among the peoples of Europe, to work to end divisions based upon religion, ethnic origin or perceived national identity and to promote a new international order of peace and justice throughout the world

8    To contest elections in Northern Ireland with a view to securing the implementation of the following principles:

   (a)    The abolition of all forms of discrimination based upon religion, gender, disability, ethnic origin, class, political belief or sexual orientation and the promotion of equality amongst all our citizens

   (b)    The promotion of culture and arts with a special responsibility to cherish and develop all the diverse aspects of our national cultures

   (c)    The public ownership and democratic control of such essential industries and services as the common good requires

   (d)    The protection of the environment with sustainable development and the achievement of social and economic justice for all our people.

### 1.7 Ulster Unionist Party

The party's objectives, summarised in the constitution of the Ulster Unionist Council (UUC), were as follows up to 1939.[10]

   (a)    To bring together all Local Unionist Associations with a view to consistent and continuous political action;

   (b)    To act as a further connecting link between Ulster Unionists and their parliamentary representatives;

   (c)    To settle in consultation with them the parliamentary policy;

   (d)    To be the medium of expressing Ulster Unionist opinion, as current events may from time to time require, and

   (e)    Generally to advance and defend the interests of Unionism.

By 1943, two new additional objectives had been inserted in front of these, and the revised statement remained valid up to the early 1970s.[11]

- to maintain Northern Ireland as an integral part of the United Kingdom
- to uphold and defend the Constitution and Parliament of Northern Ireland

In 1974 the party's objectives were reformulated to take account of the suspension of Stormont.[12]

> The objects of the [Ulster Unionist] Council shall be:
> (i)   To maintain Northern Ireland under the Crown as an integral part of the United Kingdom and to uphold democratic institutions of government for Northern Ireland
> (ii)  To safeguard the British citizenship of the people of Northern Ireland
> (iii) To act as a further connecting link between Ulster Unionists and their parliamentary representatives, to settle in consultation with them the parliamentary policy and to be the medium of expressing Ulster Unionist opinion as current events may from time to time require, and generally to advance and defend the interests of Ulster Unionism
> (iv)  To promote the principles and aims of the Ulster Unionist Party and to encourage membership amongst those of all ages who share these objectives.

By 2002, the first two of these objectives remained unaltered, but the third and fourth had been replaced (Ulster Unionist Party, 2002).

> 3   To uphold the right of the people of Northern Ireland to self-determination based upon the democratic requirement for the consent of the majority of the people of Northern Ireland to any constitutional change
> 4   To promote a democratic system of local government in Northern Ireland.

## 1.8 Democratic Unionist Party

The party's constitution, as passed by its central delegate assembly in May 1982, defined its objectives as follows (Ulster Democratic Unionist Party, 1982).

> 1   To uphold and maintain the constitution of Northern Ireland as an integral part of the United Kingdom as at present constituted
> 2   To impose and maintain the rule of law in all areas of Northern Ireland so that all citizens are not only equal under the law, but are equally subject to it
> 3   To devise and urge a policy of social betterment and equal opportunity for all sections of the community in the economic, educational and social welfare spheres.

## 1.9 Progressive Unionist Party

From the mid-1990s the party's constitution defined its aims as follows (the second objective was not part of the original statement of aims; and an additional, more specific statement of objectives has coexisted with this).[13]

1     To organise and maintain in parliaments, national and regional, a Political Labour and Unionist Party

2     To watch over, promote and protect the constitutional position of Northern Ireland as an integral part of the United Kingdom

3     To cooperate with appropriate community, labour and or other kindred organisations, in joint political or other action, in harmony with the party constitution and standing orders

4     To give effect as far as may be practicable to the principles from time to time approved by the party conference

5     To secure for the workers by hand or by brain the full fruits of their industry and the most equitable distribution thereof that may be possible upon the basis of common ownership of the means of production, distribution and exchange, and the best obtainable system of popular administration and control of each industry or service

6     Generally to promote the political, social and economic emancipation of the people of Northern Ireland, and more particularly those who depend directly upon their own exertions by hand or brain for the means of life

7     To cooperate with labour and trades union organisations in the United Kingdom with a view to promoting the purposes of the party, and to take common action for the promotion of a higher standard of social and economic life for the working population of our respective regions.

## 1.10  Alliance Party

The original party constitution required it 'to promote in every way the aims and principles of the Party as defined by its "Statement of Principles" (appended hereto) and policies of the Party as defined from time to time by the Council of the Party.' The party's principles are appended to its constitution.[14]

Statement of principles upon which the Alliance Party was founded on 21 April 1970:

1     We support the constitutional position of Northern Ireland as an integral part of the United Kingdom. We know that this belief is shared by the overwhelming majority of our people and that provocative debate about it has been the primary cause of all our most fundamental troubles. The union is in the best economic and social interest of all citizens of the state. It also implies British standards of democracy and social justice which will be energetically secured and steadfastly upheld. We are firmly committed to the principle of devolved government and would not support any attempt to suspend or dissolve the Northern Ireland Parliament.

2     Our primary objective is to heal the bitter divisions in our community by ensuring:

(a)  Equality of citizenship and human dignity;

(b)  The rooting out of discrimination and injustices;

(c)  The elimination of prejudice by a just and liberal appreciation of the beliefs and fears of different members of the community;

(d)  Equality of social, economic and educational opportunities

(e)  Highest standards of democracy at both parliamentary and local government level

(f)  Complete and effective participation in our political, governmental and public life at all levels by people drawn from both sides of our present religious divide.

3  Our economic policies will not be shackled by any economic dogma, whether socialist or conservative. The Alliance Party will never accept any such socio-economic allegiance. Nor is there any intention or desire whatsoever to affiliate with any other party.

4  We firmly believe that without universal respect for the law of the land and the authorities appointed to enforce it, there can be no measurable progress. We, therefore, intend to secure the rapid achievement of such respect and the absolutely equal enforcement of the law without fear or favour, in every part of the state. Equal justice will be guaranteed to all citizens regardless of their political or religious persuasion.

## 1.11  Northern Ireland Women's Coalition

The party constitution, adopted in 1999, defines the party's aims as follows (Northern Ireland Women's Coalition, 2002).

(a)  To promote the principles of inclusion, equality and human rights in every sphere of politics

(b)  To promote and defend the participation of women in politics

(c)  To promote and defend the civil, social, economic, human and cultural rights of women, men and children

(d)  To promote openness and transparency in politics through greater public participation.

# 2  An evolving nationalist consensus?

The steady shift in nationalist thinking is illustrated powerfully in documents produced by three different cross-party bodies. The first is the All-Party Anti-Partition Conference, which in 1949 summarised conventional nationalist thinking in the relatively stable form that it assumed during the first 50 years of the life of independent Ireland. The second is the New Ireland Forum, which signalled a significant shift in this thinking in the mid-1980s, showing a considerable openness to a range of possible models for a settlement, though coming down in favour of one close to the traditional nationalist position. The third is the Forum for Peace and Reconciliation in the mid-1990s, which substantially abandoned the traditional nationalist emphasis on the right to unity and redefined the notion of self-determination.

## 2.1 The All-Party Anti-Partition Conference (1949)

The All-Party Anti-Partition Conference was established by Taoiseach John A. Costello with inter-party agreement in 1949, and in its propagandist work took over where the North-East Boundary Bureau (1922–6) had left off. The 46th and apparently last meeting of its standing committee, commonly known as the Mansion House Committee, took place in Áras an Uachtaráin on 26 October 1971, chaired by John A. Costello and attended by most of its original members.[15] At that time it was still interested in the partition issue, but it had been sidelined by other developments. A document it produced in 1949 accurately summarised traditional nationalist thinking on the partition issue.[16]

- The essence of democracy lies in the right of a people freely to determine how they are to be governed.
- The unit for this self-determination is the nation.
- Ireland through a nationhood never questioned in almost 2,000 years has that right.
- Partition is the denial of the right to self-determination.
- It is a refusal to accept the majority will of a people in choosing the government they themselves desire.
- No group, party, or political organisation in Ireland sought for or desired partition.
- It was imposed by the British Government against the passionate protest of the overwhelming majority of the Irish people.
- First established by force, it is now maintained by British support and by flagrant manipulation with British consent of electoral boundaries within the area.
- The perpetual interference in Ireland's internal affairs by an outside power sets an example destructive of the rule of law among the nations.
- Partition gravely injures both parts of Ireland; it injures Britain too, for as long as it lasts Britain cannot sustain her claim to stand for democracy in Western Europe.

## 2.2 The New Ireland Forum (1983–4)

The New Ireland Forum was established on the proposal of the SDLP by the Taoiseach, Garret FitzGerald, with inter-party agreement in 1983 and comprised representatives of the three major parties in the Republic and of the SDLP. Chapter 5 of its report (1984) summarised a new consensus on the national question. Cross-references are omitted from the extract below.[17]

5.1   The major realities identified in the Forum's analysis of the problem, as set out in earlier chapters, may be summarised as follows:

(1)   Existing structures and practices in Northern Ireland have failed to provide either peace, stability or reconciliation. The failure to recognise and accommodate the identity of Northern nationalists has resulted in deep and growing alienation on their part from the system of political authority.

(2)   The conflict of nationalist and unionist identities has been concentrated within the narrow ground of Northern Ireland. This has prevented constructive interaction between the two traditions and fostered fears, suspicions and misunderstandings.

(3)   One effect of the division of Ireland is that civil law and administration in the South are seen, particularly by unionists, as being unduly influenced by the majority ethos on issues which Protestants consider to be a matter for private conscience and there is a widespread perception that the South in its laws, attitudes and values does not reflect a regard for the ethos of Protestants. On the other hand, Protestant values are seen to be reflected in the laws and practices in the North.

(4)   The present formal position of the British Government, namely the guarantee, contained in Section 1 of the Northern Ireland Constitution Act, 1973, has in its practical application had the effect of inhibiting the dialogue necessary for political progress. It has had the additional effect of removing the incentive which would otherwise exist on all sides to seek a political solution.

(5)   The above factors have contributed to conflict and instability with disastrous consequences involving violence and loss of life on a large scale in Northern Ireland.

(6)   The absence of political consensus, together with the erosion of the North's economy and social fabric, threatens to make irreversible the drift into more widespread civil conflict with catastrophic consequences.

(7)   The resulting situation has inhibited and placed under strain the development of normal relations between Britain and Ireland.

(8)    The nationalist identity and ethos comprise a sense of national Irish identity and a democratically founded wish to have that identity institutionalised in a sovereign Ireland united by consent.

(9)    The unionist identity and ethos comprise a sense of Britishness, allied to their particular sense of Irishness and a set of values comprising a Protestant ethos which they believe to be under threat from a Catholic ethos, perceived as reflecting different and often opposing values.

(10)    Irish nationalist attitudes have hitherto in their public expression tended to underestimate the full dimension of the unionist identity and ethos. On the other hand, unionist attitudes and practices have denied the right of nationalists to meaningful political expression of their identity and ethos.

(11)    The basic approach of British policy has created negative consequences. It has shown a disregard of the identity and ethos of nationalists. In effect, it has underwritten the supremacy in Northern Ireland of the unionist identity. Before there can be fundamental progress Britain must re-assess its position and responsibility.

5.2    Having considered these realities the Forum proposes the following as necessary elements of a framework within which a new Ireland could emerge:

(1)    A fundamental criterion of any new structures and processes must be that they will provide lasting peace and stability.

(2)    Attempts from any quarter to impose a particular solution through violence must be rejected along with the proponents of such methods. It must be recognised that the new Ireland which the Forum seeks can come about only through agreement and must have a democratic basis.

(3)    Agreement means that the political arrangements for a new and sovereign Ireland would have to be freely negotiated and agreed to by the people of the North and by the people of the South.

(4)    The validity of both the nationalist and unionist identities in Ireland and the democratic rights of every citizen on this island must be accepted; both of these identities must have equally satisfactory, secure and durable, political, administrative and symbolic expression and protection.

(5)    Lasting stability can be found only in the context of new structures in which no tradition will be allowed to dominate the other, in which there will be equal rights and opportunities for all, and in which there will be provision for formal and effective guarantees for the protection of individual human rights and of the communal and cultural rights of both nationalists and unionists.

(6)    Civil and religious liberties and rights must be guaranteed and there can be no discrimination or preference in laws or administrative practices, on

grounds of religious belief or affiliation; government and administration must be sensitive to minority beliefs and attitudes and seek consensus.

(7) New arrangements must provide structures and institutions including security structures with which both nationalists and unionists can identify on the basis of political consensus; such arrangements must overcome alienation in Northern Ireland and strengthen stability and security for all the people of Ireland.

(8) New arrangements must ensure the maintenance of economic and social standards and facilitate, where appropriate, integrated economic development, North and South. . . .

(9) The cultural and linguistic diversity of the people of all traditions, North and South, must be preserved and fostered as a source of enrichment and vitality.

(10) Political action is urgently required to halt disillusionment with democratic politics and the slide towards further violence. Britain has a duty to respond *now* in order to ensure that the people of Northern Ireland are not condemned to yet another generation of violence and sterility. The parties in the Forum by their participation in its work have already committed themselves to join in a process directed towards that end.

5.3   It is clear that the building of a new Ireland will require the participation and co-operation of all the people of Ireland. In particular, it is evident that the people of the South must whole-heartedly commit themselves and the necessary resources to this objective. The parties in the Forum are ready to face up to this challenge and to accommodate the realities and meet the requirements identified by the Forum. However, Britain must help to create the conditions which will allow this process to begin. The British Government have a duty to join in developing the necessary process that will recognise these realities and give effect to these requirements and thus promote reconciliation between the two major traditions in Ireland, and to make the required investment of political will and resources. The British and Irish Governments should enter into discussions to create the framework and atmosphere necessary for this purpose.

5.4   Among the fundamental realities the Forum has identified is the desire of nationalists for a united Ireland in the form of a sovereign, independent Irish state to be achieved peacefully and by consent. The Forum recognises that such a form of unity would require a general and explicit acknowledgement of a broader and more comprehensive Irish identity. Such unity would, of course, be different from both the existing Irish State and the existing arrangements in Northern Ireland because it would necessarily accommodate all the fundamental elements in both traditions.

5.5 The Parties in the Forum are convinced that such unity in agreement would offer the best and most durable basis for peace and stability. In particular, it would have a number of advantages and attractions:

- It would restore the historic integrity of Ireland and end the divisions in the country.
- It would enable both traditions to rediscover and foster the best and most positive elements in their heritages.
- It would provide the most promising framework for mutual interaction and enrichment between the two traditions.
- It would give unionists the clearest sense that all of Ireland, in all its dimensions, and not just Northern Ireland, is their inheritance and the opportunity to share in the leadership and to shape the future of a new Ireland.
- It would end the alienation and deep sense of injustice felt by nationalists.
- It would provide a framework within which agreed institutions could apply economic policies suited to the particular and largely similar circumstances and interests of both parts of the country, and in which economies of scale and the possibilities of integrated planning could be fully exploited.
- It would best allow for the advancement internationally of the particular and largely common interests of Ireland, North and South and for the contribution, based on distinctive shared values, which the people of all traditions can make to the European and international communities.
- It would end the dissipation of energies in wasteful divisions and redirect efforts towards constructive endeavour, thus giving a major impetus to the social, cultural and economic development of the entire country.

5.6 The Parties in the Forum will continue to work by peaceful means to achieve Irish unity in agreement. There are many varying constitutional and other structures of political unity to be found throughout the world, for example, Australia, France, Italy, Spain, Switzerland and the United States of America which recognise to the extent necessary the diversity as well as the unity of the people concerned and ensure constitutional stability. It is essential that any structures for a new Ireland must meet both these criteria.

5.7 The particular structure of political unity which the Forum would wish to see established is a unitary state, achieved by agreement and consent, embracing the whole island of Ireland and providing irrevocable guarantees for the protection and preservation of both the unionist and nationalist identities. A unitary state on which agreement had been reached would also provide the ideal framework for the constructive interaction of the diverse cultures and values of the people of Ireland. . . .

5.8 Constitutional nationalists fully accept that they alone could not determine the structures of Irish unity and that it is essential to have unionist agreement and participation in devising such structures and in formulating the guarantees they required. In line with this view, the Forum believes that the best people to identify the interests of the unionist tradition are the unionist people themselves. It would thus be essential that they should negotiate their role in any arrangements which would embody Irish unity. It would be for the British and Irish governments to create the framework and atmosphere within which such negotiations could take place.

5.9 The Forum in the course of its work, in both public and private sessions, received proposals as to how unionist and nationalist identities and interests could be accommodated in different ways and in varying degrees in a new Ireland. The Forum gave careful consideration to these proposals. In addition to the unitary state, two structural arrangements were examined in some detail – a federal/confederal state and joint authority. . . .

5.10 The Parties in the Forum also remain open to discuss other views which may contribute to political development.

## 2.3 The Forum for Peace and Reconciliation

The Forum for Peace and Reconciliation was set up in the aftermath of the Downing Street Declaration of 1993 and the paramilitary ceasefires in 1994 and comprised representatives of 12 political groups (including Sinn Féin, the SDLP and the Alliance Party). Its proceedings showed further evolution in the thinking of the mainstream nationalist parties, though its final summary of the position failed to gain the assent of all of them (with Sinn Féin objecting to some of its central points). Its analysis of the contemporary position and proposals as to the way forward are reproduced below (Forum for Peace and Reconciliation, 1996).

PRESENT REALITIES

Arising from its discussions on the nature of the problem, the Forum has identified the following key realities as, in its view, requiring to be addressed:

(a) The most urgent and important challenge facing the people of Ireland, North and South, and the British and Irish Governments together, is to remove the causes of conflict, to overcome the legacy of history and to heal the divisions which have resulted.

(b) The peace process provides an unprecedentedly favourable climate in which to face this challenge. The opportunity now available needs to be grasped to the full.

(c)    Most of the divisions within Northern Ireland and within the island, which are a persisting source of pain and distrust, are part of the enduring historic legacy of wider British-Irish relations. The origins and context of those divisions, therefore, transcend Northern Ireland itself and encompass the totality of relationships involved – i.e. those within Northern Ireland, within the island of Ireland as a whole and between the peoples of these islands.

(d)    In terms of the way ahead, a central role rests with the Irish and British Governments. Building on the evolution of agreed arrangements and positions – starting with the Sunningdale communiqué, followed by the 1980 Summits, which placed the relationship on a formal footing, and leading over time to the deepened level of co-operation represented by the Anglo-Irish Agreement, the Joint Declaration, the Joint Framework Document and the Twin-track Approach – the two Governments have accepted that they have a responsibility to lead the process of overcoming the divisions of the past and the search for a new accommodation acceptable to all. Both Governments having acknowledged their responsibility, it will be essential that they discharge it actively and fully. In the Joint Declaration, the British Government, having declared that it has no selfish strategic or economic interest in Northern Ireland, has accepted that its role will be to encourage, facilitate and enable the achievement of agreement among the people of Ireland through a process of dialogue and co-operation and that it will legislate for any such agreement, while the Irish Government has committed itself to the principle that the democratic right of self-determination by the people of Ireland as a whole must be achieved and exercised with and subject to the agreement and consent of a majority of the people of Northern Ireland.

(e)    The Forum also notes that the Irish Government has said that no individual party can have a veto over negotiations and discussions over their outcome, and the British Government has said no group or organisation has a veto over the policy of a democratically elected government. The two Governments have also agreed that in political dialogue no outcome is either predetermined or ruled out and that other positions, apart from theirs, will be given full consideration in all-party talks.

(f)    The engagement of the political parties, together with the two Governments, in all- inclusive talks, commencing at the earliest possible date, will also be crucial to the achievement of a comprehensive agreement. The political parties will bring to the talks their own analysis and positions on the political and constitutional changes required for the achievement of a new accommodation acceptable to all. To ensure their success, such talks will require careful, sensitive and urgent preparation.

(g)    Violence, from whatever source and whatever its rationale, served – particularly in Northern Ireland, but also as between North and South – to deepen divisions, reinforce the barriers of fear and hatred, retard cross-community contact and reconciliation, and has impeded the search for agreement. It caused immense human suffering. For many, the burden of that suffering remains a living and profoundly difficult reality. A compassionate acknowledgement of that reality and a commitment to devote sufficient resources to necessary treatment and support programmes will be important elements of building a true process of reconciliation. Moreover, the cost of violence in economic terms was also on an enormous scale.

(h) By the same token, the ceasefires announced in Autumn 1994 have profoundly altered the situation in Northern Ireland and represent a strongly positive contribution to the process of establishing an agreed settlement. The bringing about of the ceasefires was made possible through the climate created by the commitment of the two Governments to a common approach on core issues, by the work of many individuals and groups within the republican and wider nationalist communities and within the loyalist and wider unionist communities, and by the support and influence of the United States and the European Union. In a more general sense, tribute should also be paid to the many groups and individuals, including within the Churches, who during the years of conflict maintained and developed links across the community divisions, seeking to break down barriers of mistrust and misunderstanding. At a wider level, the ceasefires, and the new climate which they have helped create, have given rise to a deep determination throughout Ireland, North and South, that the advances that have been made must be consolidated and built upon.

(i) Conflict and division now in Northern Ireland primarily result from profound disagreement on its status and on what shape a durable political settlement should take. The absence of consensus on these issues gives rise to many other divisions, including on policing, the administration of justice and also on social, cultural and economic issues. There is however a more open acknowledgement than in the past of the depth and complexity of divisions that exist and a greater awareness of the need to address them.

(j) The profound disagreement amongst the people of Ireland on the constitutional status of Northern Ireland derives from the fact that the two major traditions there define their identities, allegiances and aspirations in terms which transcend Northern Ireland, viz looking broadly to Britain and Ireland. The Joint Declaration acknowledges that there can be no stability under a system rejected on grounds of identity by a significant minority and there is widespread acceptance of the need for both traditions to feel secure about their future.

(k) The issues of self-determination and consent are fundamental. While it is a view shared by a majority of the people of this island, though not by all its people, that the Irish people as a whole have a right to national self-determination, the exercise of self-determination is a matter for agreement between the people of Ireland and must be based on consent. There is not full agreement about how the principles of self-determination and consent should be exercised. Given their central role in the process overall, the approach reflected in the agreed position of the two Governments on this crucial matter is of particular importance. The British Government recognise that it is for the people of Ireland alone, by agreement between the two parts respectively and without external impediment, to exercise their right to self-determination on the basis of consent freely and concurrently given, North and South, to bring about a united Ireland if that is their wish; the Irish Government accept that the democratic right of self-determination by the people of Ireland as a whole must be achieved and exercised with and subject to the agreement and consent of a majority of the people of Northern Ireland. This integrated approach by the two Governments to the issues of self-determination and consent has been accepted by the majority – though not all – of the political parties, North and South, representing a large majority of the people of Ireland as a whole. Two further realities apply in this regard: (1) Northern Ireland's current constitutional status reflects and relies upon the present wish of a majority of people there and (2) nationalist support for the above approach to the principle of consent does not imply that the existing status of Northern Ireland commands nationalist consent.

(l) Current attitudes to the constitutional status of Northern Ireland, therefore, may be summarised as follows: The present wish of a majority of the people in Northern Ireland is for no change in its constitutional status. Conversely, a substantial minority wish for a sovereign united Ireland, overwhelmingly on the basis that this objective is achieved by peaceful, democratic means. It is recognised that the option of a sovereign united Ireland, which is also the preferred option of a majority of the people in Ireland, does not command the consent of the unionist tradition, nor, as indicated, does the existing status of Northern Ireland, which is the preferred option of a majority of people there, command the consent of the nationalist tradition. Against this background, and addressing the totality of relationships involved, there is a need for new arrangements and for new structures not simply based on majoritarianism which, on the basis of a new and balanced constitutional accommodation, will reflect the reality of diverse aspirations, reconcile as fully as possible the rights of both traditions, promote co-operation between them, and afford each, on the basis of equality of treatment, secure and satisfactory expression and protection in all spheres of public life.

(m) The divisions between the two communities in Northern Ireland, and between the two traditions on the island as a whole, have been perpetuated and accentuated by an absence, to a large extent, of mutual understanding, of contact and of dialogue between them. This absence of trust, which in some areas of Northern Ireland in particular is compounded by a mutual sense of threat, represents a major obstacle to the negotiation in good faith of an overall political settlement.

(n) The lesson of history is that only through an even-handed and just compromise, achieved without violence or coercion and acceptable to both communities and to both traditions on the island, can a lasting and stable settlement be reached. While the accommodation of the two major traditions remains the primary requirement, such a settlement must also take account of the minority of people, particularly in Northern Ireland, who define themselves as neither unionist nor nationalist in any traditional sense (the 'third strand').

(o) There are severe forms of deprivation in Northern Ireland within both communities. Historically, there has been particular discrimination against nationalists and Catholics which has meant the persistence of economic and social disadvantage. All this, apart from its intrinsic unacceptability, represents a barrier to the search for a lasting and comprehensive political settlement. The coming of peace will undoubtedly be of substantial economic benefit to Northern Ireland and the island of Ireland as a whole. The Forum's own study of the social and economic consequences of peace and economic reconstruction suggests that the 'peace dividend' will be substantially greater in the context of a political settlement than in that of simple continuation of the ceasefires. It will be essential to ensure that the economic benefits of peace are fully realised, that they accrue to communities, families and individuals most severely affected by the conflict, that they promote social inclusion and that economic discrimination is redressed.

(p) In North/South terms, the numerous common economic interests, the convergence between the structures of the two economies and the increasing inter-action in the context of peace between the business communities in both parts, in other economic spheres and indeed across a broad range of human activity, bear testimony in practical terms to the need for joint or common approaches.

(q) Major economic, social and cultural changes have taken place in the South over recent decades. These have led to the creation of a more prosperous, diverse and pluralistic society, very different from that which existed prior to 1969. One consequence of this is a development in understanding among many towards the situation in Northern Ireland and a greater willingness to accept unionists in terms of their own self-perception.

(r) The development of European integration will require new approaches between the two parts of the island to serve their economic interests. Participation in the process of European integration has been a significant ingredient in Ireland's recent political and economic development. While the effects of membership have not been felt to the same extent in Northern

Ireland, the European Union's supportive response to the ceasefires has served to highlight the positive potential of the European dimension. Already, co-operation on social and economic issues in the EU context has helped to bring people together across the divide in Northern Ireland. Common involvement in the European Union has injected new and constructive elements into relations between Ireland and Britain. European integration holds enormous potential for an accommodation in Ireland, both as a model for the resolution of deep-seated conflicts and as an incentive for a more co-operative approach to the many shared economic, environmental and social problems confronting the two parts of the island.

PRINCIPLES AND REQUIREMENTS

Having identified and considered these Realities, the Forum proposes the following Principles and Requirements as necessary elements of a political accommodation and settlement – and the process of achieving them – acceptable to all the people of Ireland, North and South.

1. The first principle must be the right to peace, based on justice. Flowing from this right is the principle that the pursuit of all political goals, including the establishment of an overall political settlement, must be undertaken by exclusively democratic and peaceful means, characterised by dialogue and free from violence and coercion.

2. An essential requirement of an approach based exclusively on dialogue, negotiation and non-coercion will be the building of a true process of trust and reconciliation. Such an approach must take particular account of, and be sensitive to, the position of those who have suffered directly from violence and injustice – from whatever source. In building trust and reconciliation, appropriate action will also be important on the various issues relating to those who have been imprisoned in the context of the conflict.

3. A new beginning, if it is to lead to a comprehensive, lasting resolution of the conflict, must adequately address the totality of the three central relationships involved – within Northern Ireland, within the island of Ireland and between the peoples of these islands.

4. It will be essential that the commitment of the Irish and British Governments to a common approach, as identified in paragraph d in 'Present Realities' above, is met and that they work in close partnership and collaboration. In addition to their shared functions, each Government will have important separate roles in the process also, some of which were set out in the Joint Declaration and the two Framework Documents. Above all, both Governments must actively and fully honour their commitment to foster agreement and reconciliation, leading to a new political accommodation founded on consent and encompassing all the relationships involved.

5    The achievement of such a new accommodation will require the urgent establishment of an inclusive talks process – carefully and sensitively prepared – involving the political parties as well as the two Governments. Addressing all the relationships involved, the task of the process will be to secure agreement and the maximum degree of consensus on the nature and form of future constitutional, political and institutional arrangements and structures. Having regard, inter alia, to practical and legal requirements, the agreed outcome of this process will have to be ratified by the people of Ireland, North and South.

6    The objective of the talks process must be a new political dispensation, representing an honourable, democratic accommodation between the two major traditions with which both can live and which is based on consent and on full respect for the concerns, rights and identities of all. There must be a rejection of any concept of victory or defeat.

7    Agreement on an overall settlement will require, inter alia, a balanced accommodation of the differing views of the two main traditions, which takes full account of the conflict of identities and allegiances. In terms of specific constitutional legislation, the two Governments must, on a balanced and even-handed basis, discharge the commitments they have undertaken respectively in this regard in paragraphs 20 and 21 of 'A New Framework for Agreement'. In particular, they must ensure that, in regard to the people of Northern Ireland, the constitutional changes proposed should be such as not to diminish in any way their existing citizenship rights and their birthright to be accepted as being British or Irish – or both – as appropriate and desired.

8    In determining the nature and extent of constitutional change, the issues of self-determination and consent will be crucial. The Forum believes that in this respect the following principles and requirements should apply:

It is for the people of Ireland alone, North and South, to determine their own future by agreement and consent. While there continues to be disagreement on how the principle of self-determination is to be exercised, a substantial consensus has developed, as indicated in paragraph k in 'Present Realities' above, around the approach reflected in the agreed position of the British and Irish Governments, viz: the British Government recognise that it is for the people of Ireland alone, by agreement between the two parts respectively and without external impediment, to exercise their right of self-determination on the basis of consent, freely and concurrently given, North and South, to bring about a united Ireland, if that is their wish; the Irish Government accept that the democratic right of self-determination by the people of Ireland as a whole must be achieved and exercised with and subject to the agreement and consent of a majority of the people of Northern Ireland.

Full account must be taken of the realities (a) that Northern Ireland's current constitutional status reflects and relies upon the present wish of a majority of people there and (b) that nationalist support for the above approach to the principle of consent does not imply that the existing status of Northern Ireland commands nationalist consent.

Securing an agreement which can earn and enjoy the allegiance of the different traditions on the island will be a core task of the comprehensive, all-party talks described in paragraph 5 above. Should these talks result in an agreement, and if that agreement were democratically ratified North and South, then the result of that ratification process will represent a valid and legitimate exercise by the people of Ireland as a whole of their right to self-determination.

9    Agreed arrangements based on a new and balanced constitutional accommodation must reflect the reality of diverse aspirations, reconcile as fully as possible the rights of both major traditions, and promote co-operation between them. They must even-handedly afford both traditions parity of esteem and equality of treatment in all spheres. They must enhance and facilitate the development of a truly pluralist ethos throughout the island of Ireland. While the central requirement of a lasting settlement is the forging of an accommodation between the two major traditions, the construction of new arrangements and structures must, against the foregoing background, take due account also of the position of the minority of people, particularly in Northern Ireland, who define their identity in terms which are not reflected by either of those traditions.

10   The consent of the governed is essential to the stability and legitimacy of any political arrangements. Institutions and structures forming part of new political arrangements must be accepted by both major traditions as essential elements of an overall settlement which is honourable and balanced, and must therefore enjoy widespread public support from within both traditions. In this context, and in the context of the totality of relations, it is widely accepted that there can be no exclusively internal Northern Ireland settlement. The precise structuring of relationships within Northern Ireland and their institutional expression will be a matter for the all-inclusive talks process. Equally, the securing of the endorsement and consent of both traditions will require the process to address relationships within Ireland and between Ireland and Britain. In this regard, institutions and structures will be needed which, while respecting both the requirements of identity and the diversity of the people of Ireland, would enable them to work together in all areas of common interest. Such structures would, of course, include institutional recognition of the special links that exist between the peoples of Britain and Ireland as part of the totality of relationships, while taking account of newly forged links with the

rest of Europe (see also paragraph 15 below). Such institutions must be democratically accountable and must in their functions be open and transparent.

11    The comprehensive, systematic, effective and entrenched protection of human rights – civil, political, economic and social – should underpin the establishment and operation of agreed institutions and structures. Human rights should be guaranteed, including, if necessary, internationally, on a basis of equivalence throughout all of Ireland, for example, by incorporation of the European Convention on Human Rights and Fundamental Freedoms into domestic law, irrespective of the constitutional context and of any possible future changes to it. Critical issues in this regard, particularly, but not exclusively, in relation to Northern Ireland, will be the administration of justice and policing – specifically, the development in each case of changes and reforms which will secure the unequivocal support, participation and confidence of all sections of the community. The cultural and linguistic diversity of the people of all traditions, North and South, should be safeguarded and fostered as a source of enrichment and vitality.

12    Particular attention must be paid to the protection of the rights and identity of any community which in consequence of the applying of the principle of consent finds itself in a minority position, whether in the North, or in the South, or in the island as a whole. It should be the duty of the state in such a situation vigorously, imaginatively and sensitively to protect and promote the interests of such a community, while also upholding the equal rights of the majority tradition.

13    The achievement of greater and more equally-shared prosperity, the promotion of equality of opportunity and fair participation in education and the labour market, the eradication of discrimination, and the empowerment and inclusion of marginalised and deprived communities and groups, are not only vital in themselves, but also have the capacity to create a more stable social environment, in which new political arrangements are more likely to take root and command public confidence. These goals should be, and must be, vigorously pursued.

14    Mutual understanding and contact between individuals, groups, communities, organisations and institutions have an important role in the elimination of barriers of suspicion, in the creation of mutual trust and in the building of confidence and should be further promoted and supported, including financially. Education will have a particularly significant function in this regard. In the matter of schooling, parental choice should be respected and facilitated, including the preferences of those parents who choose integrated and Irish-medium education for their children. There is a need to extend and strengthen programmes that increase contact between pupils and teachers within Northern Ireland and between schools North and South and in Britain. In addition, greater emphasis must be devoted to

exchange and mutual understanding programmes and to making the history and full cultural heritage of the people of the island in all their strands, and in its relationship with Britain and with the rest of Europe, available in all schools throughout Ireland.

15   New arrangements should also incorporate a strong European dimension. Changes are mooted in the character and nature of the European Union at political, economic, social and indeed many other levels which will have profound implications for its member states and regions. New approaches will be required to address the evolving common challenges and opportunities which these developments will hold for both parts of the island and for Ireland and Britain as partners in Europe. A further requirement, therefore, of new arrangements and structures emerging from a comprehensive settlement must be the capability of embracing such a process of evolving change.

16   Each of the foregoing principles and requirements would apply and have equal validity in all constitutional situations, and under all of the institutional frameworks, which may be envisaged.

## 3   An evolving unionist consensus?

Direct counterparts to nationalist consensus-building are not to be found on the unionist side. However, the report of the Northern Ireland Constitutional Convention (1975), which reflected the views of that body's unionist majority, summarise the traditional perspective. Later documents reflected change within particular parties, but the report of the Joint Unionist Task Force (1987), though lacking the broad support of the Convention report and ultimately failing to win the endorsement of the two main unionist parties who had set it up, is a valuable indication of new thinking within the unionist community.

### 3.1 The Northern Ireland Constitutional Convention, 1975

The Convention was elected in 1975 and the 'Loyalist Coalition' (UUP, DUP, Vanguard and others) controlled 47 of its 78 seats and determined the content of its report. Parts I and IV (dealing respectively with the background and summarising recommendations) are reproduced below; headings from the relevant portions of parts II and III have been inserted in italics in part IV to enhance legibility (Northern Ireland Constitutional Convention, 1975). Crown copyright material is reproduced with the permission of HMSO and the Queen's Printer for Scotland.

PART I. THE HISTORICAL BACKGROUND

2    The Convention considers it desirable, before dealing with the main content of its Report, to go briefly into the historical background. There is

a tendency to project the values and controversies of the present into the past. It is important before dealing with present problems to explain the historical context more adequately.

### Composition of the Community

3    To look simply in the seventeenth century for the roots of recent conflict in Northern Ireland is quite unrealistic. The absence in the small pre-Plantation population of a modern nationalistic sense of identity, and hence a low resistance to social, linguistic, cultural and religious absorption, the intermingling of people, the continuous arrival of numerous immigrants from Britain, and a considerable influx of later-newcomers from other parts of Ireland, have all united to obliterate the lines of division which existed in 1610. Earlier this year (1975), Professor J. C. Beckett, Professor of Irish History at Queen's University, Belfast, a scholar always dissociated from party politics, took a public opportunity, in a contribution on the political situation to the Annual Report of the General Synod of the Church of Ireland, to dismiss as quite fallacious the application to the contemporary social and political scene of a theory of 'planters' and 'natives'.

4    Equally to be dismissed is a social theory of 'two communities', based on a supposed long-standing identity of political orientation with religious affiliation. All over the world political movements have sought to strengthen themselves by making common cause with sectarian movements and vice versa, and this has certainly occurred in Ulster. But the facts of history refute the notion that there has been anything like the complete identification which might be thought to indicate a separate 'community'.

### Past Patterns of Political Response

5    A government publication of this year sets out some easily obtainable research material bearing on this matter. In a blue book entitled 'The Northern Ireland General Elections of 1973' (Cmnd. 5851) it is shown that, in all the Northern Ireland general elections from 1929 to 1969 inclusive, the average vote for the Nationalist and Republican candidates – the candidates seeking to unite Northern Ireland with the Irish Free State or Republic – was only 14.6 per cent of the total vote. Even if it is assumed that all who voted for those candidates were Roman Catholics, this would indicate that only two-fifths of the Roman Catholic voters were at that time positively oriented towards the Republic in political aspirations.

6    This position is confirmed by Northern Ireland results in Westminster elections, particularly those in which every seat was contested, as in 1959 when the Republican vote was only 11 per cent, or in 1964 when it was 15.9 per cent. And an opinion poll in 1973 showed only 39 per cent. of Roman Catholic respondents desiring 'a united Ireland'.

*Towards United Community Participation*

7    There is also evidence that there is in Northern Ireland a shared sense of identity which cuts across religious differences. When Professor Richard Rose published, in his book 'Governing without Consensus' (1971), the results of a widely based social survey made in 1968, he showed that a very large majority of the Roman Catholic respondents regarded their Protestant neighbours as more like themselves than their own co-religionists in the Irish Republic and an equally large majority of the Protestants regarded their Roman Catholic neighbours as more like themselves than Protestants in Britain. There is ample reason to believe that this is still true.

8    These historical and social facts made it clear that the type of constitution which, in certain other countries, has been devised to provide for two or more communities, which are clearly separated from one another by language or race or geographical location, would be quite inappropriate for Northern Ireland. Indeed to impose such a constitution, or any constitution devised on a theory of 'two communities', would be disruptive and divisive in effect and widely unacceptable.

9    These considerations lie behind the view, embodied in concrete proposals in this Report, that the right form of constitution is one which will give every member of the legislature not only the opportunity, but also the responsibility and duty of becoming much more fully involved in parliamentary decision-making, supervision of administration and scrutiny of new legislation than is the case at Westminster.

*Relations with the Irish Republic*

10    A further aspect of the historical past is also highly relevant to the present task of constitution making. This is the history of the Ulster community's relations with its nearest neighbour. In the Government's White Paper of July, 1974, entitled 'The Northern Ireland Constitution' (Cmnd. 5675), there is a Part devoted to 'The Problem'. In this there is no mention of the Irish Republic. Relations with the State which shares the same island with Northern Ireland are, however, an important factor in Northern Ireland's problem.

11    Northern Ireland and the Republic have never in the historical past been under one and the same effective government except under British rule. Under the Government of Ireland Act 1920, they were given separate governments, of which only that in Northern Ireland survived the next few years unchanged. A stabilisation of the situation was achieved after the establishment of the Irish Free State and the confirmation in 1925 of a tripartite agreement in which the Governments of the United Kingdom, of the Irish Free State and of Northern Ireland all participated. This agreement settled the frontier between Northern Ireland and the Free State. It recorded the resolve of the signatories 'mutually to aid one another in the spirit of

neighbourly comradeship' and provided a basis for meetings between the cabinets of the Belfast and Dublin governments. In effect the agreement provided for mutual recognition, mutual consultation and mutual co-operation.

*A regretted change of policy*

12    Unhappily a subsequent Dublin government dishonoured these undertakings and, in a constitution adopted in 1937, laid claim to sovereignty over Northern Ireland. Although no Dublin government has attempted to enforce this claim, a vigorous international propaganda campaign has been carried on by Dublin governments, seeking to give impetus to the claim, often by representing conditions in Northern Ireland as being other than they are.

13    Under the cover and pretext of this doctrine of nationalist irredentism on the side of the Republic, terrorist organisations have from time to time attacked Northern Ireland from the territory of the Republic and have been directed in their activities by headquarters in the Republic. It is this, and not any internal differences of religious denomination, that has been the main cause of violent disturbances in Northern Ireland. It has undoubtedly resulted in the Republic being regarded by a large section of the public in Northern Ireland as an enemy country.

14    These events have made concern for its national identity and for security against external attack or internal sedition a major factor in the political life of the Ulster community. This in turn sets important conditions as to what is acceptable in a future form of government. It rules out as widely unacceptable any scheme that involves the imposition of divided allegiance at the highest level of government.

*Events before the Convention*

15    Events leading up to the establishment of the Constitutional Convention require little further comment. A referendum showed that 98 per cent of those voting desired Northern Ireland to remain in partnership with Britain within the United Kingdom. Two Westminster general elections and the Convention election showed that a majority rejected imposed power-sharing and divided allegiance at the top level of government, as provided in the Northern Ireland Constitution Act 1973, hereinafter referred to as the 1973 Constitution Act, and also rejected an institution relationship with the Irish Republic involving joint organs of administration.

[PARTS II and III omitted]

PART IV. LIST OF CONCLUSIONS REACHED BY THE CONVENTION
Consistent with Section 2(1) of the Northern Ireland Act 1974 the Convention worked for the provision of a government of Northern Ireland on the basis of the

only constraint therein i.e., that likely to command the most widespread acceptance throughout the community in Northern Ireland.

It was noted with approval that in the Northern Ireland Act 1974 the United Kingdom Parliament did not impose any constraints such as power sharing in an executive or all-Ireland institutions.

Therefore it concluded.

### Constitutional basis

1   That Northern Ireland should be administered by an elected body and an executive empowered to legislate and govern and to be known as the Parliament and Government of Northern Ireland.

### Governor

2   That legislation affecting devolved matters should be enacted by the Queen in Parliament and Her Majesty should be represented in Northern Ireland by a Governor appointed by Her Majesty to exercise such constitutional functions and perform such ceremonial duties as She is not able to fulfil in person.

### Privy Council

3   That there should be a Privy Council of Northern Ireland in which some places should be offered to leading members of major opposition parties.

### Representation at Westminster

4   That the number of Northern Ireland Members of Parliament at Westminster should be increased to between 20 and 24, the boundaries and exact number of the constituencies to be determined by judicial commission on a basis and scale similar to comparable parts of the United Kingdom.

### Office of Secretary of State

5   That the office of the Secretary of State for Northern Ireland should lapse and those services not directly administered by the devolved administration should be the concern of a Secretary of State for the devolved regions or other senior Cabinet Minister.

### Form of legislature and franchise

6   That the Parliament of Northern Ireland should be unicameral and a term should not exceed five years. The Chamber should consist of not less than 78 and not more than 100 members who are British citizens.

7   That the Parliament of Northern Ireland should be able to legislate in matters affecting the franchise, elections and disqualification for membership of that Parliament.

### Functions to be devolved

8　That the devolved government for Northern Ireland should have powers broadly similar to those conferred by the Government of Ireland Act 1920.

### Formation of Northern Ireland government

9　That the formation and operation of the executive should conform to the practices and precedents of the Parliament of the United Kingdom.

10　That the Queen's Representative should invite the leader of the largest parliamentary party or group to form a government.

11　That the selection and dismissal of ministers should be at the discretion of the Prime Minster, who should not be compelled to include members of any particular party or group.

12　That no country ought to be forced to have in its Cabinet any person whose political philosophy and attitudes have revealed his opposition to the very existence of that State.

13　That the Government should be responsible to Parliament and the Cabinet should be collectively responsible for its decisions.

14　That the Prime Minister should be entitled to remain in office until he has ceased to retain the support of a majority in Parliament.

15　That the number of Cabinet Ministers should not exceed eight.

### Committees

16　That a Committee system should be devised to give real and substantial influence to an opposition and to make Parliament more effective.

17　That covering each Department of Government there should be a Departmental Committee of 8 or 10 backbenchers drawn equally from Government and opposition supporters with normal parliamentary voting rights.

18　That each Committee would be involved in the legislative process and scrutiny of Government action relating to its Department.

19　That there should be a Rules Committee drawn from the whole House.

### United Kingdom – Northern Ireland financial relationship: Northern Ireland social and economic priorities

20　That it should be the role of a strong regional government to deal with economic and social problems.

21　That it should be the responsibility of a strong regional government to determine economic and social priorities.

22　That the systems which existed in the latter years of the Northern Ireland Parliament and during the brief lifetime of the Northern Ireland Assembly were unduly restrictive and inhibited local variations.

23　That there should be provision for divergences in approach to spending as compared to the rest of the United Kingdom.

24 That there should be supplementary financial assistance related to Northern Ireland needs from the United Kingdom Government.

25 That there should be scope for some Northern Ireland variations in taxation.

*Human rights*

26 That there should be a Bill of Constitutional Rights to guarantee the stability and integrity of the Northern Ireland Constitution and a general Bill of Rights and Duties to protect the rights of the individual citizen.

*External relations*

27 That external relations should be the responsibility of the Government at Westminster in consultation with the Government of Northern Ireland.

28 That good neighbourly relations should be welcomed but that imposed institutionalised associations with the Republic of Ireland should be rejected.

*The way ahead: continuing political activity*

29 That Her Majesty's Government should make all haste to end the political vacuum, defeat terrorism, and, recognising the political realities, restore devolved Government to Northern Ireland: in the interim the Convention should continue in being as a representative forum of the people of Northern Ireland until the administration is formed, and tender advice to the Secretary of State.

This Convention puts forward these conclusions in the belief that they offer a firm basis upon which all the inhabitants of Northern Ireland can live and work together under the rule of law in peace and justice, participating democratically in all decisions which affect the future of themselves and their families; of Northern Ireland; and of Northern Ireland's position within the United Kingdom.

### 3.2 The Joint Unionist Task Force, 1987

Although it has been described as 'a unionist version of the New Ireland Forum' (Cochrane, 2001: 227), and it was based on extensive consultation with wide sections of the unionist community, the task force comprised only two members of the UUP and one of the DUP, and its report had the status of a confidential document for the leaders of the two parties (only an abridged version was published), who did not embrace it with enthusiasm. It nevertheless offers an important insight into a new strand of unionist thinking, and the main parts of the abridged version are reproduced below (Joint Unionist Task Force, 1987).

HISTORICAL BACKGROUND

Since the late 1960s Unionism has lost a series of vital rounds in the battle to preserve Northern Ireland's position within the United Kingdom.

Much ground was lost during the Civil Rights crisis itself. The highly simplistic notion of Protestant 'guilt' and Catholic 'grievance' persists to the present day, and this despite the fact that since 1972 the government of Northern Ireland has been the exclusive preserve of the Westminster Parliament.

This dismantling of our security base and the fall of Stormont paved the way for a Whitehall machine unashamedly neutral on the issue of the constitutional position. All that has followed since is symptomatic of the policy carved and created by Lord Carrington on behalf of Edward Heath: *'Her Majesty's Government has no desire to impede the realisation of Irish unity'.*

The minority Labour Government of James Callaghan offered a brief respite.

Increased parliamentary representation and a more robust security policy did much to reassure Unionists: Direct Rule was apparently giving way to gradual integration and the Conservative Party in Opposition had elected a leader who seemed set to complete the process.

However, Article One of the Anglo-Irish Agreement confirms that under Mrs Thatcher's administration the wheel has turned full circle.

It is a matter of record that Airey Neave's Ulster policy died with him just weeks before the 1979 General Election.

Mr Atkins' round table conference, followed by Mr Prior's scheme for Rolling Devolution, were a far cry from the Regional Council promised in the Conservative Party's 1979 Manifesto.

But if some Unionists were slow to accept even this evidence of a move away from Integration, Mrs. Thatcher's rhetoric and her ability to distance herself from decisions of her own Government, provide at least part explanation.

For a long time Mrs Thatcher's pragmatism was kept well concealed from her own natural Conservative supporters. Having declared herself *'rock firm for the Union'* and Northern Ireland *'as British as Finchley'*, it isn't hard to see why beleaguered Unionists chose for so long to give her the benefit of the doubt.

Mrs Thatcher, some rationalised, was consumed by economic concerns and would hardly have addressed herself to the peripheral issue of Northern Ireland; policy pursued in her name certainly didn't reflect her personal view and in all probability had not obtained her seal of approval.

When Mrs Thatcher forthrightly rejected the principal findings of the Forum Report, the exponents of this view proclaimed themselves well satisfied.

The Union appeared once more secure!

With hindsight it may be said that Mrs Thatcher did Northern Ireland few favours with her famous '*out, out, out*' declaration. Whilst significant policy initiatives were signalled by the two Unionist parties in 'The Way Forward' and 'Ulster The Future Assured', they were not pursued with sufficient vigour.

Meanwhile the Anglo-Irish dialogue was continuing and by the time Mr Molyneaux and Dr Paisley offered their alternative British/Irish scenario in August 1985, the dye was cast.

Mrs Thatcher was set on confrontation with the Unionist community, and media critics, quite unjustifiably, said Unionists had offered too little, too late.

To Unionists themselves of course the opposite appeared all too obviously the case.

Few outsiders can understand the bitterness and indignation of Unionists unfairly characterised as the guilty party in the Ulster conflict.

A supporter of the police and a devotee of the democratic process, the average Unionist has had to witness the impotence of lawful authority and the inadequacy of democratic safeguards in face of violent political rebellion.

The Stormont Parliament had been successfully discredited as the keeper of Protestant privilege. Its demise paved the way for a form of colonial rule which violates the fundamental rights and entitlements of all the people of Northern Ireland as citizens of the United Kingdom.

Security powers were removed from Stormont and the RUC placed under the direct control of a Westminster which more than once has sanctioned negotiations with the Provisional IRA.

In Town Halls across the province the denial of real local democracy pales beside the presence of an army of Sinn Fein Councillors bent on the destruction of Northern Ireland '*with an armalite in one hand and a ballot paper in the other*'.

The catalogue of injury and insult is endless. The net effect is a community increasingly confused as to what is and what is not acceptable in a democratic society; a community torn between loyalty to the law and established order, and the compelling conclusion that violence and anarchy are the likeliest route to political reward.

At various times in the past eighteen years it has looked as if the populous might take matters into their own hands. Indeed they did so in 1974. Unfortunately the

Sunningdale Agreement fell without any understanding or agreement as to what should take its place.

Murder at Darkley and a succession of other atrocities brought the province periodically back to the brink. However no single issue or event captured the public mood or provided the dynamic for change evidenced in 1974 until the Anglo-Irish Agreement.

The Unionist leadership in Northern Ireland reacted to the Agreement with clarity and conviction.

On the evening of 15 November 1985 Mr Molyneaux described it as '*the beginning of the end of the Union as we have known it*'. He and Dr Paisley pledged to resist to the end 'an emergent joint authority' and that same evening set in motion a chain of events designed to manifest the absence of Unionist consent for the system by which Northern Ireland was to be governed.

Any doubt about the attitude of the community generally was effectively dispelled at the City Hall on Saturday 23 November 1985.

Some 203,000 people rallied to the joint leadership's call and gave an emphatic 'NO' to the Agreement. Less than two months later Unionist candidates received the endorsement of 420,000 electors for their proposed campaign of resistance.

The leadership and the community were united in an historic purpose, and it is salutary to recall that those most hostile to Unionist unity conveniently and consistently ignore the fact that Unionist politicians have acted at all times in accordance with a policy put to, and endorsed by, the people. All those we met confirmed their view that this unity of purpose is entrenched in the community at large.

CONCLUSIONS

We have found absolutely no lessening in the Unionist community's antipathy to the Anglo-Irish Agreement. At the same time our investigations have unearthed deep disquiet about the current protest campaign and a simple disbelief that on its own it can or will persuade Mrs Thatcher to change course.

There is recognition that Northern Ireland's position within the Union has been steadily and successfully undermined since the late 1960s.

Our various discussions pointed to the need for action to arrest a widely perceived drift in our affairs. This demand for action is tempered by a realistic appraisal of the limits of Unionism's negotiating strength and, on the other hand, by anxiety that a commitment to negotiate 'a reasonable alternative' should not be construed, in London or elsewhere, as evidence of a willingness to come to terms with the Agreement itself.

The temptation in such circumstances might be to do nothing. However we would consider this the ultimate abdication of responsibility.

It seems to us that those who counsel against negotiation must make plain the alternative means by which they propose to determine the future of the people of Northern Ireland. Reliance on other people to undertake a campaign of violence which can be disowned, but from which can be extracted political advantage, would be disreputable and dishonest in the extreme.

For our part we are confident that Unionists have the ability to recognise the point in negotiation beyond which the search for consensus about the future government of Northern Ireland becomes damaging to the Unionist interest.

Negotiation need not be the precursor to 'sell out' or 'betrayal'. Indeed the assumption that Unionists must inevitably be bested in any negotiations can only reflect the judgment of those who have already sold out and accepted defeat. We must give hope to a community dangerously immune to disappointment and defeat.

Our opinion survey confirmed that the policy of total integration continues to attract substantial support in the Unionist community. However, the survey also confirms our view that the Whitehall establishment is strongly opposed to such a course and that devolution is the more attainable objective.

All the principal parties in Britain favour Irish unity, which cause has been advanced and enhanced by fifteen years of Direct Rule.

We cannot believe that constitutional security is to be found in a campaign to persuade mainland political parties to extend their organisation to Northern Ireland. We believe that only a government representative of and answerable to the people of the province can properly understand and respond to the continuing terrorist campaign. Devolved-government therefore is our objective and whilst we hope this will prove attainable within the context of the United Kingdom, Unionists would be wise and prudent to anticipate that it might not.

We are convinced and agreed that the Anglo-Irish Agreement represents a fundamental and unacceptable change in the constitutional relationship between Great Britain and Northern Ireland. We have no doubt that the Anglo-Irish Conference is tantamount to joint authority and that its early demise is vital if we are to arrest a quickening process leading to our inevitable absorption in an Irish unitary State. *Having sworn never to accept the Agreement as a basis for continued membership of the United Kingdom, we must ascertain what alternative terms for the Union can be found.*

Recognising the inadequacies of the existing protest campaign we propose the creation of a Unionist Convention to construct and lead a renewed campaign to manifest the absence of consent for the arrangements by which Northern Ireland is presently governed.

In addition we suggest that the Unionist Convention be invited to endorse the demand for an alternative to and replacement of the Anglo-Irish Agreement, and the commencement of 'without prejudice' discussions with Her Majesty's Government thereto.

We see a clear distinction between such discussions and formal negotiations, and ask you to appoint a panel to establish whether a base for formal negotiations exists or can be established.

In order to protect and reserve your position we recommend that the said panel be appointed *only* to consult and report.

In the course of our investigation it has become apparent that some people fail to understand the nature and basis of negotiation. We repeat our view that Unionists would be foolhardy to reveal their hand ahead of negotiation and whilst two of the parties, Her Majesty's Government and the SDLP, continue to set the pre-condition that political development in Northern Ireland must fall within the framework of the Anglo-Irish Agreement.

However we submit that in earnest of your desire to find a reasonable alternative you should signal that *no matter* could or should be precluded from any negotiations.

In addition, and in order to prevent any misunderstanding or confusion amongst your own supporters, we believe you should draw public notice to plans and proposals you have previously offered as a base for negotiation.

Specifically in this regard we have in mind the Catherwood Plan in which both Unionist parties abandoned pure majority rule as the price for Devolution, and your correspondence with the Prime Minister in August and September 1985 in which you pledged your willingness to negotiate a British/Irish framework for the promotion of friendship and co-operation within these islands.

In our opinion this emphasis on Unionist flexibility must be balanced by clear and repeated warning that the expedient of compromise and barter can only succeed if it is a two way process.

In advance of any negotiation we feel it must be made plain that failure to arrive at consensus would leave the Unionist leadership no alternative but to seek an entirely new base for Northern Ireland *outside* the present constitutional context.

To this end it should be observed that Article 1 of the Anglo-Irish Agreement itself purports to recognise and safeguard the right of the people of Northern Ireland to self-determination.

In reality of course Article 1 concerns itself only with a decision by the majority of the people of Northern Ireland either to remain within the United Kingdom or alternatively to join the Irish Republic. However it seems to us inescapable that the same Article could be invoked to give effect to a majority decision in favour of some other alternative.

We offer no precise or definite suggestion as to what that alternative might be. But we are convinced that, whatever the intentions of the Governments in London and Dublin, membership of the United Kingdom or membership of an Irish Republic are *not* the only options available to the people of Northern Ireland.

In this regard we propose the appointment of a Special Commission to consider and advise upon those alternative constitutional models, their implications vis à vis future relationships with Britain and the Irish Republic, and the steps by which an alternative constitutional arrangement might be secured and sustained.

# Notes

*Chapter One    Introduction (pp. 1–29)*

Acknowledgement: I would like to thank Paul Arthur, Richard English, Tom Garvin and Jennifer Todd for comments on an earlier draft.

1  A number of biographical and autobiographical accounts also reflect on the peace process; see, for example, Mitchell, 1999.

2  From 1922 to 1979, unionists on average won nine more seats than nationalists at Westminster elections; but this reduced to a net advantage of six seats in the two most recent elections. The significance of this obviously depends on the balance of power in the House of Commons; and account must be taken of the fact that Sinn Féin MPs refuse to sit there.

3  The Irish government decision to open consulates in Edinburgh and Cardiff may be seen as recognition of this new reality; on the implications of devolution, see Aughey, 2001; Bogdanor, 2001.

4  Dáil debates, vol. 13, 7–10 Dec. 1925, cols. 1313–1673. For the views of the anti-Treaty opposition, see *An Phoblacht*, 11 Dec. 1925; in its own reaction and in its reports on speeches (including one by de Valera) at a major protest meeting, the issue of the Council of Ireland was entirely overshadowed by more general attacks on partition and on the boundary commission. The Northern Ireland Labour Party protested against the fate of the council, at some cost to itself in terms of hostility from its pro-union support base (Mitchell, 1974: 221).

5  The only non-Unionist members ever appointed were Harry Midgely, an independent who had been a member of the Northern Ireland Labour Party (1944–9), David Bleakley of the Northern Ireland Labour Party (1971–2) and Gabriel Newe, an independent pro-Union junior minister and the only Catholic to hold government office (1971–2).

6  Unionists in Leinster, Munster and Connacht organised after 1885 as the Irish Loyal and Patriotic Union (later, Irish Unionist Alliance); separate developments in Ulster culminated in the foundation of the Ulster Unionist Council in 1905; see Buckland, 1972, 1973.

7  Very close party-state relations (leading to a near equation of the state with the party) were a pronounced characteristic of the former Communist-governed states; within liberal democracies, the positions of the Christian Democrats in Italy (1945–94) and the Liberal Democrats in Japan (1955–93, and subsequently) were similar.

8  Sinn Féin, Republican Sinn Féin and the Workers' Party all claim to have been founded in 1905, and continued to number their annual conventions accordingly. The history of Sinn Féin is covered unevenly in the many studies of the IRA; see Bell, 1997, for a recent overview.

9  For discussions of the IRA, see Bell, 2000; Coogan, 1995; O'Brien, 1995; Patterson, 1997; Taylor, 1997.

10   O'Brien was elected to the Northern Ireland Forum of 1996–8 as a representative of the anti-agreement United Kingdom Unionist Party led by Robert McCartney, but resigned in 1998 (though he subsequently held the position of honorary president of the party) after suggesting that Irish unity might be the most appropriate long-term solution for Northern Irish unionists.

11   For the text of the Downing Street declaration, see Cox, Guelke and Stephen, 2000: 327–30; on the peace process, see Mansergh, 2000; de Bréadún, 2001.

12   For a reassessment of the significance of Lemass's remark, which sets it in the context of attitudes towards a particular constitution rather than towards constitutionalism as such, see Horgan, 1997: 55–7.

13   Between 1927 and 1933, the Fianna Fáil share of the combined 'ex-Sinn Féin' vote rose from 48 per cent to 62 per cent; between the Westminster elections of 1997 and 2001, the Sinn Féin share of the combined nationalist vote rose from 40 per cent to 51 per cent.

14   On the early biconfessional character of Alliance, which the party managed subsequently to maintain, see McAllister and Wilson, 1978.

## Chapter Nine    *The growth of new unionism (pp. 95–105)*

1   Clearly, there are some unionist politicians who despise Trimble-style politics, but who are themselves extremely articulate and able (McCartney, 2001b); and clearly there are scholars sceptical about precisely how new the 'new unionism' will actually prove to be (O'Dowd, 1998).

2   Sammy Wilson, interview with Feargal Cochrane, 20 November 1991, quoted in Cochrane, 1997: 71.

3   For one such set of defences, see Foster, 1995.

4   As Ian Paisley put it: 'we have in embryo a condominium in the [1985] Anglo-Irish Agreement and in the [1993] Downing Street Declaration' (interview with the author, Belfast, 21 February 1994).

## Chapter Ten    *The emergence of new loyalism (pp. 106–22)*

1   I wish to acknowledge an ESRC grant (Award L327253058) that I received with Jon Tonge from the University of Salford to carry out this work. Some of the interview material included in this chapter was carried out under this project.

2   Interview with David Ervine, Belfast, summer 2000

3   *Ibid.*

4   See various editions of *The Orange Standard* in 2001 and the DUP website: http://www.dup.org.

5   For further discussion of the character of new loyalism, see Democratic Dialogue, 1996; Jacobson, 1997; McAuley, 1994a, 1994b, 1995, 1996, 1997b, 1997c, 1998, 1999, 2000; Sales, 1997a, 1997b, 1998; Rooney, 1992, 2000.

6   See various editions of *The Volunteer, Leading the Way, The Wright View.*

*Chapter Twelve    Conclusion (pp. 132–54)*

Acknowledgement: I would like to thank Paul Arthur, Yvonne Galligan, Tom Garvin, Allan Leonard, Claire Mitchell and Jennifer Todd for comments on an earlier draft.

1    In a late echo of this perspective, one Sinn Féin supporter is reported to have shouted 'Free State b\*\*\*s!' as Fianna Fáil narrowly defeated the Sinn Féin candidate for the last seat in Dublin Central in the general election of May 2002; see Frank McNally in *The Irish Times*, 20 May 2002.

2    For a systematic analysis of Paisley's theology from a committed Protestant perspective, see Cooke, 1996; see also Smyth, 1987: 115–35 for an empathetic but detached discussion of Paisleyism as a marriage of Scottish Protestant radicalism with Ulster loyalism (or Orangeism), with some influence from American fundamentalism.

3    For early expressions, see Ulster Vanguard, 1972, and Lindsay, 1972; for a discussion of later cultural developments, see Nic Craith, 2002, especially pp. 93–113.

4    For more detailed analysis, see Bruce, 1986: 292–7.

5    It also registered a by-election victory in Derry City in 1913. Liberal Unionists were rather more successful, normally holding four seats after 1892.

6    Between 1914 and 1959, the Liberals contested only one Westminster election in Northern Ireland (that of 1929, when they put forward six candidates); they put forward one candidate in 1959, four in 1964, three in 1966, and two in 1970, the last general election contested by the party. The party first contested an election to the Northern Ireland House of Commons in 1929 (with four candidates), and contested the Queen's University seat from 1958 until its abolition in 1969 (Sheelagh Murnaghan held one of the four seats here for the Liberals from 1961 to 1969); it contested three additional seats in 1962 and in 1965 and two in 1969 (calculated from Walker, 1978, 1992).

7    On the history of the party in Northern Ireland, see Farr, 2002; the overlap between the last days of the Liberals and the early days of the Alliance Party is discussed in Loretto, 2002.

8    David Trimble was unable to obtain the required majority among those members of the assembly designated 'unionist', and was elected only following a decision first by the Women's Coalition and then by the Alliance Party to redesignate from 'other' to 'unionist' or 'nationalist'; the 'unionist' members of these parties then supported Trimble, securing him the required communal majority.

9    On divisions within the old Northern Ireland Labour Party, see Cradden, 1993: 30–3; the departure of an earlier pro-union tendency led by Harry Midgley is discussed in Walker, 1985: 114–46

10    The NILP seats since 1949 have all been in Belfast, in the unionist constituencies of Oldpark (1958–69), Pottinger (1958–65), Victoria (1958–62) and Woodvale (1958–62), with a further seat in the nationalist Falls constituency (1969; won by Paddy Devlin); see Elliott, 1973.

11    See Northern Ireland Labour Party, 1976. The closest that it came to defining its position on the national question at this time was expressed in clause II, point 5 of which specified as an aim: 'to establish a government for the people founded on the principles of social justice, sustained by democratic institutions, which will guarantee full civil and religious liberties to all citizens'.

12    Following the merger of the Women's Alliance in Iceland with other parties in 1999, no national parliament in Western Europe has a women's party.

13    For a detailed overview, see Urquhart, 2000: 46–84; for an outline of this movement in the context of the development of the Unionist Party, see Harbinson, 1973: 61–3.

14  On the background to this tendency within unionism, see Coulter, 1996.

15  For a discussion of these reactions, see Aughey, 1989, especially pp. 99–189.

16  For a perceptive analysis of Sinn Féin's capacity to carry its supporters down this new political path, see Feeney, 2002: 429–42.

17  Already in 1983, 34 per cent of respondents in the Republic saw the Irish nation as constituting 26 counties (63 per cent saw it as comprising 32); and only 41 per cent saw the people of Northern Ireland as 'Irish'; see Cox, 1985.

18  For example, in the course of an election campaign in late 1982 Garret FitzGerald's support for an all-Ireland police force was used vigorously against him by a Fianna Fáil opposition that sought to play on southern fears of police from the north exercising authority in the south; see FitzGerald, 1991: 419–20.

19  See, for example, Sheehy, 1955; for early expressions of the 'two nations' perspective, see, on the nationalist side, Chanel, 1907, and, on the unionist side, Monypenny, 1913.

20  See Irish Communist Organisation, 1969, 1970, 1972, which document the development of Ulster's distinctiveness; this body later became the British and Irish Communist Organisation.


*Appendix (pp. 155–95)*


1   The founding ard-fheis had decided 'that the economic programme of the First Dáil be embodied in the constitution of Fianna Fáil' (*An Phoblacht*, 17 Dec. 1926); the final wording cited here is from Fianna Fáil, 1929. The first sentence was later changed to 'Fianna Fáil is a National Movement. Its aims are'.

2   Irish Labour Party and Trade Union Congress, *Official report of proceedings of the twenty-seventh annual meeting held in the Mansion House, Dublin, Aug. 1, 2, 3 and 4, 1921* (Dublin: National Executive, 1921). A minor verbal change was made in 1925, and in 1929 further minor changes were made; see Irish Labour Party and Trade Union Congress, *35th Annual Report, 1928–9*.

3   Irish Labour Party, *First Annual Report 1930–1* (Dublin: Labour Party, 1931)

4   This was authorised at the 1934 congress; see Labour Party, *Fourth Annual Report for 1934*; for the new text, see *Eighth annual report for 1938*; in addition, clause (d), now renumbered as (f), was amended so that the reference to unity by agreement was dropped: the first 15 words now read: 'to secure in a Workers' Republic the political union of Northern Ireland with the Saorstát'. In 1940, this was replaced by the words 'to secure the political union of Ireland', and at the same time clause (b) was deleted and the expression 'a Worker's Republic' in clause (a) was replaced by 'a Republican form of government'; Labour Party, *Ninth Annual Report for 1939*.

5   This is the text as it was in 1963; see Chubb, 1964: 226–8. By 1972, the word 'socialist' had been inserted in front of 'republican' in clause (a). No other changes of significance had occurred by 1979; see Chubb, 1983: 142–3.

6   This was followed by a statement of more detailed aims, omitted here; see *Sinn Féin* (weekly newspaper), 7 Sept. 1907.

7   Sinn Féin, 1924. This was preceded by a preamble that referred to the proclamation of the republic during the 1916 rising and the declaration of the republic by the first Dáil in 1919.

8   Workers' Party, 1993. At the same time, the secessionist Democratic Left made only oblique reference to Northern Ireland in its new constitution, in which it called for 'the

development of a democratic pluralist, socialist society in Ireland' and committed itself to 'an active commitment to peace and political reconciliation in Ireland in accordance with international conventions on human rights both individual and collective'; Democratic Left, 1993.

9   See Sinn Féin, 1970. It also included the standard preamble referring to 1916 and 1919 and defined as fundamental principles 'that the allegiance of Irishmen and Irishwomen is due to the sovereign Irish Republic proclaimed in 1916' and 'that the sovereignty and unity of the Republic are inalienable and non-justiciable'. A fourth aim was later added: '(d) to promote the restoration of the Irish language and Irish culture and the widest knowledge of Ireland's history; to make Irish citizens conscious and proud of their traditional and cultural heritage; and to educate the citizens of the Republic in their rights and responsibilities as citizens'. In 1983, the reference to 'Christian principles' in clause (c) was replaced by a reference to 'Irish republican and socialist principles'. The constitution of Republican Sinn Féin had almost identical objectives, though with some variation in emphasis. It called for 'the establishment of a *federal* democratic socialist republic' (emphasis is added; the word 'federal' had appeared for some years in the Provisional Sinn Féin constitution, but had been dropped by the early 1980s). Its fourth aim was also rather stronger: '(d) to establish the Irish language as the primary means of communication in the Republic, to teach Irish history in such as way as will foster pride in our cultural heritage and a sense of rights and responsibilities in our people as citizens of the Republic'.

10   Harbinson, 1973: 35; Ulster Unionist Council, *Yearbook*, 1938, 1939.

11   Ulster Unionist Council, *Yearbook*, 1943, 1974.

12   Ulster Unionist Council, *Yearbook*, 1976, 1980.

13   Progressive Unionist Party, 1996; an earlier version varied slightly from this, and did not contain clause 2 (Progressive Unionist Party, 1985). A parallel statement of aims is more specific:

> To secure peace and reconciliation within this region of the United Kingdom
> To establish a local parliament in this region, representative of all interested parties and groups
> To work actively for political, social and economic advancement to secure a better life for all our people
> To secure the termination of the Anglo-Irish agreement through the introduction of new agreed structures, within an elected devolved government
> To pursue new and established policies through a broadly representative committee system of government i.e. sharing responsibility
>
> (Progressive Unionist Party, 1997).

14   Alliance Party of Northern Ireland, 1974. In 1999 the constitution was amended as follows:

> 1.2 The Party was founded on the basis of the statement of principles dated 21 April 1970.
> 1.3 The objectives of the Party shall be to heal the bitter divisions in our community and to promote the policies of the party as determined by the Council.

15   Aiken papers, UCD archive, P104 /8670. The others attending the 1971 meeting were President de Valera, Frank Aiken and Sean MacBride. The fund administered by the committee continued after this date.

16   'Summary', in All-Party Anti-Partition Conference, 1949: 16.

17   Chapter 5, 'Framework for a new Ireland: present realities and future requirements', in New Ireland Forum, 1984.

# References

Adams, Gerry (1982) *Falls memories.* Dingle: Brandon.

Adams, Gerry (1986) *The politics of Irish freedom.* Dingle: Brandon.

Adams, Gerry (1996) *Before the dawn: an autobiography.* London: Heinemann.

Alliance Party of Northern Ireland (1974) *Constitution and rules. Adopted October 23, 1970; amended March 1974.* Belfast: Alliance Party.

Alliance Party of Northern Ireland (1988) *Governing with consent.* Belfast: Alliance Party.

All-Party Anti-Partition Conference ([1949]) *Ireland's right to unity: the case stated by the All-Party Anti-Partition Conference, Mansion House, Dublin, Ireland.* 2nd ed. Dublin: Mansion House Committee, n.d.

Anderson, James and James Goodman, eds (1998) *(Dis) Agreeing Ireland: contexts, obstacles, hopes.* London: Pluto.

Apter, David (1992) *Democracy, violence and emancipatory movements: notes for a theory of inversionary discourse.* Geneva: UNRISD paper, no. 44.

Apter, David, ed. (1997a) *The legitimization of violence.* London: Macmillan, in association with UNRISD.

Apter, David (1997b) 'Political violence in analytical perspective', pp. 1–32 in Apter, 1997a.

Arthur, Paul (1995) 'Some thoughts on transition: a comparative view of the peace processes in South Africa and Northern Ireland', *Government and Opposition* 30 (1): 48–59.

Arthur, Paul (1997) '"Reading" violence: Ireland', pp. 234–91 in Apter, 1997a.

Arthur, Paul (2000) *Special relationships: Britain, Ireland and the Northern Ireland problem.* Belfast: Blackstaff.

Aughey, Arthur (1989) *Under siege: Ulster unionism and the Anglo-Irish agreement.* London: Hurst.

Aughey, Arthur (1991) 'Unionism and self-determination', pp. 1–16 in Roche and Barton, 1991.

Aughey, Arthur (2001) *Nationalism, devolution, and the challenge to the United Kingdom state.* London: Pluto.

Aughey, Arthur and Duncan Morrow, eds (1996) *Northern Ireland politics.* London: Longman.

Ballymacarret Arts and Cultural Society (1999) *Orangeism and the Twelfth: what it means to me.* Newtownabbey: Island Pamphlets no. 24.

Ballymacarret Think Tank (1999a) *Puppets no more.* Newtownabbey: Island Pamphlets, no. 21.

Ballymacarret Think Tank (1999b) *Beyond King Billy?* Newtownabbey: Island Pamphlets, no. 22.

Bartlett, Thomas (1998) 'Ulster 1600–2000: posing the question?', *Bullán* 4 (1): 5–18.

Bell, J. Bowyer (1990) *IRA tactics and targets. an analysis of tactical aspects of the armed struggle 1969–1989.* Dublin: Poolbeg.

Bell, J. Bowyer (1997) *The secret army: the IRA.* 3rd ed. New Brunswick, NJ: Transaction Publishers.

Bell, J. Bowyer (2000) *The IRA 1968–2000: analysis of a secret army.* London: Frank Cass.

Bew, Paul, Peter Gibbon and Henry Patterson (1996) *Northern Ireland, 1921–1996: political forces and social classes.* Rev. ed. London: Serif.

Bew, Paul and Gordon Gillespie (1999) *Northern Ireland: a chronology of the troubles 1968–1999.* New ed. Dublin: Gill & Macmillan.

Birrell, Derek and Alan Murie (1980) *Policy and government in Northern Ireland: lessons of devolution.* Dublin: Gill & Macmillan.

Bloomfield, David (1998) *Political dialogue in Northern Ireland: the Brooke Initiative, 1989–92.* Basingstoke: Macmillan.

Boal, Fred, J. A. Campbell and D. N. Livingstone (1991) 'The Protestant mosaic: a majority of minorities', pp. 99–129 in Roche and Barton (1991).

Bogdanor, Vernon (2001) *Devolution in the United Kingdom.* New ed. Oxford: Oxford University Press.

Bowman, John (1982) *De Valera and the Ulster question, 1917–1973.* Oxford: Clarendon.

Boyle, J. W. (1962) 'The Belfast Protestant Association and the Independent Orange Order, 1901–10', *Irish Historical Studies* 13 (50): 117–52.

Brady, Ciaran (1994) *Interpreting Irish history.* Dublin: Irish Academic Press.

Breen, Richard (1996) 'Who wants a united Ireland? Constitutional preferences among Catholics and Protestants', pp. 33–48 in Richard Breen, Paula Devine and Lizanne Dowds, eds, *Social attitudes in Northern Ireland: the fifth report.* Belfast: Appletree.

Brewer, John D., with Gareth I. Higgins (1998) *Anti-Catholicism in Northern Ireland, 1600–1998: the mote and the beam.* Basingstoke: Macmillan.

Bruce, Steve (1986) *God save Ulster! The religion and politics of Paisleyism.* Oxford: Clarendon.

Bruce, Steve (1992) *The red hand: Protestant paramilitaries in Northern Ireland.* Oxford: Oxford University Press.

Bruce, Steve (1994) *The edge of the union: the Ulster loyalist political vision.* Oxford: Oxford University Press.

Bryan, Dominic, T. G. Fraser and Seamus Dunn (1995) *Political rituals: loyalist parades in Portadown.* Coleraine: University of Ulster.

Buckland, Patrick (1972) *Irish unionism: one: the Anglo-Irish and the new Ireland 1885–1922.* Dublin: Gill & Macmillan.

Buckland, Patrick (1973) *Irish unionism: two: Ulster unionism and the origins of Northern Ireland 1886–1922.* Dublin: Gill & Macmillan.

Burton, Frank (1978) *The politics of legitimacy: struggles in a Belfast community.* London, Routledge & Kegan Paul.

CAIN (2002a) A chronology of the conflict – 1968 to the present. Available http://cain.ulst.ac.uk/othelem/chron.htm [2002–03–15].

CAIN (2002b) Background on the Northern Ireland conflict. Available http://cain.ulst.ac.uk/othelem/index.html [2002–03–15].

Campbell, T. J. (1941) *Fifty years of Ulster.* Belfast: The Irish News.

Carty, Anthony (1998) 'The Irish constitution, international law and the northern question: the need for radical thinking', pp. 97–105 in Tim Murphy and Patrick Twomey, eds, *Ireland's evolving constitution, 1937–97: collected essays.* Oxford: Hart.

Chanel [pseud. Arthur Clery] (1907) *The idea of a nation.* Dublin: James Duffy.

Chubb, Basil (1964) *A source book of Irish government.* Dublin: Institute of Public Administration.

Chubb, Basil, ed. (1983) *A source book of Irish government.* Rev. ed. Dublin: Institute of Public Administration.

Coakley, John (1998) 'Religion, ethnic identity and the Protestant minority in the Republic', pp. 86–106 in William Crotty and David E. Schmitt, eds, *Ireland and the politics of change*. London: Longman.

Coakley, John and Michael Gallagher, eds (1999) *Politics in the Republic of Ireland*. 3rd ed. London: Routledge.

Cochrane, Feargal (1997) *Unionist politics and the politics of unionism since the Anglo-Irish agreement*. Cork: Cork University Press.

Cochrane, Feargal (2001) *Unionist politics and the politics of unionism since the Anglo-Irish agreement*. Rev. ed. Cork: Cork University Press.

Constitution Unit (2002) Monitoring devolution: quarterly reports. Available http://www.ucl.ac.uk/constitution-unit/leverh/index.htm [2002–03–15].

Coogan, Tim Pat (1995) *The IRA*. New ed. London: HarperCollins.

Cooke, Dennis (1996) *Persecuting zeal: a portrait of Ian Paisley*. Dingle: Brandon.

Coulter, Colin (1996) 'Direct rule and the unionist middle classes', pp. 169–91 in English and Walker, 1996.

Cox, Michael, Adrian Guelke and Fiona Stephen, eds (2000) *A farewell to arms? From 'long war' to long peace in Northern Ireland*. Manchester: Manchester University Press.

Cox, W. Harvey (1985) 'Who wants a united Ireland?', *Government and Opposition* 20 (1): 29–47.

Cradden, Terry (1993) *Trade unionism, socialism and politics: the labour movement in Northern Ireland 1939–1953*. Belfast: December Publications.

Cunningham, Michael (1997) 'The political language of John Hume', *Irish Political Studies* 12: 13–23.

Cusack, Jim and Henry McDonald (1997) *UVF*. Dublin: Poolbeg.

Davis, Richard P. (1974) *Arthur Griffith and non-violent Sinn Fein*. Dublin: Anvil.

de Bréadún, Deaglán (2001) *The far side of revenge: making peace in Northern Ireland*. Cork: Collins.

Democratic Dialogue (1996) *Power, politics, positionings: women in Northern Ireland*. Report 4, Belfast: Democratic Dialogue.

Democratic Left (1993) *Constitution and rules (as adopted at founding conference and confirmed at the 1993 ADC)*. Dublin: Democratic Left.

Democratic Left (1994) *Setting a new agenda: a framework for agreement on Northern Ireland*. Dublin: Democratic Left.

Donoghue, D. (1981), 'Inside the Maze: legitimizing heirs to the men of 1916', *The Listener*, 3 Sept.

Dunn, Seamus and Valerie Morgan (1994) *Protestant alienation in Northern Ireland: a preliminary survey*. Coleraine: Centre for the Study of Conflict, University of Ulster.

Elliott, Marianne (2000) *The Catholics of Ulster: a history*. London: Allen Lane, Penguin.

Elliott, Sydney (1973) *Northern Ireland parliamentary election results 1921–1972*. Chichester: Political Reference Publications.

Elliott, Sydney (1997) 'The referenda and assembly elections in Northern Ireland', *Irish Political Studies* 14: 138–49.

Elliott, Sydney (1999) 'The Northern Ireland Forum / entry to negotiations election 1996', *Irish Political Studies* 12: 111–22.

Elliott, Sydney and W. D. Flackes (1999) *Northern Ireland: a political directory, 1968–1999*. 5th ed. Belfast: Blackstaff.

English, Richard (1996) 'The same people with different relatives? Modern scholarship, unionism and the Irish nation', pp. 220–35 in English and Walker, 1996.

English, Richard (1998) *Ernie O'Malley: IRA intellectual.* Oxford: Oxford University Press.

English, Richard and Graham Walker, eds (1996) *Unionism and modern Ireland: new perspectives on politics and culture.* Basingstoke: Macmillan.

English, Richard and Michael Kenny, eds (2000) *Rethinking British decline.* Basingstoke: Macmillan.

Errera, Roger (1999) 'Memory, history and justice in divided societies: the unfinished dialogue between Mnemosyne and Clio', paper read at a Conference on 'Constitution-making, conflict and transition in divided societies', Bellagio, Italy, Feb.

Evans, Geoffrey and Brendan O'Leary (2000) 'Northern Irish voters and the British-Irish Agreement: foundations of a stable consociational settlement?', *Political Quarterly* 71: 78–101.

Fanning, Ronan (2001) 'Playing it cool: the response of the British and Irish governments to the crisis in Northern Ireland, 1968–69', *Irish Studies in International Affairs* 12: 57–85.

Farr, Berkley (2002) 'Liberalism in unionist Northern Ireland', *Journal of Liberal Democrat History* (33): 29–32.

Farrell, Michael (1980) *Northern Ireland: the Orange state.* London: Pluto.

Farren, Sean and Robert F. Mulvihill (2000) *Paths to a settlement in Northern Ireland.* Gerrards Cross: Colin Smythe.

Fearon, Kate (1999) *Women's work: the story of the Northern Ireland Women's Coalition.* Belfast: Blackstaff.

Fearon, Kate, and Monica McWilliams (2000) 'Swimming against the mainstream: the Northern Ireland Women's Coalition', pp. 117–37 in Carmel Roulston and Celia Davies, eds, *Gender, democracy and inclusion in Northern Ireland.* Basingstoke: Palgrave.

Feeney, Brian (2002) *Sinn Féin: a hundred turbulent years.* Dublin: O'Brien.

Fianna Fáil (1929) *Córiú Fhianna Fáil* [as passed by the Ard-fheis in 1929], UCD, Aiken papers, P104/1968.

Fianna Fáil (1996) *Córú agus rialacha: constitution and rules revised 1996.* Dublin: Fianna Fáil.

Fine Gael (1963) *Constitution and rules.* Dublin: Fine Gael National Council.

Fine Gael (1979) *Ireland: our future together.* Dublin: Fine Gael.

Finlay, Fergus (1998), *Snakes and ladders.* Dublin: New Island Books.

FitzGerald, Garret (1991) *All in a life: an autobiography.* Dublin: Gill & Macmillan.

Forde, Michael (1987) *Constitutional law of Ireland.* Cork: Mercier.

Fortnight (1988) Coopers and Lybrand poll for *Fortnight* and UTV, reported *Fortnight* no. 261.

Forum for Peace and Reconciliation (1996) *Paths to a political settlement: realities, principles and requirements. Final paper of the drafting committee of the Forum for Peace and Reconciliation.* Dublin: Forum for Peace and Reconciliation; available http://www.irlgov.ie/iveagh/angloirish/forum/final.html [2002–05–10].

Foster, John Wilson, ed. (1995) *The idea of the union: statements and critiques in support of the union of Great Britain and Northern Ireland.* Vancouver, BC: Belcouver Press.

Gallagher, Michael (1982) *The Irish Labour Party in transition 1957–82.* Manchester: Manchester University Press.

Gallagher, Michael (1990) 'Do Ulster unionists have a right to self-determination?', *Irish Political Studies* 5: 11–30.

Galligan, Yvonne, Eilís Ward and Rick Wilford, eds (1999) *Contesting politics: women in Ireland, North and South*. Boulder, CO: Westview.

Garland, Roy (2001) *Gusty Spence*. Belfast: Blackstaff.

Garvaghy Residents (1999) *Garvaghy: a community under siege*. Belfast: Beyond the Pale.

Garvin, Tom (1996) *1922: the birth of Irish democracy*. Dublin: Gill & Macmillan.

Garvin, Tom (2000) 'A quiet revolution: the remaking of Irish political culture', pp. 187–203 in Ray Ryan, ed., *Writing in the Irish Republic*. London: Macmillan.

Gilligan, Chris and Jon Tonge, eds (1997) *Peace or war? Understanding the peace process in Northern Ireland*. Aldershot: Ashgate.

Girvin, Brian (1999) 'Northern Ireland and the Republic', pp. 220–41 in Mitchell and Wilford, 1999.

Graham, Brian (1997) 'Ireland and Irishness: place, culture and identity', pp. 1–16 in Brian Graham, ed., *In search of Ireland: a cultural geography*. London: Routledge.

Hall, Michael (1994) *Ulster's Protestant working class: a community exploration*. Belfast: Island Pamphlets.

Hall, Michael (1995) *Beyond the fife and drum*. Belfast: Island Pamphlets.

Hall, Michael (1996) *Reinforcing powerlessness: the hidden dimension to the Northern Ireland 'troubles'*. Belfast: Island Pamphlets.

Harbinson, John F. (1973) *The Ulster Unionist Party, 1882–1973: its development and organisation*. Belfast: Blackstaff.

Harnden, Toby (2000) *'Bandit country': the IRA and South Armagh*. London: Coronet.

Harris, Mary (1993) *The Catholic Church and the foundations of the Northern Irish state*. Cork: Cork University Press.

Hayes, Bernadette and Ian McAllister (1999) 'Ethnonationalism, public opinion and the Good Friday Agreement', pp. 30–48 in Ruane and Todd, 1999.

Healy, Cahir (1945) *The mutilation of a nation*. Derry: Derry Journal.

Hennessey, Thomas (2000) *The Northern Ireland peace process: ending the troubles?* Dublin: Gill & Macmillan.

Hinds, Bronagh (1999) 'Women working for peace in Northern Ireland', pp. 109–29 in Galligan, Ward and Wilford, 1999.

Horgan, John (1997) *Seán Lemass: the enigmatic patriot*. Dublin: Gill & Macmillan.

Howarth, David, Aletta J. Norval and Yannis Stavrakakis, eds (2000) *Discourse theory and political analysis: identities, hegemonies and social change*. Manchester: Manchester University Press.

Hume, John (1986) 'A new Ireland: the acceptance of diversity', *The Irish Times*, 13 Sept.

Hume, John (1988) 'Letter to Gerry Adams', *Sinn Féin/SDLP talks*. Belfast: Sinn Féin.

Hume, John (1996) *John Hume: personal views*. Dublin: Townhouse.

Irish Communist Organisation (1969) *The economics of partition*. Dublin: Irish Communist Organisation.

Irish Communist Organisation (1970) *The birth of Ulster unionism*. Dublin: Irish Communist Organisation.

Irish Communist Organisation (1972) *The home rule crisis*. Dublin: Irish Communist Organisation.

Jackson, Alvin (1993) *Sir Edward Carson*. Dundalk: Dundalgan Press.

Jackson, Alvin (1995) *Colonel Edward Saunderson: land and loyalty in Victorian Ireland.* Oxford: Oxford University Press.

Jacobs, Susie, Ruth Jacobson and Jen Marchbank, eds (2000) *States of conflict: gender, violence and resistance.* London: Zed Books.

Jacobson, Ruth (1997) 'Whose peace process? Women's organisations and political settlement in Northern Ireland, 1996–1997'. Bradford: University of Bradford Peace Studies Papers.

Jacobson, Ruth (2000) 'Women and peace in Northern Ireland: a complicated relationship', pp. 179–98 in Jacobs, Jacobson and Marchbank, 2000.

Jarman, Neil (1997) *Material conflicts: parades and visual displays in Northern Ireland.* Oxford: Berg.

Jarman, Neil and Dominic Bryan (1996) *Parades and protest: a discussion of parading disputes in Northern Ireland.* Coleraine: University of Ulster.

Joint Unionist Task Force (1987) *An end to drift: an abridged version of the report presented to Mr Molyneaux and Dr Paisley, 16th June, 1987.* Belfast: n.p.

Kearney, Richard (1976) 'Myth and terror', *Crane Bag* 2 (1–2): 273–87.

Kearney, Richard (1997) *Postnationalist Ireland: politics, culture, philosophy.* London: Routledge.

Keating, Geoffrey (1723) *The general history of Ireland,* translation by Dermod O'Connor. Dublin: J. Carson [Irish title: Seathrún Céitinn, *Foras Feasa ar Éireann*].

Keating, Michael (1998) *The new regionalism in western Europe: territorial restructuring and political change.* Cheltenham: Edward Elgar.

Kelly, J. M. (1994) *The Irish constitution.* 3rd ed., by Gerard Hogan and Gerry Whyte. Dublin: Butterworth.

Kennedy, Dennis (1988) *The widening gulf: northern attitudes to the independent Irish state 1919–49.* Belfast: Blackstaff.

Kennedy, Michael (2001) '"This tragic and intractable problem": the reaction of the Department of External Affairs to the outbreak of the troubles in Northern Ireland', *Irish Studies in International Affairs* 12: 87–95.

Kennedy, Michael J (2000) *Division and consensus: the politics of cross-border relations in Ireland, 1925–1969.* Dublin: Institute of Public Administration.

Kohn, Leo (1928) 'Die Verfassung des Irischen Freistaats', *Archiv des öffentlichen Rechts* 15 (1): 33–83; 15 (2–3): 269–341.

Kohn, Leo (1932) *The constitution of the Irish Free State.* London: Allen & Unwin.

Kymlicka, Will (1995) *Multicultural citizenship: a liberal theory of rights.* Oxford: Clarendon.

Labour Party (1991) *Constitution of the Labour party for consideration by National Conference, Killarney 1991.* Dublin: Labour Party.

Laclau, Ernesto and Chantal Mouffe (1985) *Hegemony and socialist strategy: towards a radical democratic politics.* London: Verso.

Laffan, Michael (1999) *The resurrection of Ireland: the Sinn Féin party, 1916–1923.* Cambridge: Cambridge University Press.

Lee, J. J. (1989) *Ireland 1912–1985: politics and society.* Cambridge: Cambridge University Press.

Leonard, Allan (1999) 'The Alliance Party of Northern Ireland and power sharing in a divided society'. Dublin: unpublished MA thesis, University College Dublin.

Lindsay, Kennedy (1972) *Dominion of Ulster?* Belfast: Ulster Vanguard Publications.

Longley, Edna (1994) 'From Cathleen to anorexia: the breakdown of Irelands', pp. 173–95 in *The living stream: literature and revisionism in Ireland.* Newcastle upon Tyne: Bloodaxe.

Loretto, Denis (2002) 'Alliance, Liberals and the SDP: a personal memoir', *Journal of Liberal Democrat History* (33): 33–8.

Lyne, Tom (1987) 'The Progressive Democrats 1995–97', *Irish Political Studies* 2: 107–14.

Lynn, Brendan (1997) *Holding the ground: the Nationalist Party in Northern Ireland, 1945–72.* Aldershot: Ashgate.

MacDonagh, Oliver (1983) *States of mind: a study of Anglo-Irish conflict 1780–1980.* Cambridge: Cambridge University Press.

MacNeill, Eoin (1919) *Phases of Irish history.* Dublin: Gill.

Mac Stiofáin, Seán (1975) *Memoirs of a revolutionary.* Edinburgh: Gordon Cremonesi.

McGuire, Maria (1973) *To take arms: a year in the Provisional IRA.* London: Quartet Books.

Mallie, Eamonn and David McKittrick (1997) *The fight for peace: the secret story behind the Irish peace process.* Rev. ed. London: Mandarin.

Mansergh, Martin (2000) 'The background to the Irish peace process', pp. 8–23 in Cox, Guelke and Stephen, 2000.

McAllister, Ian (1977) *The Northern Ireland Social Democratic and Labour Party: political opposition in a divided society.* London: Macmillan.

McAllister, Ian and Brian Wilson (1978) 'Bi-confessionalism in a confessional party system: the Northern Ireland Alliance Party', *Economic and Social Review* 9 (3): 207–25.

McAuley, James W. (1994a) *The politics of identity: a loyalist community in Belfast.* Aldershot: Avebury.

McAuley, James W. (1994b) 'Loyalists and their ceasefire', *Parliamentary Brief* 3 (1): 14–16.

McAuley, James W. (1995) 'The changing face of new loyalism', *Parliamentary Brief* Spring: 45–7.

McAuley, James W. (1996) '(Re)constructing Ulster loyalism: political responses to the "peace process"', *Irish Journal of Sociology* 6: 165–82.

McAuley, James W. (1997a) '"Flying the one-winged bird": Ulster unionism and the peace process', pp. 158–75 in Shirlow and McGovern, 1997.

McAuley, James W. (1997b) 'The Ulster loyalist political parties: towards a new respectability', *Etudes Irlandaises* 22 (2): 117–32.

McAuley, James W. (1997c) 'Divided loyalists, divided loyalties: conflict and continuities in contemporary unionist ideology', pp. 37–53 in Gilligan and Tonge, 1997.

McAuley, James W. (1998) 'A process of surrender? Loyalist perceptions of a settlement', pp. 193–210 in Anderson and Goodman, 1998.

McAuley, James W. (1999) '"Very British rebels": politics and discourse within contemporary Ulster unionism', pp. 106–25 in P. Bagguley and J. Hearn, eds, *Transforming politics: power and resistance.* Basingstoke: Macmillan.

McAuley, James W. (2000) 'Mobilising Ulster Unionism: new directions or old?', *Capital and Class* 70: 37–64.

McAuley, James W (2002, forthcoming) 'Ulster Unionism after the Peace', in J. Neuheiser and S. Wolff, eds, *Breakthrough to peace? The Impact of the Good Friday Agreement on Northern Irish politics and society.* Oxford: Berghahn (in press).

McAuley, James W. and Scott Hislop (2000) 'Many roads forward: politics and ideology within the Progressive Unionist Party', *Études Irlandaises* 25 (1): 173–92.

McAuley, James W. and Jon Tonge (2001) ESRC Award L327253058 'The role of "extra-constitutional" parties in the Northern Ireland Assembly', Final report to the ESRC, Jan.

McCartney, R. L. (2001a) 'Gerry pandering?', *Belfast Telegraph*, 4 Oct.

McCartney, R. L. (2001b) *Reflections on liberty, democracy and the Union.* Dublin: Maunsel.

McDonald, Henry (2000) *Trimble.* London: Bloomsbury.

McGarry, John, ed. (2001) *Northern Ireland and the divided world: post-agreement Northern Ireland in comparative perspective.* Oxford: Oxford University Press.

McGarry, John and Brendan O'Leary (1995) *Explaining Northern Ireland: broken images.* Oxford: Basil Blackwell.

McMahon, Deirdre (1984) *Republicans and imperialists: Anglo-Irish relations in the 1930s.* New Haven, CT: Yale University Press.

Miller, David (1995) *On nationality.* Oxford: Clarendon.

Miller, David, ed. (1998) *Rethinking Northern Ireland.* London: Longman.

Miller, Kerby A. (1990) 'Emigration, capitalism and ideology in post-famine Ireland', in R. Kearney, ed., *Migrations. the Irish at home and abroad.* Dublin: Wolfhound.

Mitchell, Arthur (1974) *Labour in Irish politics, 1890–1930: the Irish labour movement in an age of revolution.* Dublin: Irish University Press.

Mitchell, George J. (1999) *Making peace.* London: Heinemann.

Mitchell, Paul and Rick Wilford, eds (1998) *Politics in Northern Ireland.* Boulder, CO: Westview.

Moloney, Ed and Andy Pollak (1986) *Paisley.* Dublin: Poolbeg.

Moneypenny, W. F. (1913) *The two Irish nations.* London: Murray.

Morgan, Austen (1991) *Labour and partition: the Belfast working class 1905–23.* London: Pluto.

Moss, David (1993), *Italian political violence, 1969–1988: the making and unmaking of meanings.* Geneva: UNRISD paper.

Moss, Warner (1933) *Political parties in the Irish Free State.* New York: AMS.

Moxon-Browne, Edward (1983) *Nation, class and creed in Northern Ireland.* Aldershot: Gower.

Munck, Ronnie and Bill Rolston, eds (1987) *Belfast in the thirties: an oral history.* Belfast: Blackstaff.

Murray, Gerard (1998) *John Hume and the SDLP: impact and survival in Northern Ireland.* Dublin: Irish Academic Press.

Nelson, Sarah (1984) *Ulster's uncertain defenders: Protestant political, paramilitary and community groups and the Northern Ireland conflict.* Belfast: Appletree.

New Ireland Forum (1984) *Report.* Dublin: Stationery Office.

New Ulster Political Research Group (1979) *Beyond the religious divide.* Belfast: New Ulster Political Research Group.

Nic Craith, Máiréad (2002) *Plural identities – singular narratives: the case of Northern Ireland.* Oxford: Berghahn.

Northern Ireland Constitutional Convention (1975) *Report.* Belfast: HMSO.

Northern Ireland Labour Party (1976) *The constitution and rules of the Northern Ireland Labour Party.* Belfast: Northern Ireland Labour Party.

Northern Ireland Women's Coalition (2002) *Aims and objectives.* Available http://www.niwc.org/files/aimsobs.htm [2002–05–10].

Ó Brádaigh, Ruairí (1976) 'Introduction', in *Aisling 1916–1976.* Dublin: Sinn Féin.

O'Brien, Brendan (1995) *The long war: the IRA and Sinn Féin from armed struggle to peace talks.* New ed. Dublin: O'Brien Press.

O'Brien, Conor Cruise (1972) *States of Ireland.* London: Hutchinson.

O'Brien, Conor Cruise (1994) *Ancestral voices: religion and nationalism in Ireland.* Dublin: Poolbeg.

Ó Broin, Leon (1976) *Revolutionary underground: the story of the Irish Republican Brotherhood, 1858–1924*. Dublin: Gill & Macmillan.

O'Dowd, Liam (1998) '"New unionism", British nationalism and the prospects for a negotiated settlement in Northern Ireland', pp. 70–93 in Miller, 1998.

Ó Faoláin, Seán (1938) *King of the beggars*. London: Nelson.

Ó Faoláin, Seán (1942) *The Great O'Neill*. London: Longmans, Green.

O'Halloran, Clare (1987) *Partition and the limits of Irish nationalism: an ideology under stress*. Dublin: Gill & Macmillan.

O'Higgins, Brian ([1932]) *Gair-chatha Gaedheal: Sinn Fein and freedom*. Dublin: Sinn Féin Bureau, n.d.

O'Leary, Brendan (2000) 'Albion retains the right to be perfidious', *Sunday Business Post*, 30 Apr.

O'Leary, Cornelius, Sydney Eliott and R. A. Wilford (1988) *The Northern Ireland Assembly, 1982–1986: a constitutional experiment*. London: C. Hurst.

Olson, Mancur (1982) *The rise and decline of nations*. New Haven: Yale University Press.

Paisley, Rev. Ian (1970) *Northern Ireland: what is the real situation. Message delivered at Bob Jones University Friday, September 12, 1969*. Greenville, SC: Bob Jones University Press.

Paisley, Rev. Ian (1998) *The fruits of appeasement* (DUP press statement, 3 Sept.). Belfast: DUP.

Paisley, Rev Ian (2001) Vote DUP: Eve of Poll Message, http://www.dup.org/ [2001–11–1].

Patterson, H. (1980) 'Independent orangeism and class conflict in Belfast: a reinterpretation', *Proceedings of the Royal Irish Academy* 80 C: 1–27.

Patterson, Henry (1989) *The politics of illusion: republicanism and socialism in modern Ireland*. London: Hutchinson Radius.

Patterson, Henry (1997) *The politics of illusion: a political history of the IRA*. New ed. London: Serif.

Phoenix, Eamon (1994) *Northern nationalism: nationalist politics, partition and the Catholic minority in Northern Ireland 1890–1940*. Belfast: Ulster Historical Foundation.

Porter, Norman (1996) *Rethinking unionism: an alternative vision for Northern Ireland*. Belfast: Blackstaff.

Porter, Norman, ed. (1998) *The republican ideal: current perspectives*. Belfast: Blackstaff.

Progressive Democrats (1996) *Constitution*. Dublin: Progressive Democrats.

Progressive Unionist Party (1985) *Constitution and standing orders of the Progressive Unionist Party of Northern Ireland as agreed by the party conference*. Belfast: PUP.

Progressive Unionist Party (1996) *Constitution*. Belfast: PUP, n.d. [*c*.1996].

Progressive Unionist Party (1996a) *Manifesto for the Forum Election*. Belfast: PUP.

Progressive Unionist Party (1996b) *Dealing with reality* (Press Statement issued by Billy Hutchinson, 31 Mar.). Belfast: PUP.

Progressive Unionist Party (1996c) *Support the Progressive Unionists* (Forum election communication). Belfast: PUP.

Progressive Unionist Party (1997) *Aims and objectives* [dating from 1974; revised 1997] Belfast: PUP.

Progressive Unionist Party (1998) Election material. http://www.pup.org/ [1998–11].

Progressive Unionist Party (1999) The hard bitter experience. http://www.pup.org/ [1999–09].

Progressive Unionist Party (2000) Speech by David Ervine. http://www.pup.org/ [2000–06].

Purdie, Bob (1986) 'The Irish Anti-partition League, South Armagh and abstentionism', *Irish Political Studies* 1: 67–77.

Purdie, Bob (1990) *Politics in the streets: the origins of the civil rights movement in Northern Ireland*. Belfast: Blackstaff.

Purvis, Dawn (1998) North West freedom address: Gay Pride North West. http://www.pup.org/ [1998–11].

Pyne, Peter (1969) 'The third Sinn Féin party 1923–1926: I: narrative account', *Economic and Social Review* I (I): 29–50.

Regan, John (1999) *The Irish counter-revolution 1919–1936: treatyite politics and settlement in independent Ireland*. Dublin: Gill & Macmillan.

Robinson, Peter (1996) 'Wake up Ulster, you're being sold!', http://www.dup.org/ [1999–09–21].

Robinson, Peter (1999) Speech to DUP annual conference 1998, Omagh. http://www.dup.org/ [1999–09–21].

Roche, Patrick J. and Brian Barton, eds (1991) *The Northern Ireland question: myth and reality*. Aldershot: Avebury.

Rooney, Eddie (1984) 'From republican movement to Workers' Party: an ideological analysis', pp. 79–98 in Chris Curtin, Mary Kelly and Liam O'Dowd, eds, *Culture and ideology in Ireland*. Galway: Galway University Press.

Rooney, Eilis (1992) 'Women, community and politics in Northern Ireland: isms in action', *Journal of Gender Studies* I (4): 475–91.

Rooney, Eilis (2000) 'Women in Northern Irish politics: difference matters', pp. 164–86 in Roulston and Davies, 2000.

Rose, Richard (1971) *Governing without consensus: an Irish perspective*. London: Faber & Faber.

Roulston, Carmel and Celia Davies (2000) *Gender, democracy and inclusion in Northern Ireland*. Houndmills: Palgrave.

Ruane, Joseph and Jennifer Todd (1996) *The dynamics of conflict in Northern Ireland: power, conflict and emancipation*. Cambridge: Cambridge University Press.

Ruane, Joseph and Jennifer Todd (2001) 'The politics of transition: explaining the crises in the implementation of the Belfast Agreement', *Political Studies* 49: 923–40.

Ruane, Joseph and Jennifer Todd, eds (1999) *After the Good Friday Agreement: analysing political change in Northern Ireland*. Dublin: University College Dublin Press.

Ryan, Mark (1994), *War and peace in Ireland: Britain and the IRA in the new world order*. London: Pluto.

Ryder, Chris and Vincent Kearney (2001) *Drumcree: the Orange Order's last stand*. London: Methuen.

Sales, Rosemary (1997a) *Women divided: gender, religion and politics in Northern Ireland*. London: Routledge.

Sales, Rosemary (1997b) 'Gender and Protestantism in Northern Ireland', pp. 140–57 in Shirlow and McGovern, 1997.

Sales, Rosemary (1998) 'Women, the peace makers?', pp. 141–61 in Anderson and Goodman, 1998.

Seeds of Hope (2000) ['Seeds of Hope' Ex-Prisoner Project] *Seeds of hope*. Newtownabbey: Island Pamphlets, no. 27.

Shankill Think Tank (1995) *A new beginning*. Newtownabbey: Island Publications.

Shankill Think Tank (1998) *At the crossroads?* Newtownabbey: Island Pamphlets, no. 18.

Sheehy, Michael (1955) *Divided we stand: a study of partition*. London: Faber & Faber.

Shirlow, Peter and Mark McGovern, eds (1997) *Who are the people? Unionism, Protestantism and loyalism in Northern Ireland*. London: Pluto.

Sinn Féin (1917) *Córughadh*. Dublin: Sinn Féin.

Sinn Féin (1924) *Córughadh*. Dublin: Sinn Féin (UCD, Aiken papers, P104/1453).

Sinn Féin (1970) *Bunreacht agus rialacha: constitution and rules*. Dublin: Sinn Féin.

Sinn Féin (1988) *Towards a strategy for peace*. Dublin: Sinn Féin.

Sinn Féin (1992) *Towards a lasting peace in Ireland*. Dublin: Sinn Féin.

Smith, M. L. R. (1995), *Fighting for Ireland? The military strategy of the Irish republican movement*. London: Routledge.

Smyth, Clifford (1987) *Ian Paisley: voice of Protestant Ulster*. Edinburgh: Scottish Academic Press.

Smyth, Marie (2000) 'The human consequences of armed conflict: constructing 'victimhood' in the context of Northern Ireland's troubles', pp. 118–35 in Cox, Guelke and Stephen, 2000.

Social Democratic and Labour Party ([1972]) *Towards a new Ireland: proposals by the Social Democratic and Labour Party*. Belfast: Social Democratic and Labour Party, n.d.

Social Democratic and Labour Party (1995) *Constitution*. Belfast: SDLP.

Sofer, Sasson (1997) 'The diplomat as a stranger', *Diplomacy and statecraft* 8 (3): 179–86.

Spence, Gusty (1995) *Speech to the PUP conference, 11th February* [document in possession of James McAuley].

Staunton, Enda (2001) *The nationalists of Northern Ireland 1918–1973*. Blackrock, Co Dublin: Columba Press.

Tamir, Yael (1993) *Liberal nationalism*. Princeton: Princeton University Press.

Tamir, Yael (1995) 'The enigma of nationalism', *World Politics* 47 (3): 418–40.

Taylor, Peter (1997) *Provos: the IRA and Sinn Féin*. London: Bloomsbury.

Taylor, Peter (2000) *Loyalists*. New ed. London: Bloomsbury.

Thirty Two County Sovereignty Movement (2002) *Constitution*. Available http://www.geocities.com/thirtytwocounty/constitution1.html [2002–03–19].

Todd, Jennifer (1987) 'Two traditions in unionist political culture', *Irish Political Studies* 2: 1–26.

Todd, Jennifer (1990) 'Northern Irish nationalist political culture', *Irish Political Studies* 5: 31–44.

Todd, Jennifer (1999) 'Nationalism, republicanism and the Good Friday Agreement', pp. 49–70 in Ruane and Todd (1999).

Tóibín, Colm (1998) 'Erasures', *London Review of Books*, 30 July.

Trimble, David (2001) *To raise up a new Northern Ireland: articles and speeches 1998–2000*. Belfast: Belfast Press.

Trouillot, Michel-Ralph (1995) *Silencing the past: power and the production of history*. Boston: Beacon Press.

Ulster Democratic Unionist Party (1982) *Constitution and rules*. Belfast: UDUP.

Ulster Democratic Unionist Party (1984a) *The unionist case: the Forum report answered*. Belfast: UDUP.

Ulster Democratic Unionist Party (1984b) *Ulster: the future assured*. Belfast: UDUP.

Ulster Democratic Unionist Party (1996a) *Our covenant with the Ulster people: manifesto for the Forum election*. Belfast: UDUP.

Ulster Democratic Unionist Party (1996b) *The unionist team you can trust* (Forum election communication) Belfast: UDUP.

Ulster Democratic Unionist Party (1996c) *UDUP election special*. Belfast: UDUP.

Ulster Democratic Unionist Party (1996d) *The framework of shame and sham: yes the framework document is a one way road to Dublin.* Belfast: UDUP.

Ulster Democratic Unionist Party (1997a) *DUP rebuff Trimble remarks* (DUP press statement, 24 Mar.). Belfast: UDUP.

Ulster Democratic Unionist Party (1997b) *Peter Robinson's speech to united unionist rally* (DUP press release, 27 Oct.). Belfast: UDUP.

Ulster Democratic Unionist Party (1998) *The real Drumcree issue* (DUP press release, 1 July). Belfast: UDUP.

Ulster Democratic Unionist Party (1999) The tragedy of a false peace. http://www.dup.org [1999-01-21].

Ulster Political Research Group (1987) *Common sense: Northern Ireland – an agreed process.* Belfast: Ulster Political Research Group.

Ulster Unionist Council (1984) *Devolution and the Northern Ireland Assembly: the way forward. A discussion paper presented by the Ulster Unionist Assembly Party's Report Committee.* Belfast: Ulster Unionist Council.

Ulster Unionist Party (2002) *Aims.* Available http://www.uup.org/policy/index.shtml [2002-05-10].

Ulster Vanguard (1972) *Ulster – a nation.* Belfast: Ulster Vanguard Publications.

Ultach (1943) 'The real case against partition', *The Capuchin Annual* 1943: 283–312.

Urquhart, Diane (2000) *Women in Ulster politics 1890–1940: a history not yet told.* Dublin: Irish Academic Press.

Walker, Brian M., ed. (1978) *Parliamentary election results in Ireland, 1801–1922.* Dublin: Royal Irish Academy.

Walker, Brian M., ed. (1992) *Parliamentary election results in Ireland 1918–92: Irish elections to parliaments and parliamentary assemblies at Westminster, Belfast, Dublin, Strasbourg.* Dublin: Royal Irish Academy; Belfast: Institute of Irish Studies, Queen's University.

Walker, Graham (1985) *The politics of frustration: Harry Midgley and the failure of labour in Northern Ireland.* Manchester: Manchester University Press.

Walker, Graham (1995) *Intimate strangers: political and cultural interaction between Scotland and Ulster in modern times.* Edinburgh: John Donald.

Walsh, Dick (1986) *Des O'Malley: a political profile.* Dingle: Brandon.

Ward, Eileen (1998) *Free Presbyterian Church moral committee in a moral dilemma* (PUP Press Statement, 6 Feb.) Belfast: PUP.

Whyte, J. H. (1973) 'Intra-unionist disputes in the Northern Ireland House of Commons, 1921–72', *Economic and Social Review* 5 (1): 99–104.

Whyte, John (1990) *Interpreting Northern Ireland.* Oxford: Oxford University Press.

Wilford, Richard, ed. (2001) *Aspects of the Belfast Agreement.* Oxford: Oxford University Press.

Wilford, Rick and Yvonne Galligan (1999) 'Gender and party politics in Northern Ireland', pp. 169–84 in Galligan, Ward and Wilford, 1999.

Wilford, Rick and Robin Wilson (2000) 'A "bare knuckle ride": Northern Ireland', pp. 79–116 in Robert Hazell, ed., *The state and the nations: the first year of devolution in the United Kingdom.* Devon: Imprint Academic.

Wilson, Robin and Rick Wilford (2001) 'Northern Ireland: endgame', pp. 77–105 in Alan Trench, ed., *The state of the nations 2001: the second year of devolution in the UK.* Devon: Imprint Academic.

Wilson, Robin, ed. (2001) *Agreeing to disagree? A guide to the Northern Ireland Assembly.* London: Stationery Office.

Workers' Party (1993) *Constitution. Agreed at a special delegate conference 13 Nov 1993.* Dublin: Workers' Party.

# Index